The Architectural Guidebook to New York City

SALT LAKE CITY

THE ARCHITECTURAL GUIDEBOOK TO NEW YORK CITY

FRANCIS MORRONE ■ PHOTOGRAPHY BY JAMES ISKA

To my wife, Patricia

Revised Edition
06 05 04 03 02 5 4 3 2 1

Published by
Gibbs Smith, Publisher
P.O. Box 667
Layton, Utah 84041

1.800.748.5439 orders
www.gibbs-smith.com

Project editor: Suzanne Gibbs Taylor
Production editor: Linda Nimori
Interior design and production: Scott Van Kampen
Printed and bound in the United States of America

Library of Congress Cataloging-in-Publication Data

Morrone, Francis, 1958-
The architectural guidebook to New York City / Francis Morrone ; photographs by James Iska.—Rev. ed.
p. cm.
Includes bibliographical references and index.
ISBN 1-58685-211-6
Includes bibliographical references and index.
1. Architecture—New York (State)—New York—Guidebooks.
2. New York (N.Y.)—Buildings, structures, etc.—Guidebooks.
3. New York (N.Y.)—Guidebooks. I. Title.
NA735.N5M64 2002
720'9747'1—dc21

2002009267

Contents

Introduction

When I told people I was writing an architectural guidebook to New York City, the inevitable response was "How will it differ from the *AIA Guide?*" This was a good question and easy to answer. The first edition of Norval White's and Elliot Willensky's *AIA Guide to New York City,* the guide with the imprimatur of the American Institute of Architects, came out in 1967. Updated editions arrived in 1978, 1988, and 2000. It is a dense, encyclopedic guide packed with information, insight, and wit. I doubt there is a better guide of its kind in the world. But its kind is that primarily of a reference book, albeit one that is inordinately pleasurable to read. It is a starting point for more-interpretive guidebooks. I would not even have considered writing my book if I did not have the *AIA Guide* close at hand.

In 1979, Paul Goldberger, then architectural critic for the *New York Times,* came out with *The City Observed: New York,* a leisurely, opinionated, interpretive guide covering only a fraction of the buildings in the *AIA Guide.* He never conceived of it as an alternative to the *AIA Guide,* but rather as a supplement to it. The fact that *City Observed* remained in print for many years without being updated demonstrates the need for such a book. It seemed to me the time was ripe for a new, up-to-date guide along the lines of Goldberger's book, and rather than continuing to wait for Goldberger to update *City Observed,* I decided to write my own book.

I have lived in New York for the last twenty-three years, and in that time I have worked as a freelance writer, a teacher, a lecturer, and a tour guide, specializing in architecture and New York history in all of these areas. My experience of sharing my knowledge with people in the classroom and on walking tours has afforded me what I like to think is an acute sense of the sorts of things people want to know, and should know, about the urban environment. In this book, I have tried to present information in as contextual a way as possible, including what I feel to be pertinent historical and cultural background, making extensive use of comparisons, and quoting liberally.

I discuss approximately six hundred buildings, and I could easily have included another twelve hundred. There is hardly a structure in the city that cannot yield a whole history of ideas. Indeed, those of us who love being in cities do so for the very reason of their inexhaustible, many-layered historicity. What we city lovers love is the day-to-day mental stimulation of peeling back some of those layers. So it is that while mine is not the first architectural guide to New York, it will not be, and should not be, the last.

In the years I have lived in New York, I have walked the city's streets, explored the city's neighborhoods, eaten in its restaurants and drunk in its bars, browsed in its secondhand bookstores—all in measures far exceeding what anyone would consider normal or healthy. I am quite certain that I have sacrificed a large part of my potential for worldly success to the daily lure of the urban trail. In its small way, mine is a hedonistic existence (small because I am much more concerned with owning a pair of good walking shoes than an automobile, the latter being a means of conveyance that is worse than useless in New York City.)

I have limited myself in this volume to the borough of Manhattan. This is not because I do not think there are worthy things in the other four boroughs. To have included them, however, would have made this book unmanageably bulky. I have instead written another book on the architecture of Brooklyn (*An Architectural Guidebook to Brooklyn,* Gibbs Smith, Publisher, 2001), of which borough I am a proud resident.

Most of the major buildings erected in Manhattan in the frenzied real-estate boom of the 1980s are included in the present guide. If I have not dealt with them in as much detail as I have many older buildings, that is because it takes a certain amount of time for a building to achieve its identity. This is the problem faced by architectural critics in the periodical press. Don't forget that Lewis Mumford panned Rockefeller Center and the Chrysler Building.

As great a critic as Mumford was, in my opinion much of what he championed in the pages of *Architectural Record* and the *New Yorker* in the 1920s through the 1950s now seems strangely more antiquated than the *haute bourgeois* Beaux-Arts classicism of 1880 to 1930 that he found so distasteful. My own taste leans considerably, though not excludingly, to the classical. Unlike Henry Hope Reed, whom I unreservedly admire, I do believe there is such a thing as great modern architecture, though there are in New York fewer great, and far fewer good, modern buildings than buildings in a classical mode. I noted in the introduction to the first edition of this book in 1994 that I thought John Barrington Bayley's 1977 addition to the Frick Collection was the best work of post–World War II architecture in Manhattan. I still think that.

When I first wrote this book in the early nineties, New York seemed in the doldrums. The 1980s boom had ended, a major real-estate recession had set in, crime was soaring to new record levels, and cutbacks in municipal services left our streets filthy and our walls, statues, and subway cars covered in graffiti. My, how things have changed. Within only a few years, the city has taken a turn for the better in the quality of its public environment. As I write this, the homicide rate is the lowest it has been since the city started keeping records in the 1930s. In almost all categories of crime, New York ranks lower than London. The image of the city soared in the 1990s. Visitors to the city, with whom I am in constant contact, never fail to mention how much cleaner and more salubrious they find the city's streets and public places. The Central Park Conservancy undertook a major refurbishment of Central Park that, because it was systematically carried out over many years, may not register with many people as what it in fact has been, namely one of the most monumental urban restoration and reclamation projects in history. Once a symbol of municipal ineffectuality, Central Park today looks better than it has at virtually any point in its history. Grand Central Terminal, once considered beyond hope, similarly shines anew. On and on, great buildings and places in New York have come back to life. Why? How? Those questions are beyond the scope of this book, and the answers are hotly debated. Some say it had mostly to do with the roaring economy of the 1990s. That answer seems wrong to me, for we have had other booms that did not affect the city in the same way. Many, of course, give much of the credit to Mayor Giuliani, who campaigned on "quality of life" issues, and who only the very foolish would not credit with the city's dramatic drops in crime. The Business Improvement Districts (34th Street Partnership, Grand Central Partnership, Times Square Business Improvement District, and many others) should partly be credited with the elevated standard of cleanliness and orderliness in many of our streets. The city's image received a boost from one of the recurrent phenomena in our history: the rediscovery of the city by a fresh generation of young people, who saw New York exemplified in the warm and gently humorous presentation of the city and its oddball characters in television series like *Seinfeld*.

As I write this in the spring of 2002, there is something else that obviously bears mentioning. Last September 11, terrorists deliberately crashed two hijacked jetliners into the twin towers of the World Trade Center. Thousands of gallons of burning jet fuel melted the steel supports of the towers, which imploded in images seared into the memories of all Americans. Nearly three thousand people perished, many of them city workers—policemen, firefighters, emergency medical personnel—who so valiantly attempted to save lives, and who succeeded in saving tens of thousands of lives in acts of bravery that are also indelibly etched in our memories. These acts of bravery and the responses of New Yorkers in general are, to an infinitely greater degree than the restorations of Central Park and Grand Central Terminal, a testament to the resiliency and the greatness of New York and New Yorkers, and tell us as nothing else could that, whatever new and as yet unimagined horrors the future may hold in this frighteningly uncertain world, New Yorkers will not allow their city to pass uncontested into oblivion.

I must mention a few people who have helped this book see the light of day. I thank John Frazier, who started Urban Center Books, New York's outstanding architectural bookstore, for putting me in touch with Gibbs Smith, the publisher of this book. I thank Gibbs Smith. Suzanne Taylor, editorial director at Gibbs Smith, Publisher, does magnificent work, and this book's infelicities are entirely those of its author. Mostly I thank Patricia Rainsford, my wife, without whom I would be Bartleby the scrivener.

CHAPTER 1

The Financial District

1 *U. S. Custom House*

Chapter 1
The Financial District

1 U.S. CUSTOM HOUSE

1 Bowling Green, between State and Whitehall streets
1907, Cass Gilbert

One of New York's great experiences of the classical is the walk up State Street along the east side of Battery Park from the Staten Island Ferry to Bowling Green and Broadway. The long south and west sides of the Custom House loom into view, walls of beguiling sumptuousness that make this, with the intersection of Riverside Drive and 116th Street (19.4), one of the two spots on Manhattan Island that most make me feel like I am in Paris. This is New York's third Custom House, after what is now the Federal Hall National Memorial (1.12) and 55 Wall Street (1.8), Doric and Ionic respectively. (The fourth Custom House is in the World Trade Center.) This granite building would be monumental enough were it only for its massive Corinthian columns rising from its rusticated base. What makes it the heady, powerfully sensuous experience it is, however, as well as what makes it so Parisian, are its elaborate mansard and its superabundance of architectural sculpture. The main elevation is on Bowling Green. Along the cornice are twelve figures representing different civilizations. From east to west, these figures are: *Greece* and *Rome* by Frank Edwin Elwell; *Phoenicia* by Frederick Wellington Ruckstull; *Genoa* by Augustus Lukeman; *Venice* and *Spain* by Mary Lawrence Tonetti; *Holland* and *Portugal* by Louis Saint-Gaudens; *Denmark* by Johannes Gelert;

2 *26 Broadway*

Belgium by Albert Jaegers; and *France* and *England* by Charles Grafly. In the center is Karl Bitter's cartouche of the U.S. seal, topped by an eagle and flanked by *Peace* and *Strength*. The four sculptures in front of the base—*Asia, America, Europe,* and *Africa*—are by Daniel Chester French. The wealth of symbolism and the sensuous beauty of the modeling make these among the most exquisite sculptures in New York.

The rotunda has a fresco by Reginald Marsh, dating from 1937, called *An Ocean Liner Entering New York Harbor.* Few people enter New York Harbor by ocean liner anymore, but I like to think of arrival by the Staten Island Ferry as a symbolic formal entrance to Manhattan. Though the ferry facilities themselves have all the aesthetic character of a parking garage, to move from that setting across a swath of green and be met by the perfectly sited walls of an exceptionally well-crafted Beaux Arts building is about as stirring a welcome to a city as I can imagine.

2 26 BROADWAY

Northeast corner of Beaver Street
1922, Carrère & Hastings, and Shreve, Lamb & Blake

The Beaux-Arts former headquarters of John D. Rockefeller's Standard Oil Company of New Jersey, faced in beautiful Indiana limestone, maintains the promise of the Custom House. Again siting is everything. The main body, with a rusticated base and an Ionic colonnaded attic, hugs the curve of Broadway, and like Schwartz and Gross's Colosseum apartments on Riverside Drive and 116th Street (19.4), pulls in the eye with all the sinuous momentum of a Beaux-Arts roller coaster. But this is not the only way 26 Broadway works in the cityscape. The tower, rising to twenty-seven stories, is not like the base set to Broadway's curve, but is set instead to the uptown grid, so that it aligns with the rest of the skyline, and does not present an off-angle when the skyline is viewed as a whole. And what does it add to that skyline? A four-sided Corinthian colonnade topped by a pyramidal crown. As Henry Hope Reed says of American cities, "Nowhere else in the world are found columns hundreds of feet in the air." This, and not the Chrysler Building (11.4) or the Empire State Building (19.4), is my idea of the quintessential New York building.

3 25 BROADWAY

Southwest corner of Morris Street
1921, Benjamin Wistar Morris and Carrère & Hastings
Great Hall converted to post office, 1977

The handsome neo-Renaissance limestone façade of the 23-story former Cunard Building is the perfect complement to the sweeping 26 Broadway across the street. The glory of this building, however, is inside. The domed Great Hall is one of the city's monumental interiors. It is based on Raphael's Villa Madama (begun 1516) in Rome, and its spectacular frescoes, by Ezra Winter, are the best in New York. There are also maps by Barry Faulkner and ironwork by Samuel Yellin. Some sense of the stupendous scale of the Great Hall can be inferred from the fact that nearby Trinity Church (1.17), minus its tower, would fit inside it. Alas, the United States Postal Service, while doing no permanent damage to this space, has nonetheless cluttered it up in such a way as to make any proper experience of it impossible.

3 *Former Cunard Building on right*

4 *Broad Financial Center*

4 BROAD FINANCIAL CENTER

33 Whitehall Street, northeast corner of Pearl Street
1986, Fox & Fowle

This twenty-seven-story reflective glass wedge is noted for its flamboyant corner atrium lobby with its crazy clock.

5 BANCA COMMERCIALE ITALIANA

1 William Street, southeast corner of Hanover Square
1907, Francis H. Kimball and Julian C. Levi
Renovated and expanded in 1984, Gino Valle

This twelve-story, Anglicized Baroque office building, with fully rusticated façades and Ionic colonnades just below the top, was for fifty years the headquarters of Lehman Brothers. The rounded corner, with an elaborate entrance at the bottom and a domed tower at the top, is one of the Financial District's romantic high points. This building is curiously comparable to Carrère and Hastings's First Church of Christ, Scientist (16.26) on Central Park West of four years earlier.

6 DELMONICO'S

56 Beaver Street, southwest corner of South William Street
1891, James Brown Lord

Established in 1827, Delmonico's is perhaps the most famous name in New York's restaurant history. Like the Banca Commerciale Italiana, with which it shares one of the Financial District's most picturesque intersections, it features a powerful, rounded corner entrance.

7 20 EXCHANGE PLACE

Between William Street and Hanover Square
1931, Cross & Cross

The slender shaft of this fifty-seven-story Art Deco office building is a conspicuous element on the lower Manhattan skyline, while the rear corner entrance of the vaguely Renaissance base adds another element to the beguiling intersection that includes the Banca Commerciale Italiana and Delmonico's.

6 *Delmonico's Restaurant*

7 *20 Exchange Place*

8 55 WALL STREET

Between William and Hanover streets
1836–42, Isaiah Rogers
Remodeled and heightened in 1907, McKim, Mead & White

The lower, Ionic portion was built as the Merchants' Exchange and, in 1863, became the U.S. Custom House. When the new Custom House was built at Bowling Green, the upper, Corinthian portion was added, and the building became the headquarters of the First National Bank, which in 1955 merged with the City Bank Farmers Trust Company, then headquartered at 20 Exchange Place, to become Citibank, today America's largest bank. This building became a particularly splendid Citibank branch, offering an especially notable banking room, with a domed and coffered ceiling and high, arched windows framed by majestic Corinthian columns. This is an outstanding example of the skill and sensitivity with which architects once were able to add to old buildings.

9 MORGAN BANK HEADQUARTERS

60 Wall Street, between Nassau and William streets
1988, Kevin Roche John Dinkeloo & Associates

This immense, fifty-five-story, 1.7 million-square-foot building is another of the 1980s string of Egyptoid designs spewed forth by Roche Dinkeloo. The three hundred-foot-long, four-story granite colonnade at its base is a bow to the Greek Revival Citibank across the street, whose air rights made the Morgan building possible. Like Roche Dinkeloo's Leo Burnett Building in Chicago, the inspiration here may have been Adolf Loos's columnar-skyscraper entry in the 1922 *Chicago Tribune* competition. The vast lobby is in a style that can only be called *tropical kitsch.*

10 BANK OF NEW YORK BUILDING

48 Wall Street, northeast corner of William Street
1928, Benjamin Wistar Morris

The rusticated base with its high, arched windows makes for a dignified street presence. The Bank of New York was founded in 1784 by Alexander Hamilton, and it is that history that inspired Morris's choice of a Federal-style cupola to top this thirty-one-story building. When you think about it, a Federal cupola thirty-one stories in the air is the perfect symbol for

12^A *Federal Hall*

12^B *Interior of Federal Hall*

much of what Alexander Hamilton represented. The overall style of the building is almost stripped classical.

11 40 WALL STREET

Between William and Nassau streets
1929, H. Craig Severance and Yasuo Matsui

At seventy stories and over a million square feet, still a giant in these parts. Originally the headquarters of the Bank of the Manhattan, this was intended to be the world's tallest building, but William Van Alen, who had worked for Severance, surprised everyone by making his Chrysler Building (11.4) taller than the announced plans had indicated. The distinctive pyramidal crown is wedded to modernistic massing to create a typically romantic tower of the roaring twenties. Insofar as the style can be called stripped classical, this is the tallest such building in the world.

12 FEDERAL HALL NATIONAL MEMORIAL

28 Wall Street, northeast corner of Nassau Street
1834–42, Town & Davis with John Frazee and Samuel Thompson

This marble Doric temple, the most distinguished Greek Revival building in New York, was originally the U.S. Custom House. It became, after the Custom House moved to 55 Wall Street, and remained until 1925, the U.S. Sub-Treasury Building. Since 1955 it has been a National Park Service memorial to George Washington, for it was on this site that, fifty-three years before the completion of this building, in the old City Hall, he took his oath of office as the first president of the United States. In front of the building is John Quincy Adams Ward's bronze statue of Washington, dating from 1883. It is one of the best American sculptures of its period. The severe exterior of Federal Hall belies the rich, domed rotunda within.

13 MORGAN GUARANTY TRUST BUILDING

23 Wall Street, southeast corner of Broad Street
1913, Trowbridge & Livingston

So sharp angled it almost hurts to look at it. The only comparably sharp-edged building in New York is the Metropolitan Club (17.2), although the Morgan Library (9.11) comes close. Here J. Pierpont Morgan expressed conspicuous consumption by the very act of erecting a mere

14 *New York Stock Exchange*

four-story building on one of the most expensive plots of real estate in the world. J. P. Morgan and Company was instrumental in the founding of such businesses as General Electric, AT&T, and U.S. Steel. Morgan Stanley and Drexel Burnham were outgrowths of J. P. Morgan.

14 NEW YORK STOCK EXCHANGE

8 Broad Street, between Wall Street and Exchange Place
1903, George B. Post
1923 addition, Trowbridge & Livingston

The nerve center of the American economy is housed in a marble Roman temple. It is a remarkable work of urban architecture, a façade of enormous power that gives away nothing to the much larger buildings that bear down on it from every side. Post achieved such strength by three principal means. First, he gave the building a two-story base, rather than the customary one-story base, and enriched that base with bold brackets and balconies. Second, he set the base with massive, magnificent, fifty-two-foot-high, fluted Corinthian columns. Third, he gave the building a huge pediment crammed with a hyperactive group of sculptural figures designed by John Quincy Adams Ward. (Alas, the figures we see today are copies of the marble originals, which had to be removed because they were disintegrating.) The achievement of such monumentality in such a tight space is an object lesson in the infinite flexibility of the vocabulary and grammar of classicism.

15 BANKERS TRUST BUILDING

16 Wall Street, northwest corner of Nassau Street
1912, Trowbridge & Livingston

The distinctive pyramidal top of this thirty-seven-story building is modeled on the tomb of Mausolus at Halicarnassus (355–350 B.C.), one of the seven wonders of the world, in which a pyramid surmounts a base of Ionic columns. The top of Roche Dinkeloo's Morgan Bank Headquarters (1.6) up the street is a highly abstracted variation on the very popular motif inspired by this tomb.

16 ONE WALL STREET

Southeast corner of Broadway
1932, Voorhees, Gmelin & Walker
1965 addition, Smith, Smith, Haines, Lundberg & Waehler

This sleek, fifty-story, limestone mass is as reminiscent as any Manhattan building of Hugh Ferriss's visionary drawings of the 1920s. Ralph Walker was perhaps the 1920s' most revolutionary experimenter in the plastic molding of skyscraper form, in the process inventing the Art Deco skyscraper, i.e., the mating of the 1916 zoning regulations, mandating setbacks, with the then-fashionable Parisian decoration. As in the Chrysler Building (11.4), there is more than a hint here of *The Cabinet of Dr. Caligari* in the faceted form of the tower and especially in the spidery entrance. The spectacular red mosaics in the first-floor banking room are by Hildreth Meiere, whose work is prominent at St. Bartholomew's Church (10.10) and at Temple Emanu-El (17.7). One Wall Street was built as the headquarters of the Irving Trust Company, which became part of the Bank of New York in 1989.

17 *Trinity Church*

17 TRINITY CHURCH (Episcopal)

Broadway at the head of Wall Street
1846, Richard Upjohn
Chapel: 1913, Thomas Nash
1965 addition, Adams & Woodbridge

This is the oldest Episcopal congregation in a city where Episcopalianism was once the official religion. It is the wealthiest congregation of any denomination in New York. Trinity Church once owned—lock, stock, and barrel, and by royal decree—all the land bounded by Fulton and Christopher streets, Broadway, and the Hudson River. No one ever made more money in Manhattan real estate than Trinity Church. Since 1846, the church building itself has remained ensconced amid its bucolic churchyard, more than holding its architectural own against the towering office buildings that impose on it from every side. When built, Trinity's tower, at 280 feet, was the tallest structure in Manhattan—the World Trade Center of its day. (The twin towers of the World Trade Center, 1,350 feet high, are only two blocks away, 3.5.) Trinity is set at the head of Wall Street, famously closing its western vista in a dramatic, though not an overbearing, manner. It is also probably the most important Gothic Revival building in America.

Upjohn was inspired by the ideas of Augustus Welby Northmore Pugin and the ecclesiological movement, the artistic arm of the Oxford Movement, which under such leaders as John Henry Newman sought to reinvigorate the Church of England by recalling its roots in medieval Catholicism. Pugin and Newman ended up converting to Catholicism, but not until the Gothic Revival, precisely because of its association with Catholicism, had come to dominate Anglican and Episcopal church design in England and America. Pugin's Gothic was based on a clear expression of liturgical functions, reflecting the hierarchy the Oxford Movement sought to restore, in opposition to the Protestant trend of turning churches into community meeting halls, a tendency reaching its stylistic apogee in the Georgian church designs of James Gibbs, on which Trinity's neighbor, St. Paul's Chapel (2.6), is based. Upjohn's design for Trinity is strikingly similar to a drawing of an "ideal church" that appeared in Pugin's *True Principles of Pointed or Christian Architecture* of 1841. Pugin's church was in the perpendicular Gothic mode of the late fourteenth century. It had a high tower and spire; a nave roof rising over side aisles on a high, dramatic clerestory; crenellated and pinnacled parapets along the exterior walls of the nave and aisles; and a chancel as wide as, but lower than, the nave. Trinity closely resembles the Pugin drawing, lacking only the high degree of articulation of Pugin's chancel and the steep pitch of his roof. Upjohn's ideas paralleled those of the English Gothic Revivalists, and with Trinity he produced a work that was comparable in quality to any of the Gothic Revival churches of the day in England.

Given the religious and economic conditions in Manhattan in the 1840s, Upjohn's church was as authentically Gothic as a church could possibly be. For example, a highly articulated chancel, as in Pugin's ideal church, is an important element in true Gothic church architecture. While Upjohn was forced to eschew the high degree of articulation employed by Pugin, the chancel of Trinity is nonetheless as articulated as it could possibly have been, given the biases of the Trinity vestry. There was at first great reluctance to allow an articulated chancel at all, for such a thing smacked of Catholicism. By the 1830s, however, the Oxford Movement was effecting a kind of counter-reformation within the Anglican church. Those involved in this counter-reformation sensed a deep malaise in the church, and felt that the only remedy lay in a return to, rather than a continuing flight from, medieval, basically Roman Catholic principles and practices, including and especially Gothic architecture. Pugin and Upjohn believed that a church building should forthrightly express its religious functions. They believed, for example, that the chancel should be clearly differentiated from the nave. The neoclassicists, following Wren and Gibbs, had completely done away with the chancel in their boxlike churches, and the first goal of the medievalists was to revive the chancel. To the proponents of counter-reformation, as to the Catholics, the chancel was the domain of the clergy, the most sacred part of the church, and the nave was the domain of the laity. The presence of a chancel expressed the belief in a clear, hierarchical differentiation of church functions, something which in Anglicanism, as in other Protestant sects, had been diminishing as they moved ever further from the ways of the Roman church.

Thus it was that the vestry rejected Upjohn's proposed chancel as too "popish." Upjohn, however, insisted on his chancel, and a compromise was reached. Instead of the highly articulated chancel of Pugin's ideal church, Trinity's chancel is *subtly* marked off from the nave. In the interior, the separation is marked by the use of steps leading up from the nave to the chancel, and by an enlargement of the wall piers at the line of demarcation, the piers continuing across the ceiling as a heavy transverse arch. The chancel culminates in an enormous perpendicular-style window. On the exterior, the chancel is also marked off, again subtly, by an increase in the size of the second buttress from the end on both the north and south sides, corresponding to the placement of the heavy piers on the interior walls. The projecting side aisles terminate at these enlarged buttresses, so that the chancel, whose roof line remains continuous with that of the nave, is nonetheless unmistakably distinguished from the main body of the building. Would that we could reconcile some of our present "culture wars" by such elegant compromise!

Inside, Trinity has a ceiling of lath and plaster suspended from wooden trusses, as opposed to one made entirely of stone in the prescribed ecclesiological manner of true Gothic construction. The exterior buttresses are therefore structurally unnecessary. The buttresses are, however, *functionally* necessary to differentiate the nave from the chancel.

Buried in the churchyard are such luminaries as Alexander Hamilton (1755?–1804), Robert Fulton (1765–1815), and Albert Gallatin (1761–1849). In the northeast corner of the yard is the Gothic Revival Martyrs Monument, designed by Upjohn and erected in 1852 as a memorial to the Continental soldiers who died while in captivity in the present-day Liberty Street, which before the revolution was called Crown Street.

The bronze doors on the east, south, and north sides of the base of the tower were added in 1894 and were designed by Richard Morris Hunt. They were modeled on the famous bronze doors by Lorenzo Ghiberti for the Baptistery (1401) of the Florence Cathedral. All Saints Chapel, designed by Thomas L. Nash, was appended to the west side of the chancel in 1913. Note how Nash retained the chancel separation by keeping the roof of his chapel lower than the roof of the aisle to the east.

The very design of Trinity Church is a text describing the battle of ideas taking place within the Episcopal church in the 1830s and '40s. I believe that the functional articulation championed by the Gothic Revival is as direct a forerunner as we have of the later "functionalism" of Louis Sullivan's "religion of democracy," in which a new paradigm of social relations is seen as compensating for the decline of religion.

18 TRINITY and U.S. REALTY BUILDINGS

111 and 115 Broadway at Thames Street
1905, 1907, Francis H. Kimball

Pugin, Upjohn, and others railed against the notion that the Gothic Revival should be valued for its romantic picturesqueness. Yet when half a century later Kimball designed these near-twin towers (one is twenty-one stories, the other twenty-two), he chose to enclose the Trinity churchyard with an unabashedly picturesque, romantically looming neo-Gothic wall. In these, as in many of his other works, Kimball was a superb urban architect, always respecting the street, scaling his buildings to the individual pedestrian without compromising his rich, romantic decorative schemes. Thus he created buildings of unique personality. Be sure to check out the lobbies, long corridors that are like medieval banquet halls, with hammer-beam ceilings, stained-glass clerestories, and effusive amounts of bronze, marble, and gilt.

19 BANK OF TOKYO

100 Broadway, southeast corner of Pine Street
1895, Bruce Price
Remodeled in 1975, Kajima International

About as stately and tasteful a Beaux-Arts skyscraper as can be found, fittingly so, for Price was the father of the avatar of etiquette, Emily Post. Equally tasteful is the sensitive modernization by Kajima. From the Ionic colonnaded base, topped by a row of statues, up the rusticated shaft to the relief figure-sculptures by J. Massey Rhind, to the crowning sequence of cornices, this twenty-two-story, gray granite skyscraper is one of the best groomed and most demurely beautiful buildings in Manhattan.

20 ONE EXCHANGE PLAZA

Broadway, southwest corner of Exchange Alley
1981, Fox & Fowle

45 BROADWAY ATRIUM

From Exchange Alley to Morris Street
1983, Fox & Fowle

The first is a sleek, thirty-one-story, brick-and-glass, round-cornered tower. The second is a sleek, thirty-two-story, brick-and-glass zigzag tower. They

18 *U. S. Realty and Trinity Buildings*

were intended to be one building, but for the holdout in between. Very characteristic of the spate of sleek eighties towers Fox & Fowle designed for Manhattan.

21 BARCLAY BANK BUILDING

75 Wall Street, between Water and Pearl streets
1987, Welton Becket Associates

Thirty-six stories of flamed granite meant to evoke the thirties, with a classical, arched-entry base, and a modernistic shaft with a faceted top. As with most of the recent spate of neo-thirties' towers, the intention is betrayed by the brittle granite veneer, which results in shallow detailing and an even greater sense of insubstantiality than in most high-modern steel-and-glass towers.

22 WALL STREET PLAZA

Water Street, from Pine Street to Maiden Lane
1973, I. M. Pei & Associates

It is remarkable how utterly routine a once radical building can seem only a few years later. This is one of the few pure Miesian exercises in New York, a very elegant building that advanced the Miesian idiom another technological level, in this case by its early use of mullionless structural bays. This is the last stylistic step before the advent of the completely flush skin, for example 140 Broadway (2.3E). Wall Street Plaza is a historical example of the painstaking effort to perfect Miesian modernism just prior to its dissolution.

CHAPTER 2

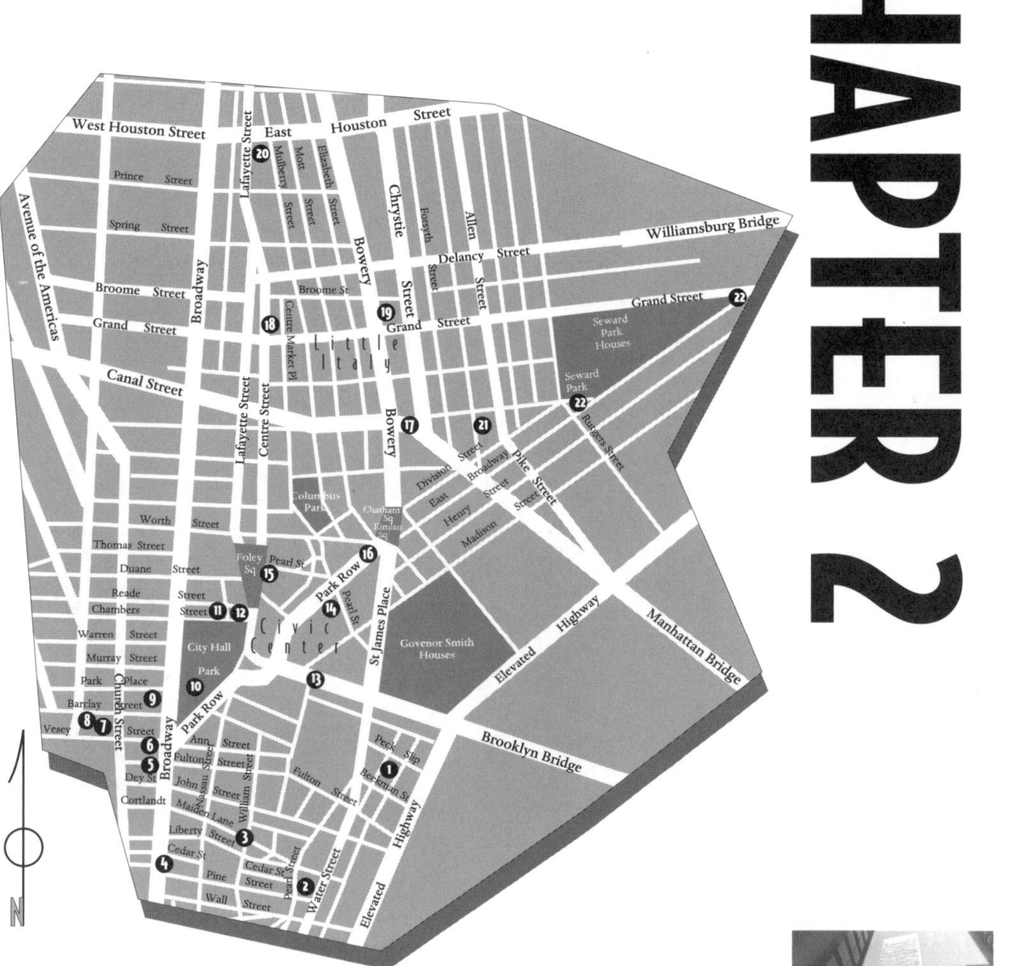

Around City Hall

3A Chase Manhattan Bank

Chapter 2

Around City Hall

1 SOUTH STREET SEAPORT

Bounded by Fulton Street on the south, Beekman Street on the north, Water Street on the west, and the East River on the east
Redeveloped in 1983–84

First it was one of the world's most bustling working waterfronts. Following its decline, it became in 1967 the South Street Seaport Museum, an endeavor to preserve the old waterfront buildings, some dating from the eighteenth century, as well as a place to exhibit historic sailing vessels. With its splendid collection of ramshackle old buildings, and the heady aroma of the still-thriving Fulton Fish Market right next door, this area exuded a funky charm through the 1970s. It was a tranquil enclave just steps from the frenetic Financial District. Sweets and Sloppy Louie's, all-American fish houses, were two of Manhattan's most venerable restaurants.

But the seventies was also the decade in which the developer James W. Rouse teamed with the architect Benjamin Thompson to work commercial wonders for the ancient waterfronts of Boston and Baltimore. Rouse and Thompson created Faneuil Hall Marketplace in Boston and Harborplace in Baltimore, "festival marketplaces" that not only pumped much-needed revenue into city coffers, but went a long way to elevate the self-image of a couple of cities from old and dowdy to youthful and energetic, more than equal to the task of rendering urban life fit for the twenty-first century. It is a little hard now to recall just how captivating those festival marketplaces seemed when they first came on the scene, and that it was perhaps inevitable that the South Street Seaport Museum would seek to replicate the achievement of Boston and Baltimore. And in the early eighties, Rouse and Thompson set out to transform the funky old waterfront of lower Manhattan into the biggest of all festival marketplaces.

Of course, one of the central tenets of the Rouse-Thompson approach is to preserve historic structures. The historic structures here are Schermerhorn Row (Fulton Street from Front to South streets). These were originally countinghouses and warehouses, built in the Federal style, later remodeled in the Greek Revival style to include storefronts. The buildings date from 1811 to 1850. Jan Hird Pokorny was the architect in charge of the restoration, which was completed in 1983. These buildings represent some of the most painstaking restoration work you're ever likely to see, and the unfortunate upshot of that is that they're so shiny and perfect they look like they belong in Disneyland. Still, these buildings date from one of those rare periods in the history of architecture when it seemed impossible for anyone to construct an ugly building. **Schermerhorn Row** is best viewed from the second floor of the **Fulton Market Building** across the street. Viewing such structures from above, especially on a rainy or snowy day, gives one a bit of the feeling that he or she has dreamily descended, as if in a children's story, upon the past.

The Bogardus Building, at the northwest corner of Fulton and Front streets, is so called because originally a cast-iron building by James Bogardus, which had been dismantled and placed in storage, was to be reerected on this site. Unfortunately, the dismantled building was stolen, presumably for scrap, and so Beyer Blinder Belle designed a building inspired by the purloined Bogardus. Benjamin Thompson & Associates designed the Fulton Market Building on Fulton Street between Front and South streets, which started out as the seaport's Quincy Market equivalent: an attempt to replicate in a somewhat more contemporary vein the traditional central-city marketplace, e.g., Lexington Market in Baltimore, Reading Terminal Market in Philadelphia, and Eastern Market in Washington, D.C. The dominant note in these new marketplaces is not farmers' stalls or ethnic groceries, but upscale fast food. Though designed in the customary high-energy, chock-a-block, Rouse-Thompson manner, the Fulton Market Building seems not to have done very well, and is now the least of the seaport's attractions.

Pier 17, fronting on the East River across South Street, opened in 1984, a year after the Fulton Market Building, and is the only seaport structure built right up to the water. Thompson designed it in a traditional waterfront-pavilion mode, with a peaked roof and outdoor decks with sweeping river vistas. At night it is lit up and is a conspicuous sight from the Brooklyn waterfront or the Brooklyn Bridge. The nicest thing to do at the seaport, in my opinion, is to sit on the outdoor deck of Pier 17 on a summer evening as dusk descends and watch the lights on the Brooklyn Bridge come on. From here there is also a superb view of the dramatic, underrated Brooklyn waterfront and skyline—a far more interesting view than that of Jersey City from Battery Park City.

Municipal, state, and federal subsidies allowed the Seaport to be redeveloped, and it was the planners' hope that it would bring diversity and excitement to the Financial District in the evenings and on weekends. The seaport has undeniably enlivened the area. Young Wall Streeters flock to the bars and restaurants after work, and on weekends the seaport has become a favored destination of suburbanites visiting the city. They seem to come because the seaport reminds them of home. After all, they crowd into the same shops that are in their mall back home, e.g., The Sharper Image, Brookstone, and The Gap. The success of festival marketplaces is based on the cultural inferiority suburbanites feel vis-à-vis the central city. These people would never live in the city because they are afraid of crime and they prefer a life based on the automobile. But when the city does something to flatter suburban sensibilities, they come running.

2 70 PINE STREET

Northwest corner of Pearl Street
1932, Clinton & Russell

A sixty-three-story skyscraper classic that once absolutely dominated the view of the lower Manhattan skyline from Brooklyn, and that remains to this day a conspicuous skyline element. This Art Deco extravaganza is the architecture of self-celebration: note the model of the building at the front entrance, as if to express the builders' utter delight at what they have wrought.

3[B] *Liberty Street looking east, with 140 Broadway (R.) and Federal Reserve Bank of New York (L.)*

3 LIBERTY STREET

From William Street to Broadway

"This small segment of New York," writes Ada Louise Huxtable, "compares in effect and elegance with any celebrated Renaissance plaza or Baroque vista."

The buildings:

3A CHASE MANHATTAN BANK BUILDING

Bounded by Liberty Street on the south, Pine Street on the north, William Street on the west, and Nassau Street on the east
1960, Skidmore, Owings & Merrill

Sixty stories of aluminum and glass in a strict Miesian design, the first such building in lower Manhattan, and the first downtown skyscraper built under the new zoning regulations allowing sheer-rise towers with plazas. It was also the first important post–World War II building in the Financial District, and came at a time when many people felt that area's days as a business center were numbered. It provided the first of four Liberty Street plazas moving west.

3B FEDERAL RESERVE BANK OF NEW YORK

33 Liberty Street, northeast corner of Nassau Street
1924, York & Sawyer

A massive, solid Florentine medieval palazzo of a kind meant for just such a street as this: narrow and tightly packed. This "bankers' bank" looks utterly impenetrable, yet its very impenetrability is expressed with a perfectly congenial street presence. Its elements are fairly simple: bold Tuscan arches, a facing of rusticated multihued Indiana limestone, Samuel Yellin's robust black ironwork. But there is nothing simple in this combination of somber dignity and urbane delight, a building that may say Keep Out but does so politely. It is the ideal wall to lend just the right note of enclosure to the sequence of plazas on the other side of Liberty Street.

3C LIBERTY TOWER

55 Liberty Street, northwest corner of Nassau Street
1909, Henry Ives Cobb

Converted to apartments in 1981, this tower was originally the headquarters of the Sinclair Oil Company. The Gothic terra-cotta decoration preceded the Woolworth Building (2.9) by four years. Cobb came to New York from Chicago, and as befitted his lineage, he gave New York one of its first tall buildings since Chicagoan Louis Sullivan's Bayard Building (6.2) so forthrightly to display its steel frame. The structural piers rise unimpeded and are seamlessly dissolved into a Gothic crown. It is a wonder that at the time of the *Chicago Tribune* competition, Sullivan was so disdainful of the Gothicizing winning entry, for in buildings such as Hood and Howells's Chicago Tribune Tower, Cass Gilbert's Woolworth Building, and Liberty Tower, Gothic decoration was shown to reveal the very "proud and soaring" qualities Sullivan believed skyscrapers should possess.

3D CHAMBER OF COMMERCE OF THE STATE OF NEW YORK

65 Liberty Street, between Nassau Street and Broadway
1901, James B. Baker

Packs quite a punch for such a compact building. A massive rusticated base supports fluted Ionic columns, above which rises one of those drippy, creamy mansards of which the Beaux-Artistes were so enamored. Like the Federal Reserve Bank, a consummately skillful essay in side-street monumentality.

3E 140 BROADWAY

Between Liberty and Cedar streets
1967, Skidmore, Owings & Merrill

One of the handful of pacesetting tall buildings to be found in New

3F *Liberty Street looking west, with Federal Reserve Bank of New York (R.) and Chase Manhattan Bank Building (L.)*

York. It's a big building: forty-nine stories and over a million square feet. Yet it seems almost as light as air—seems, indeed, almost a pure Platonic prism, anchored to this world only by the indisputably present Noguchi cube in its plaza. The matte-black-aluminum and bronze glass skin is completely flush. The development of the extremely lightweight curtain wall made such flush skins possible. With impeccable Miesian logic, the robust Miesian projecting piers became obsolete overnight. The upshot was that the Miesian mode was played out: there was utterly nowhere for it to go. Skidmore, Owings & Merrill's detailing is so refined it is invisible. This is the ideal architecture of the suburban office park, meant to be seen from a car going fifty-five miles per hour, rather than on foot going three miles per hour. Here, however, there is something quite spectacular in the way the ethereality of 140 Broadway plays off the solidity of the Federal Reserve Bank, as well as Chase Manhattan's different kind of solidity. It is all the result of superb siting: the building flares ever so slightly eastward, so that the Liberty Street vista east from Broadway is plugged magnificently by the Federal Reserve Bank. Hardly the kind of thing one would find in a suburban office park.

3F ONE LIBERTY PLAZA

Liberty Street, northwest corner of Broadway
1974, Skidmore, Owings & Merrill

Seven years after 140 Broadway, Skidmore, Owings & Merrill, the world's reigning firm of high-modern commercial architects, was clearly at an aesthetic impasse. This was the year when the Chicago office of this firm disastrously applied the flush curtain wall of 140 Broadway to the tallest building in the world, Sears Tower. In New York, they did the gigantic, fifty-three-story, two million-square-foot Liberty Plaza. Nothing's sadder than when gigantic buildings get commissioned at times of aesthetic impasse. It's particularly sad here, for Liberty Plaza replaced Ernest Flagg's Singer Tower, a charming onetime-tallest building in the world. Liberty Plaza is almost welcome as an example of the death of an aesthetic: a dark, hulking stack of flanged beams, complete with sterile plaza. And so, alas, our Liberty Street sojourn ends on a negative note.

4 120 BROADWAY (former Equitable Building)

Between Pine and Cedar streets
1915, Ernest R. Graam

The Pan Am building of the teens was designed by the same man who, working for Daniel Burnam, designed the Flatiron Building (8.3), completed thirteen years before. The immense sheer-rise bulk of this building was directly responsible for the nation's first skyscraper zoning regulations, enacted the following year and leading to the setback form that dominated tall-building design in the 1920s and '30s (to be replaced by sheer-rise towers with plazas in the 1950s and '60s, and atrium buildings in the '70s and '80s).

5 195 BROADWAY (former AT&T Building)

Fulton and Dey streets
1922, Welles Bosworth

This is to the classical skyscraper what One Liberty Plaza, a block south on Broadway, is to the modern skyscraper: the end of the line. Where Liberty Plaza is the *reductio ad absurdum* of modernism, a mountain of the stacked flanged beams, so 195 Broadway is the *reductio ad absurdum* of the classical skyscraper: a mountain of fluted columns. Is it any judgment on the respective virtues of the two skyscraper modes that one *reductio ad absurdum*—195 Broadway—is so clearly preferable to the other? The best thing about 195 is its vast lobby, an almost surreal forest of columns.

6 ST. PAUL'S CHAPEL (Episcopal)

Broadway, between Fulton and Vesey streets
1764–68
Tower, 1794

St. Paul's survived the attacks of September 11, 2001. The chapel is directly across Church Street from the site of 5 World Trade Center. In the early hours and days of that dreadful mid-September, some of us were worried for old St. Paul's. It was inconceivable that this church, long dwarfed by the twin towers, could have escaped destruction. I thought that if it were to survive, that would be a sign—a sign that our city and nation would come out of this with their spirit intact. For this building was and is not merely a local landmark, but a structure of deep national significance.

St. Paul's went up in the 1760s, and originally faced toward the Hudson River. A couple of years later, a new portico facing busy Broadway was added. Today one enters by this portico, unexpectedly on the altar side of the church. In the 1790s, St. Paul's added a marvelous tower and steeple, modeled on the Choragic Monument of Lysicrates of fourth-century B.C. Athens. The church reflects eighteenth-century English taste, showing the influence of architect James Gibbs, whose St. Martin-in-the-Fields Church had risen at London's Trafalgar Square in the 1720s.

St. Paul's is a museum of American history of the Revolutionary and early Federal periods. On the Broadway porch is a fine marble memorial to Brigadier General Richard Montgomery, felled in the Battle of Quebec in 1775. The memorial's creator was Jean-Jacques Caffiéri, one of the leading French sculptors of the late eighteenth century; other works by this sculptor can be seen in the Metropolitan Museum of Art. Inside the chapel, one finds the pew, marked by a plaque, of congregant George Washington, who worshipped here when he lived in the city as our first president. Following his inauguration on April 30, 1789, at the old Federal Hall on Wall Street, Washington and his entourage attended a service at St. Paul's. On the wall beside Washington's pew is an oil painting that is the first known representation of the Great Seal of the United States. Scholars have attributed some of the altar decoration to Pierre L'Enfant, planner of Washington, D.C. This interior is a gem of American Georgian architecture, one of the scant few such treasures to be savored within the five boroughs.

St. Paul's is doubly a survivor. In another September, that of 1776, a fire consumed some 500 buildings (about a third of the city) in New York. The fire came close to but, miraculously, did not touch St. Paul's. (The first Trinity Church at Wall Street was not so lucky.) As George Washington's church, St. Paul's is a symbol of our Founding. It is also a symbol of what Mayor Bloomberg calls our city's "unbreakable spirit."

7 20 VESEY STREET

Between Church Street and Broadway
1906, Robert D. Kohn

Undeniably the most exuberant of the few genuine Art Nouveau buildings in New York. Why, in this city where Louis Comfort Tiffany earned such renown as one of the foremost Art Nouveau decorative artists, is there such a paucity of Art Nouveau architecture, and nothing even remotely to compare with Paris's Guimard or Brussels's Horta? This

6 *St. Paul' s Chapel*

building originally housed the offices of the *New York Evening Post,* the daily begun by Alexander Hamilton.

8 ST. PETER'S CHURCH (Roman Catholic)

22 Barclay Street, southeast corner of Church Street
1838, John R. Haggerty and Thomas Thomas

With the Federal Hall National Memorial (1.12), one of the city's two best Greek temple-style buildings. It is an ambitious design. The typical Greek Revival church of the day (e.g., Minard Lafever's St. James Roman Catholic Church of 1837 at 32 James Street, where it meets Madison Street) had a portico marked by a pair of Doric columns with flanking antae or pilasters where columns would otherwise be. By contrast, St. Peter's has a full-width, projecting portico with six massive, freestanding columns. It is one of only two remaining Manhattan churches with a full set of freestanding columns, the other being the former Village Community Church of 1846, by Samuel Thompson, on 13th Street between Sixth and Seventh avenues. The columns of St. Peter's support an undecorated entablature and low-angled pediment that has a central niche containing a statue of St. Peter holding the keys to heaven. The niche and statue are the only elements compromising a façade that is otherwise as austere as anything by Mies van der Rohe more than a century later.

St. Peter's and Federal Hall are New York's greatest monuments of the national style of the era of James Monroe, Andrew Jackson, Martin Van Buren, and John C. Calhoun, and of the first, albeit short-lived, crystallization of an American national character prior to the age of mass immigration and the explosive growth it engendered. Had it not been for that explosive growth, speculates V. S. Pritchett, "one would guess that New York would have gained lastingly in architecture, for the period, especially of the Greek Revival, was excellent for design, and had not yet run into the mania for the splendacious. The city would probably have had design and a center." Go to St. Peter's for a look at what New York was destined never to be.

9 WOOLWORTH BUILDING

233 Broadway, between Park Place and Barclay Street
1913, Cass Gilbert

The search for a skyscraper style inevitably led to the use of Gothic forms. The only soaring, high structures prior to the advent of the tall office building were Gothic church and cathedral spires. The first generation of skyscraper designers conceived of the tall office building more as a classical column. Perhaps the first of the soaring, Gothicized skyscrapers to appear in New York was Henry Ives Cobb's Liberty Tower (2.3C) of 1909. Four years later, Cass Gilbert lavished extraordinary attention to detail in the decoration and massing of what was for nearly three decades the tallest building in the world. The result is a spectacular spire of a tall office building, in which rich terra-cotta Gothic ornament brilliantly accentuates, rather than hides, the steel frame, and which soars to a crown, fifty-five stories over Broadway, modeled on the Butter Tower of Rouen Cathedral. The architectural historian Carl W. Condit puts it well:

9 *Woolworth Building*

> The Woolworth, in . . . its structural engineering, and its formal design, brought the skyscraper to a climax, and it is questionable whether it has ever been surpassed. The powerful vertical movement, the upward-rising hierarchy of volumes, and the aerial delicacy, all perfectly appropriate to the overall form, make the Woolworth . . . perhaps the most imaginative transmutation of Beaux-Arts principles in existence.

The compact lobby is unquestionably the richest small public space in New York. The marble, the gilt, the carving, and especially the stunning mosaics will transport you, like a concentrated infusion of some powerfully sublimating drug. The mosaics and stained glass are the creations of two unsung masters of decorative art in New York, Otto Heinigke and Owen Bowen.

10 CITY HALL

City Hall Park, between Broadway and Park Row
1803–12, Joseph Mangin and John McComb, Jr.

The most delicately balanced building in Manhattan. Also the best. The form is basically Louis XVI (who reigned 1774–92) with Georgian detail in the manner of William Chambers. It is an imaginative fusing of two traditions. No element dominates: each is in perfect harmony with all the others. At the same time, no element—the relaxed Ionic portico, the steady rhythm of the fenestration, the graceful cupola—gives away any of the strength of its superb crafting and modeling to any other. The result is a structure at once stately and symmetrical and light as air. It expresses our founders' conception of the role of government in the American democracy better than any other building in the nation: resolute, but not overbearing. The grandiose Capitol in Washington, D.C., does not even approach it in stating the nobler aspects of the American concept of government.

10 *City Hall*

11A *Cary Building*

11 CHAMBERS STREET

From Church Street to Centre Street

Speaking of Washington, D.C., this is the part of Manhattan that comes closest to looking like it might fit in that classical city. Moving east from Church Street, there is first, at the northwest corner of Church and Chambers streets, Gamaliel King's and John Kellum's **Cary Building** (1856), said by Margot Gayle to be the oldest cast-iron building in New York. No other cast-iron building is modeled in such a stonelike manner. Note particularly the rustication, and the heavy scrolled brackets supporting the cornice. At the northeast corner of Chambers Street is **280 Broadway,** the massive marble block that was originally A. T. Stewart's dry-goods emporium. Designed by Trench and Snook and erected in 1846, it was by all accounts the largest and most luxurious dry-goods store in America, and probably the world, when built, and paved the way for Stewart's store on Broadway at Astor Place, John Kellum's cast-iron masterpiece that some historians regard as the first true *department store* in the world. **Stewart's Chambers Street "Marble Palace"** was the center of fashionable Manhattan life in the years leading up to the Civil War. Indeed, it made fashionable life in Manhattan *public* to an extent and in a way it had never before been, serving to feminize, beautify, and civilize the city's rough-hewn business district, and leading to the coinage of the universally employed term "downtown" to describe the beautiful commercial heart of a city. (Stewart's was built in the same year as Trinity Church, (1.17). The latter exemplified an aesthetic of functional expressionism that would later become a central tenet of modernism, while the dry-goods store represented a new democratic spirituality, in the form of the fashion cycle, that would in many ways supplant traditional religion. It took fifty years before the functionalist

11[B] *Surrogate's Court*

architectural mode and the religion of the fashion cycle could be fused by Louis Sullivan in his Carson Pirie Scott department store in Chicago.)

The stately, neo-Renaissance, former **New York County Courthouse,** familiarly known as the **Tweed Courthouse** after Boss William Marcy Tweed, during whose corrupt reign it was built and for which it stands as symbol, at 52 Chambers Street (between Broadway and Centre Street), was designed by John Kellum (codesigner of the aforementioned Cary Building) and Leopold Eidlitz and erected from 1858 to 1878. Its historic association with the notorious Tweed has obscured its considerable architectural merit. When looking at this near-ruin, remember that at the time it was built, it was one of the most splendid buildings in Manhattan. This area, with A. T. Stewart's Marble Palace and this courthouse, possessed a grandeur quite new to New York in the Civil War era. The former **Emigrant Industrial Savings Bank Building,** now a city office building, at 51 Chambers Street between Broadway and Elk Street was designed by Raymond F. Almirall and built in 1912. This former home of America's onetime-largest savings bank is a Beaux-Arts building with some Art Nouveau touches.

The most splendid building in the Chambers Street group is the **Hall of Records** (aka **Surrogate's Court**) at 31 Chambers Street between Centre and Elk streets. It is one of the city's finest Beaux-Arts buildings. Designed by John R. Thomas and Horgan & Slattery, it was built from 1899 to 1911. Its most striking features are its eight fluted Corinthian columns, atop a base with three high, round-arched entrances flanked by sculptural groups; and its wealth of figurative sculpture by Philip Martiny and Henry Kirke Bush-Brown. The building exudes Frenchness in every detail, and the lobby and central hall are based on Charles Garnier's Paris Opera (completed in 1875)—this despite the fact that architect Thomas never, as Henry Hope Reed points out, visited Paris. There is a delicacy and a sureness of touch here that relate beautifully to the nearby, also very French City Hall. The row of figures by Martiny along the attic of the Chambers Street elevation depict great men from the history of New York City. From west to east: David Pietersen DeVries, Caleb Heathcote, DeWitt Clinton, Abram Hewitt, Philip Hone, Peter Stuyvesant, Cadwallader Colden, and James Duane. Flanking the Chambers Street entrance are Martiny's allegorical groups representing *New York in Revolutionary Times* (west) and *New York in Its Infancy* (east). Note especially the beautiful sculpting of the folds of fabric. Martiny is considered the premier architectural sculptor of his period.

12 MUNICIPAL BUILDING

Centre Street at Chambers Street
1914, William M. Kendall for McKim, Mead & White

Henry Hope Reed says this is "the nation's finest skyscraper." By contrast, the Federal Writers Project's *New York City Guide* of 1939, which exhibits a marked disdain for ornateness, opines: "It gains dignity through the bold treatment of the intermediate stories, despite the poorly related tower and the disturbing character of the Corinthian colonnade at the base. In themselves the elements are well designed, but their combination lacks unity." While I would not go so far as Reed, I do believe this is a superb building, that it possesses exactly the unity the Federal Writers Project accused it of lacking, and that there's nothing remotely disturbing

12 *Municipal Building*

13 *Brooklyn Bridge*

about the Corinthian colonnade at the base. The functional and site requirements were staggering, and the adaptation of the Imperial Roman mode to their solution is handled with a sureness possessed by only the most talented of architects. The most noteworthy thing about the building is its siting. It is to Chambers Street, that imperial side street, what the former New York Central Building once was to Park Avenue: the simultaneous provider of closure and continuance, the vista capper that is not also a traffic stopper. It is also a gigantic building that manages to bow to its littler neighbors, genially embracing Chambers Street and politely backing off from City Hall. Meanwhile, its top, featuring a Corinthian drum adapted from the Choragic Monument of Lysicrates (Athens, 334 B.C.) surmounted by Adolph Weinman's twenty-foot-high statue of *Civic Fame*, flood-lit at night, stands unobstructed when viewed from Brooklyn, proclaiming that this indeed is the Empire City.

13 BROOKLYN BRIDGE

1867–83, John A. and Washington Roebling

What is there to say about the Brooklyn Bridge that has not already been said? It is a surpassingly beautiful structure. The best places from which to view it are Pier 17 in the South Street Seaport, the promenade in Brooklyn Heights, and a car on the Manhattan Bridge. It can, of course, be walked across. This is in all ways one of the finest sensory experiences in New York. The sweeping vistas alternate with the enveloping weblike cables to please the eye. River breezes and gentle vibration provide tactile stimulation. The Doppler effect of the passing cars is soothing meditative music. Just watch out for the bicyclists, who here, as elsewhere throughout Manhattan, behave as though they own the city.

14 POLICE HEADQUARTERS

Bounded by Park Row, Pearl Street,
and the Avenue of the Finest(!)
1973, Gruzen & Partners
M. Paul Friedberg, landscape architect

Once through the arch of the Municipal Building, Chambers Street becomes Police Plaza, a landscaped formal approach across a broad pedestrian plaza to the headquarters of the New York City Police Department, a red-brick grid overhanging a glassy base. This is functional expressionism: the upper stories are bureaucrats' offices, while at plaza level are the spaces used by the public, hence the gradation from the dense thicket of office cells down to the airy and welcoming base. That's the theory, at least. Though this is a well-detailed and generally praised work of modern architecture, it suffers mightily in comparison with the old police headquarters (2.18) (now called the Police Building) on Centre Street, which was a jolly Beaux-Arts confection reflecting the essentially benign nature of the police in a democratic society. Now the police are just another corps of bureaucrats suffering from carpal tunnel syndrome. The plaza here is dominated by structures designed by the Gruzen firm, which seems to have been remarkably adept at garnering major civic commissions.

To the north of Police Headquarters is the United States Courthouse addition, on Park Row between Police Plaza and Pearl Street, designed by Gruzen & Partners and built in 1975. **St. Andrew's Roman Catholic**

15A *New York County Courthouse*

Church (1939, Maginnis & Walsh and Robert J. Reiley), fronting on St. Andrew's Plaza (Duane Street) between Centre Street and Park Row, is sandwiched between the addition and Cass Gilbert's United States Courthouse on Foley Square. To the south of Police Headquarters, on the southeast corner of the Avenue of the Finest (that's right, *Avenue of the Finest*) and Madison Street, is the **Murray Bergtraum High School for Business Careers** (1976) by Gruzen & Partners. To the east of Police Headquarters are Chatham Green and Chatham Terrace (2.16).

15 NEW YORK COUNTY COURTHOUSE

60 Centre Street, between Pearl and Worth streets
1926, Guy Lowell

UNITED STATES COURTHOUSE

40 Centre Street, southeast corner of Pearl Street
1936, Cass Gilbert

Chambers Street culminates in the Municipal Building, at which point the imperial procession takes a left turn to head north on Centre Street. Two massive classical buildings front on an open space called Foley Square, near the site of the infamous Five Points, once the most dangerous precinct of Manhattan. It is therefore fitting that these massive classical buildings should be courthouses! The United States Courthouse is the work of the man who designed the Woolworth Building some twenty-three years earlier, though this is hard to believe. One of the stunning virtues of the earlier building was the unity Gilbert's use of Gothic ornament brought to the massing of what was then the tallest building in the world. The courthouse is a rather stolid Corinthian temple with an equally stolid neoclassical tower set atop it. Absolutely no attempt has been made to relate base to tower. Perhaps Gilbert was thinking that in New York, bases and towers live in different contexts since they are never viewed in unison; thus, the temple base, as a low, Washington, D.C.-style classical building, would relate to the street, and the tower would relate to the Lower Manhattan skyline. While this is true for tight streets, the theory has no application in the case of a building fronting an open space like Foley Square. At any rate, the gold pyramidal top of the tower is a congenial presence indeed on the skyline.

15B *U. S. Courthouse*

Much better is the New York County Courthouse, which was designed in 1913, though not built for another fourteen years. To the passerby in Foley Square, the courthouse appears as a massive, but very crisp and unusually handsome, Corinthian portico. But from the upper stories of surrounding buildings, or from Manhattan's observation decks, it is clear that dynamically appended to the three-column-deep projecting portico is a gigantic hexagonal building, the solution to an irregular site and a complex design program. This is yet another of this city's numerous examples of the infinite flexibility of the classical language of architecture, which makes it the language *par excellence* for the dense urban setting.

16 CHATHAM TOWERS

170 Park Row, between Park Row and Worth Street
1965, Kelly & Gruzen

CHATHAM GREEN

185 Park Row, between Pearl Street and St. James Place
1961, Kelly & Gruzen

Through the arch of the Municipal Building, on axis with Chambers Street, and beginning with Police Plaza, is, courtesy of Kelly & Gruzen and its successor firm of Gruzen & Partners, perhaps the most aesthetically ambitious unified assemblage of high-modern buildings in the city: Chandigarh-on-the-Hudson. Both Chatham Towers and Green are subsidized middle-income housing on the edge of Chinatown. The Towers, of which there are two, are unrepentant concrete slabs with balconies chiseled out of them. These are boldly ugly buildings that carry a conviction that makes them almost quaint period pieces. The Green is equally assertive, an undulating Great Wall of Chinatown.

17 MANHATTAN BRIDGE

Between Canal Street and the Bowery
1904–09, Carrère & Hastings and Leon Morsieff
Arch and colonnades: 1912, Carrère & Hastings

Clearly this is not the great work of art that the Brooklyn Bridge is, but it is a wonderful structure in its own right. For one thing, it is hard for any long suspension bridge not to be beautiful. But here there is fancifully sculptured steel in the idiom that also included the waiting room of the late Pennsylvania Station. A source for the design of the Manhattan Bridge, with its exposed trusswork and massive brackets, seems to have been the French neo-Gothicist Viollet-le-Duc. We move from Viollet-le-Duc's nineteenth century to the seventeenth century with Carrère & Hastings's triumphal arch, reminiscent of Nicolas-Francois Blondel's Porte Saint-Denis (begun in 1672) in Paris's tenth arrondissement, and colonnades which recall the ones Bernini designed for St. Peter's in Rome (completed in 1667).

18 POLICE BUILDING (former New York City Police Headquarters)

240 Centre Street between Grand and Broome streets
1909, Hoppin & Koen

Another monumental Beaux-Arts building tucked into a tight, complicated site. This is as grand as most state capitols, yet not till one comes

18 *Old New York City Police Headquarters*

right up to it does one see it, and the effect is instant and awesome. The street façade starts with a rusticated base, leading to a heavily modeled composition featuring fluted Corinthian columns surmounted by a massive pediment. The building is topped by a columned drum with a high dome.

19 BOWERY SAVINGS BANK

130 Bowery, between Grand and Broome streets
1894, McKim, Mead & White

Like the Police Building (2.18), this bank is an example of the way Manhattan, ever restless in the Uptown chase of fashion, is studded with magnificent buildings in the least-likely settings. Here, on one of the tawdriest stretches of road in town, is one of the city's truly palatial bank buildings. A glorious Renaissance façade, dominated by four massive, fluted Corinthian columns, is topped by one of the loveliest pediments in New York, in which a clock is flanked by female figures and lions in deep relief by Frederick MacMonnies.

19 *Bowery Savings Bank*

20 *Puck Building*

20 PUCK BUILDING

295–307 Lafayette Street, between Jersey and Houston streets
1886, 1893, Albert Wagner

This huge, robust, red-brick building owes much to the Richardsonian Romanesque. Its landmark status derives chiefly from its sheer visibility on wide, open Houston Street, dominating the east view from the heavily trafficked intersection of Broadway and Houston. It says a lot for the building that it holds up under such intense exposure, though such siting should never really have been demanded. Where this building does its best work is on its east side, on Mulberry Street, where it creates one of those romantically overbearing, tight-street walls which we visit the ruins of old towns from the Industrial Revolution to experience.

21 *Eldridge Street Synagogue*

21 ELDRIDGE STREET SYNAGOGUE

12–16 Eldridge Street, between Forsyth and Canal streets
1887, Herter Brothers

In this, the largest Jewish city on earth, one might expect to find many beautiful synagogues. This is one of the most beautiful. Again, grandeur amidst the ordinary. In this case, a flamboyantly eclectic façade, featuring Moorish, Romanesque, and Gothic elements, towers over a street of typical Lower East Side tenements. This is the oldest synagogue in the United States built by eastern European Jews, and one of the few deliberately constructed synagogues on the Lower East Side.

22 EAST BROADWAY

From Rutgers Street to Grand Street

This is the heart of the old Jewish Lower East Side. At number 175, between Rutgers and Jefferson streets, is the former **Forward Building,** which has become, in the course of ethnic succession, the New York Ling Liang Church. The *Forward* was the daily newspaper that was the intellectual epicenter of the Yiddish-speaking world, and this building, though of no great architectural import, harbors in its Beaux-Arts recesses the ghosts of a vanished culture. In its heyday, the Forward Building, which at ten stories towers above its neighbors, was topped with two neon signs proclaiming the paper's name: one faced the Manhattan Bridge and was in English; the other faced East Broadway and was in Yiddish.

Three-acre **Seward Park,** between Canal and Essex streets, was created in 1900 on the site of two blocks of tenements to bring a little light and air to the pestilential Lower East Side. Today the small park is chiefly notable as the site of a Sunday flea market, in which the goods purveyed by the elderly Jewish merchants are about as far from chic as you can get. The Art Deco **Seward Park Recreation Building** was built in 1939. **The Seward Park Branch of the New York Public Library** at

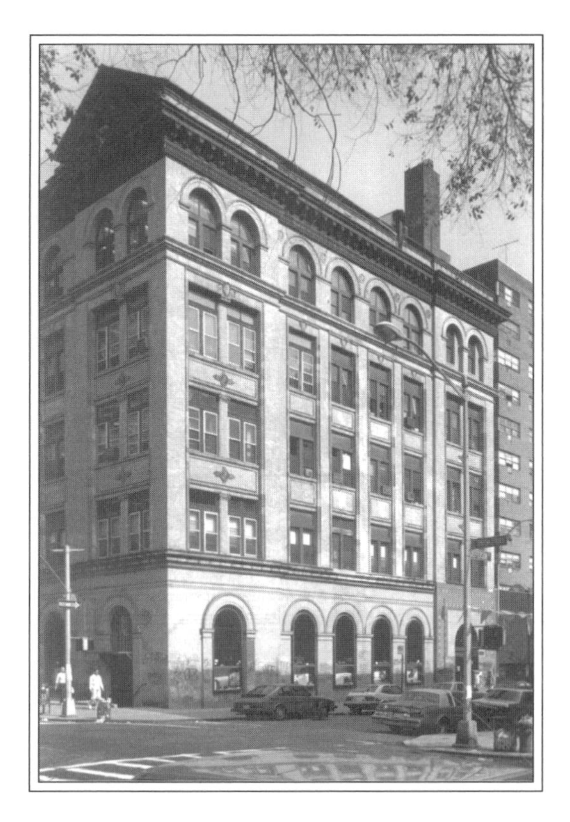

22 *Educational Alliance*

number 192, opposite Jefferson Street, is a lovely, small Beaux Arts structure designed by Babb, Cook & Welch and built in 1909. Original plans called for the roof to be used as an outdoor reading area, although this never came to pass. **The Educational Alliance** at number 197, at the southeast corner of Jefferson Street, designed by Brunner & Tryon, is a neo-Romanesque structure built in 1891 to house America's first settlement house, organized by German Jews to help assimilate their eastern European brethren. Another Art Deco structure, this one freely incorporating the Moorish elements that have achieved something of the status of traditional Jewish-American design, is the **Bialystoker Home for the Aged,** built in 1930 at number 228, east of Clinton Street.

Take a bit of a detour one block south of East Broadway to numbers 263 to 267 Henry Street, between Montgomery and Gouverneur streets, to see one of the architecturally most noteworthy groups of buildings on the Lower East Side: the **Henry Street Settlement,** a fine row of Greek Revival town houses, built from 1827 to 1834, and comparable in quality to the celebrated houses on Washington Square North (5.3). The Henry Street Settlement, like the Educational Alliance, was an early pioneer in the settlement-house movement.

Chapter 3
From The Battery to TriBeCa

1 DOWNTOWN ATHLETIC CLUB

21 West Street, southeast corner of Morris Street
1926, Starrett and Van Vleck

One of the city's most exuberant Art Deco piles, and one of the stars of Rem Koolhaas's *Delirious New York*. A polychromatic extravaganza of glazed tile. The best place from which to view it is South Cove in Battery Park City, with that exotic pocket of foliage providing the ideal forecourt to an equally exotic building.

2 BATTERY PARK CITY

Bounded by Battery Park on the south, Chambers Street on the north, West Street on the east, and the Hudson River on the west
Master plan: 1983–90, Cooper, Eckstut Associates

Battery Park City, built on a ninety-two-acre landfill created with the earth displaced by the excavation for the World Trade Center, is one of the most significant architectural and planning projects of the 1980s anywhere in the world, as well as one of the most monumental coordinated developments in Manhattan history. The master plan by Alexander Cooper and Stanton Eckstut signals a decisive break with the Corbusian superblock, which had dominated large-scale development in America since World War II. Instead, Battery Park City is conceived as an extension of lower Manhattan, the new streets made continuous with the old. The

3[B] *Winter Garden, World Financial Center*

residential sections are modeled on classic New York enclaves such as Gramercy Park and Tudor City, now thought preferable to Le Corbusier. Stanton Eckstut created design guidelines for the residential sections, ensuring a uniform commitment to the street line and traditional materials. The individual apartment buildings and town houses were designed by a number of prestigious architects, including James Stewart Polshek & Partners; Gruzen Samton Steinglass; Ulrich Franzen; Charles Moore; Mitchell/Giurgola; Conklin and Rossant; and Davis, Brody & Associates.

The first thing to do when visiting Battery Park City is to walk the length of the splendid two-mile-long Esplanade designed by Eckstut. On one side is the mighty Hudson, with outstanding views of the Statue of Liberty, Ellis Island, and the heavily developed Jersey City riverfront. On the other side are the apartments of Battery Park City and, looming behind them, the majestic Lower Manhattan skyline. The Esplanade's railings, lamps, and benches are of a traditional design, contributing to one of the most pleasant enclaves in Manhattan. Of particular note among the buildings are: **Liberty House** at 377 Rector Place at the northeast corner of the Esplanade, designed by James Stewart Polshek & Partners and completed in 1986, which in its detailing and in the manner in which it turns the corner is quite explicitly inspired by the apartment buildings of Riverside Drive (19.4); **Parc Place** at 225 Rector Place at the northeast corner of South End Avenue, designed by Gruzen Samton Steinglass and completed in 1986, which would hardly be out of place on, say, West End Avenue; and **Hudson Tower** at 350 Albany Street at the southeast corner of the Esplanade, by Davis, Brody & Associates, yet a third 1986 offering, which combines nineteenth-century oriels with 1930s corner windows by way of maximizing harbor views and sunlight. The Esplanade culminates at its southern end with the bizarre, enchanting South Cove Park, designed by Mary Miss, the British conceptual artist, with Stanton Eckstut and landscape architect Susan Child. My guess is that it is Ms. Child to whom our hats should be tipped here, for it could not have been easy to translate Mary Miss's kooky concepts into actual plots of thriving exotic foliage. From here the view of the lower Manhattan skyline is breathtaking. Indeed, what has been created is nothing less than a downtown equivalent of the classic view of the midtown skyline from the Sheep Meadow in Central Park.

3 ONE WORLD FINANCIAL CENTER (Dow Jones Building)

West Street, opposite Cedar Street
1985, Cesar Pelli

TWO WORLD FINANCIAL CENTER (Merrill Lynch World Headquarters, south building)

West Street, between Liberty and Vesey streets
1987, Cesar Pelli

THREE WORLD FINANCIAL CENTER (American Express Headquarters)

West Street, southwest corner of Vesey Street
1985, Cesar Pelli

FOUR WORLD FINANCIAL CENTER (Merrill Lynch World Headquarters, north building)

Vesey Street, southeast corner of North End Avenue
1986, Cesar Pelli

WINTER GARDEN

Between Two and Three World Financial Center
1988, Cesar Pelli, M. Paul Friedberg & Partners

The World Financial Center is the office component of Battery Park City. There are four buildings, ranging in height from thirty-four to fifty-one stories and totaling about six million square feet of space. The design guidelines were the work of Alexander Cooper. Just as residential Battery Park City attempts to evoke the best of past New York, so, too, in their way, do these office towers. As is so often the case nowadays, however, the attempt to recapture the past is betrayed by the insubstantiality and brittleness of flush granite veneers. Pelli hardly compensates with his simplistic tops, which have unfortunately become a conspicuous element on the lower Manhattan skyline.

If the exteriors of these buildings fail to deliver, though, the interiors are far more successful. Pelli establishes a sense of luxurious enclosure very close to that of the classicizing skyscraper lobbies of yore. There is within these four towers a vast extent of pedestrian public space, the design of which eschews the conventional modern atrium form as surely as the residential sections of Battery Park City eschew the Corbusian superblock. Though the pathways are lined with shops, there is not a hint of the shopping mall, but rather richly appointed office-building passages in which office workers and shoppers are not separated from each other, a type of design very reminiscent of Rockefeller Center. The principal public space, of course, is the vast Winter Garden, which functions not as a shopping mall, but as an auditorium for excellent free concerts and an exhibition space for events like the Orchid Show. The Winter Garden is 200 feet long, 120 feet wide, and 125 feet high (the concourse of Grand Central Terminal is the same exact width and height, though it is 175 feet longer). Trinity Church (1.17), minus its tower, would fit comfortably inside it.

4 5 6 WORLD TRADE CENTER

Bounded by Church, West, Liberty, and Vesey streets
1, 2, 4, 5, and 6 WTC, 1966–77, Minoru Yamasaki & Associates and Emery Roth & Sons
3 WTC, 1981, Skidmore, Owings & Merrill
7 WTC, 1987, Emery Roth & Sons

The seven World Trade Center buildings no longer stand. Fifty thousand people worked in the Center's ten million square feet of office space. In the first edition of this book, I was heavily critical of the Center. When the attacks occurred on September 11, 2001, I immediately felt I should not have said so many nasty things about the Center as I had. In the ensuing months, however, I realized that criticism of the Center's architecture had nothing to do with profound grief over the loss of so many lives. At this writing, it is yet uncertain what will rise on the site. It is therefore well that we should reflect on the architectural and urbanistic shortcomings of the World Trade Center, lest we not build something better.

When built, the twin towers were 110 stories (1,350 feet), the tallest buildings in the world. They rose from a "superblock" around an immense windswept plaza. A vast underground concourse, with much the feeling of an airport terminal, contained stores and fast-food eateries. I felt the towers were an arrogant intrusion into the jagged splendor of the lower Manhattan skyline. The best thing about the view from the observation decks of Two World Trade Center was that they were the only high vantage points in New York from which the World Trade Center itself was not visible.

Many sensitive New Yorkers share the sentiments I have just expressed. The World Trade Center represented everything that was wrong with city rebuilding in the 1960s and '70s. Yet how I wish it were still there.

Note should be made here that, given the enormousness of the devastation, the surrounding buildings were remarkably unscathed in general, a testament to the manner in which architects and engineers designed the towers to implode rather than topple sideways in the event of such a catastrophe as befell them. The Winter Garden of the World Financial Center sustained heavy damage but, at this writing, is scheduled soon to reopen. Two great landmarks of New York architecture—Cass Gilbert's gorgeous West Street Building, built in 1906–7 between Albany and Cedar streets, and McKenzie, Voorhees & Gmelin's New York

7 *New York Telephone Company Building*

Telephone Building, built in 1923–27 on West Street between Barclay and Vesey streets—were severely damaged on 9/11 but are being restored.

7 New York Telephone Building

140 West Street, between Barclay and Vesey streets
1923–27, McKenzie, Voorhees & Gmelin

An epoch-making building, along with Ely Jacques Kahn's Two Park Avenue (9, 10). Kahn and Ralph Walker, a designer for McKenzie, Voorhees & Gmelin, were the first architects to use Art Deco ornament to define the new skyscraper form envisioned in the drawings Hugh Ferriss did in response to the 1916 zoning law. There is an integration of massing and ornament that is a brilliantly imaginative updating of Louis

Sullivan's organicism (e.g., the Bayard building, 6.2). One need only compare this building to the post–World War II ziggurats on Park Avenue to realize how deeply massing relies on style.

8 Public School 234

Greenwich Street, between Warren and Chambers streets
1988, Richard Dattner

A recent public elementary-school building with fanciful, playful design elements—in particular, that fence—intended to appeal to children, and a thoroughly unintimidating polychromed brick softness. Not only is this a good design for kids, but with the neighboring Washington Market Park, it is a necessary injection of modesty and whimsy close to outscaled and cold, cold Independence Plaza. Would that our postmodern office buildings were this well designed.

8 *Public School 234*

9 *Washington Market Park*

9 WASHINGTON MARKET PARK

Greenwich Street, from Chambers Street to Duane Street
1983, Weintraub & di Domenico

A block-square, romantic, postmodern park by New York's most acclaimed landscape designers of recent years. Carter Wiseman calls it "an urban oasis as precious as any Sahara waterhole." The most striking element is the white gazebo/bandstand, a boldly homely touch at the feet of the hulking Independence Plaza apartment towers that might not have worked were it not for Weintraub & di Domenico's positively Olmstedian skill at creating a park that packs a wallop to match the city around it. In the extraordinary skill with which the designers have seamlessly incorporated a variety of landscapes into this compact space, this is, quite simply, as good an example of modern small-park design as you will find in the world.

10 HARRISON STREET ROW

Southwest corner of Greenwich Street
1796–1828
Partly relocated and restored in 1975

A prize row of Federal town houses, saved from the urban renewal that destroyed the old Washington Market and wrought Independence Plaza. In order to be saved, some of the houses had to be moved a bit, so these late eighteenth- and early nineteenth-century houses never existed as a row until 1975. They are perhaps a tad overrestored, and give no sense of the historic griminess this neighborhood possessed in its pre–urban renewal days—as indicated by the fact that these houses were converted to produce-market buildings prior to their reconversion to elegant dwellings. They are even more out of place in the shadow of Independence Plaza than is Washington Market Park.

11 SHEARSON LEHMAN PLAZA

390 Greenwich Street, southwest corner of Hubert Street
1986, Skidmore, Owings & Merrill
388 Greenwich Street, northwest corner of North Moore Street
1989, Kohn Pedersen Fox

The tower by Kohn Pedersen Fox is 1.5 million square feet in thirty-nine stories. The smaller building by Skidmore, Owings & Merrill is 750,000 square feet in nine stories. The Kohn Pedersen Fox is superscaled post-modern, and looms over TriBeCa with unwieldy bulk. The Skidmore, Owings & Merrill is a slickly detailed box.

12 Former NEW YORK MERCANTILE EXCHANGE

6 Harrison Street, northwest corner of Hudson Street
1884, Thomas R. Jackson

Originally called the Butter and Cheese Exchange, the New York Mercantile Exchange was twelve years old when it built its new home on Harrison Street. The exchange remained here until 1977, when it moved to the World Trade Center. This robust, red-brick-and-granite, Queen Anne building is not only among the city's romantic delights, but, like the Dakota (16.12) apartments, built in the same year, it is uncommonly tightly controlled for such an exuberantly picturesque building. (Compare

11 *Shearson Lehman Plaza*

the Jefferson Market Courthouse (5.9), of seven years earlier.) While most of TriBeCa impresses not with individual buildings, but with the overall effect of streets lined with massy romantic buildings, the Mercantile Exchange is well worth seeking out on its own. There is no better building in this idiom in New York.

13 DUANE PARK

Duane Street, between Greenwich and Hudson streets

This is a small triangular open space set in the middle of Duane Street and cozily enclosed by typically TriBeCan rough, but sentimental, loft buildings. It is one of the most comfortable spots on the island. The buildings were originally produce warehouses connected with the nearby Washington Market. While it is the general effect that most matters here, special note should be taken of 165 Duane Street at the northwest corner of Hudson Street, an eleven-story red-brick warehouse designed by Stephen D. Hatch and erected in 1880, a fine example of Romanesque

Revival commercial architecture. With its bottom-heavy piers and deeply recessed windows, perhaps no other building in town shouts 1880 quite so loudly. 168 Duane Street, just west of Hudson Street, is an 1886 building by Hatch, this time in a more fanciful, not nearly so robust Flemish mode. 173 Duane Street, between Greenwich and Staple streets, designed by Babb & Cook and built in 1879, is a severe and very handsome Romanesque Revival warehouse, and is said to be one of the first Romanesque Revival commercial buildings in New York. Since Hudson Street runs on a diagonal, the vista north from Duane Park is closed a block away by the Western Union Building at 60 Hudson Street between Thomas and Worth streets, a massive, but carefully sculptured, black Art Deco pile designed by Ralph Walker and dating from 1930. From every direction in Duane Park, there is just the right sense of enclosure. The architects of Battery Park City could only dream of coming up with something this good.

12 *Former New York Mercantile Exchange*

CHAPTER 4

SoHo

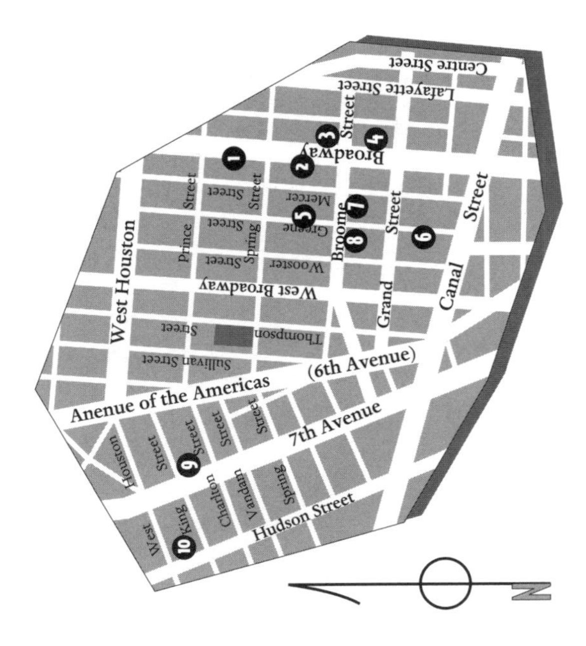

1 *Little Singer Building*

Chapter 4

SoHo

SoHo is so-called because it is the area SOuth of HOuston Street. It is roughly bounded by Houston on the north, Canal Street on the south, Broadway on the east, and Sixth Avenue on the west. SoHo is one of all-too-few areas of Manhattan that are more notable for their whole than their parts. I believe it is the most beautiful commercial district in New York, if not in all America. The peculiar beauty of the streets of SoHo comes from the area's profusion of loft buildings, dating from the last fifty years of the nineteenth century. Enough of these buildings are fronted in ornamental cast iron to allow the incontestable claim that this is the world's preeminent showcase of cast-iron architecture. What sets these buildings majestically apart is their combination of beautiful neo-Renaissance details with an unprecedented glassiness made possible by the new technology of cast iron. While in many cases the cast-iron details were rendered as stonelike as possible, it is nonetheless clear that, given the unprecedentedly broad expanses of glass, these details could not possibly be stone. There is something thrilling in this unusual juxtaposition of traditional classical detailing with a protomodern use of voids. Not until postmodernism did we begin to get anything like this again, and it was nowhere near so good, because the details were never as fully modeled or as sincere. The cast-iron-fronted commercial palazzo so amply represented in SoHo ranks just behind the Federal row house as the best vernacular style New York has ever had.

SoHo should be experienced as a whole, but here are a few buildings worth seeking out on their own:

1 LITTLE SINGER BUILDING

561 Broadway, between Prince and Spring streets
1904, Ernest Flagg

This fanciful *wrought*-iron façade is very much in the mode of the Parisian architecture of its day, which was heavily influenced by Viollet-le-Duc. It has a great deal in common with Carrère & Hastings and Leon Morsieff's Manhattan Bridge (2.17), built one year later, and even more with Flagg's Scribner Bookstore (13.5), built nine years later. This is called the *Little* Singer Building to distinguish it from Flagg's Singer Tower (1908), once the world's tallest building, which was demolished to make way for Skidmore, Owings & Merrill's hideous One Liberty Plaza (2.3F).

2 NEW ERA BUILDING

491 Broadway, between Spring and Broome streets
1897, Buchman & Deisler

With Robert D. Kohn's 1906 former Evening Post Building at 20 Vesey Street (2.7), Kohn's 1910 New York Society for Ethical Culture (16.2), and Raymond F. Almirall's 1912 former Emigrant Savings Bank on Chambers Street (2.11), the New Era is one of this city's few exercises in Art Nouveau architecture. Since it predates the earliest of the three other buildings by nine years, I reckon it is the oldest extant Art Nouveau building in Manhattan. The *très* Parisian, verdigris copper mansard is one of the highlights of SoHo.

3 HAUGHWOUT BUILDING

488 Broadway, northeast corner of Broome Street
1857, J. P. Gaynor

There are days when I feel this is the most beautiful building in Manhattan. No neo-Renaissance structure in the city, whether of stone or cast iron, is better proportioned or statelier than this. The basic window unit, in which an arch is set atop Corinthian colonnettes, flanked by Corinthian columns, is repeated ninety-two times on the Broadway and Broome Street façades, creating a tight, compressed, supremely powerful rhythm few façades anywhere can match. The precedents would seem to be Venetian, and it is interesting to compare the Haughwout with Stanford White's magnificent former Tiffany Building (9.6), built forty-nine years

2 *New Era Building*

later at Fifth Avenue and 37th Street. The façades have recently been restored to their original light color, after decades in which they were black and grimy, making the building look more like a factory than the elegant store it once was.

4 ROOSEVELT BUILDING

478–482 Broadway, between Broome and Grand streets
1874, Richard Morris Hunt

Seventeen years after the Haughwout, and twenty-one years before Hunt started on the Metropolitan Museum of Art. Cast iron, but much glassier than the Haughwout, with slender colonnettes within wide bays, framed by high Ionic columns. Around this time, cast-iron design began to open up the façade, prefiguring the glass curtain wall. The results, as here, were often beguiling.

3 *Haughwout Building*

5 72–76 GREENE STREET

Between Broome and Spring streets
1873, Isaac F. Duckworth

Greene Street from Canal to Houston streets is the area with the densest concentration of cast-iron façades in the neighborhood with the city's—and the world's—densest concentration of cast-iron façades. This building is known as the "King of Greene Street," and it is easy to see why, with its imposing, projecting central section, in which each of five floors has its own set of four fully modeled Corinthian columns in a strong *A-B-B-A* sequence, supporting a heavy cornice.

6 28–30 GREENE STREET

Between Canal and Grand streets
1872, Isaac F. Duckworth

If Duckworth's numbers 72–76 (4–5) are the "King of Greene Street," this must be the queen. SoHo's north-south streets (Mercer, Greene, and Wooster) are narrow, but that did not stop Duckworth from pushing the limits of side-street monumentality. Here, as above, is a bold projecting central section, this time culminating in a voluptuous mansard. The mansard is an explosion of ornament atop a very clean, airy façade, with widely spaced columns featuring Corinthian capitals stripped of their foliage.

7 453–55 BROOME STREET

Between Mercer and Greene streets
1873, Griffith Thomas

A powerful façade in which single high-windowed bays, flanked by heavy rusticated piers, frame rows of four similar bays separated by slender Corinthian colonnettes. The heavy outer bays and the airy inner ones combine to create a very appealing dual sense of stability and lightness.

8 469–75 BROOME STREET

Southwest corner of Greene Street
1873, Griffith Thomas

It does not quite have the sheer vitality of Louis Sullivan's Carson Pirie Scott store in Chicago, but it is well along the same path. Remarkably open façades flare out from a magnificent glazed-and-rounded corner, framed by rusticated piers. With only a few adjustments, this building would have been thoroughly modern. One of the most exciting buildings in SoHo.

9 CHARLTON, KING, and VANDAM STREETS

From Varick Street to Sixth Avenue

These streets boast some of the loveliest town houses in the city, all from that glorious age of Federal design when ugliness seems momentarily to have vanished from these parts. The earliest houses here date from the 1820s, when the Village was first developed. A few date from the 1840s. These façades are very simple and very similar to each other. But the glory of this style is that it possessed qualities—warm red brick, fine proportions, classical details, reticence, and, yes, charm—that not only prevented such replication from becoming boring, but actually made it desirable, since solid rows of these houses made for some of the most congenial streets in urban history. This was an age not of masterpieces, but of the most elegant vernacular New York has ever seen.

8 *469–75 Broome Street*

10 375 HUDSON STREET

Between King and Houston streets
1987, Fox & Fowle

This is a district of massive, handsome, utilitarian printing plants. It was a bit of a surprise when Saatchi and Saatchi, the huge international ad agency, decided to build its new headquarters down here. Fox & Fowle drew inspiration from Chelsea's Starrett-Lehigh Building (7.5), an enormous, early modern loft structure from 1931. The result is an entirely apposite modern building for its setting. The silvery-sleek façade manages both to refrain from upstaging its neighbors and create a strong presence for itself. There is perhaps nowhere else in the city where this design would have worked, but then that's what architecture is all about. Another recent building inspired by the Starrett-Lehigh is Davis, Brody's Copley (15.4) apartments, built the same year as 375 Hudson, at Broadway and 68th Street.

CHAPTER 5

Greenwich Village

5 *Elmer Holmes Bobst Library*

Chapter 5

Greenwich Village

1 WASHINGTON COURT (apartments)

Sixth Avenue, between Waverly and Washington places
1986, James Stewart Polshek & Partners

One of the good things about postmodernism was that it gave architects the green light to design contextually sensitive buildings, using traditional materials and unafraid of traditional forms and details. It is not too hard to imagine what a large apartment building on this site would have looked like if it had been built in 1966 or 1976 and not 1986. But by 1986, a modern architect like Polshek could quite unabashedly design a building that in form, scale, materials, and details bows to the Federal red-brick tradition of Greenwich Village architecture. This completely satisfying building is the *only* decent post-World War II structure on Sixth Avenue in the Village, which otherwise is a tawdry street dominated by modern "taxpayers" (one- to two-story buildings), tourist-trap shops and restaurants, and garish signage. Sixth Avenue from 8th street to 3rd street has lately taken on the appearance of a West Indian street side bazaar, such as one imagines might exist in the slums of Kingston or Port-au-Prince. Surprisingly, the major portion of the merchandise for sale is books, some stolen, some not, along with porno magazines, comic books, and Africanish craft objects. The sidewalks here are always congested with idlers, panhandlers, tourists, and dissolute teens. Enormous radios blaring rap and reggae dominate the aural environment. Underground, the West 4th Street subway station is a fair approximation of hades.

2 WASHINGTON SQUARE PARK

Bounded by Waverly Place, 4th Street, University Place, and MacDougal Street
Redesigned 1971; Robert Nichols, landscape architect

WASHINGTON MEMORIAL ARCH

Fifth Avenue and Waverly Place
1892, McKim, Mead & White

There are many reasons to disparage Washington Square Park. It attracts the motliest assortment of characters of any open space in Manhattan—drug dealers, street performers, runaway teens, aging hippies, NYU students, bridge-and-tunnel teenyboppers, and the all-too-ubiquitous homeless—all up to God knows what. Many people who do not belong to these groups therefore shun the park as unsavory. Every time the cleanup of Times Square is mentioned, someone says that all the vice concentrated there will simply make a new home for itself here in the environs of Washington Square Park. And then there are those who hate the design of the place. As a park, it is conspicuously lacking in greenery and rather dominated by concrete. Some say it is too large to be a proper square, yet too small to be an effective park.

One thing, however, is certain. Despite its varied and well-documented shortcomings, people continue to flock to this open space. Despite the presence of all the unsavory characters, it remains a fairly safe place. There is remarkably little spillover of its vice or even of its teenybopper activity into elegant lower Fifth Avenue and its even more elegant side streets. And as a spot for people watching, this park is well-nigh without peer. What other small neighborhood open space attracts so many people not only from out of the neighborhood, but also from out of the borough? There is also a generally high quality among the street performers here, for the concentration of people in this park makes it one of the city's best public showcases.

The one undeniably fine architectural element in the park is the seventy-seven-foot-high marble arch designed by Stanford White at the very foot of Fifth Avenue. The arch is a superb work of classical design, notable for the absence of any order. The pier sculptures were added later. The east pier bears Hermon A. MacNeil's sculpture of George Washington as general; it was completed in 1916. The west pier depicts

Alexander Stirling Calder's Washington as president; it was completed in 1918. It is interesting to compare these marble sculptures with Manhattan's great bronze Washingtons: John Quincy Adams Ward's statue (1883) at the Federal Hall National Memorial (1.12), and Henry Kirke Brown's equestrian image (1855) in Union Square Park (8.1). The arch itself is one of two freestanding triumphal arches in Manhattan, the other being Carrère & Hastings's entrance (1905) to the Manhattan Bridge (2.17).

3 WASHINGTON SQUARE NORTH

Waverly Place, from University Place to MacDougal Street

Numbers 1 to 13, between Fifth Avenue and University Place, date from 1832–33 (except for **number 3,** which dates from 1884), just a few years after the earliest houses in the Charlton-King-Vandam group (4.9). Here the style is somewhat more elaborate, but equally beautiful, Greek Revival. Note that these houses are contemporary with such landmark Greek Revival structures as the Federal Hall National Memorial (1.12) and St. Peter's Roman Catholic Church (2.8). **Numbers 19 to 26,** between Fifth Avenue and MacDougal Street, date from 1836–39, except for **number 20,** which dates from 1829 (with its façade altered in 1880 by Henry J. Hardenbergh). The Sloper residence in Henry James's *Washington Square* (1881) was modeled on the home of James's grandmother at number 18, demolished to make way for the apartment building at **2 Fifth Avenue.** It is worth quoting James's description:

> The ideal of quiet and genteel retirement, in 1835, was found in Washington Square, where the Doctor built himself a handsome, modern, wide-fronted house, with a big balcony before the drawing-room windows, and a flight of marble steps ascending to a portal which was also faced with white marble. This structure, and many of its neighbours, which it exactly resembled, were supposed, forty years ago, to embody the last results of architectural science, and they remain to this day very solid and honourable dwellings. In front of them was the square, containing a considerable quantity of inexpensive vegetation, enclosed by a wooden paling, which increased its rural and accessible appearance; and round the corner was the more august precinct of the Fifth Avenue, taking its origin at this point with a spacious and

confident air which already marked it for high destinies. I know not whether it is owing to the tenderness of early associations, but this portion of New York appears to many persons the most delectable.

It has a kind of established repose which is not of frequent occurrence in other quarters of the long, shrill city; it has a riper, richer, more honourable look than any of the upper ramifications of the great longitudinal thoroughfare—the look of having had something of a social history.

4 WASHINGTON MEWS

University Place to Fifth Avenue, between 8th Street and Waverly Place

MACDOUGAL ALLEY

East of MacDougal Street, between 8th Street and Waverly Place

To the generation of the 1920s and '30s, the height of urban sophistication was to live in a converted carriage house in Greenwich Village. The houses on MacDougal Alley and the north side of Washington Mews were once stables for the houses on Washington Square North. They were converted to dwellings in the twenties and thirties, and long housed artists and other creative types. The simple, stuccoed houses on the south side of Washington Mews were built as residences in 1939. MacDougal Alley with its gas lamps, Washington Mews with its Belgian-block pavement, and both with their small, picturesque houses, epitomize a certain, still-prevalent conception of Village quaintness.

5 ELMER HOLMES BOBST LIBRARY (New York University)

70 Washington Square South (4th Street) between LaGuardia Place and Washington Square East (MacDougal Street)
1972, Philip Johnson and Richard Foster

Post-International Style, pre-postmodern Philip Johnson, but edging toward the latter. The massive orange block is like a hollowed-out giant pumpkin. The glazed façade displays to the park the library's internal activities in a web of staircases, balustrades, bold lighting fixtures, intricate floor patterns, and thousands of NYU students. There's *lots* of microfilm in this pumpkin.

6 *Judson Memorial Baptist Church*

6 JUDSON MEMORIAL BAPTIST CHURCH

55 Washington Square South (4th Street), southwest corner of Thompson Street
1892, McKim, Mead & White
Tower: 1895, McKim, Mead & White

Designed by Stanford White and based on the Romanesque San Miniato al Monte in Florence, which was also the model for Goodhue's chapel at St. Bartholomew's (10.10). The church is both sensuous and dignified, and perfect as a park wall. The combination of yellow Roman brick with terra-cotta ornament always served Stanford White well in his gorgeous façades, as at the Century Club (13.3) of one year earlier. Here, the composition is enlivened by the high campanile, now NYU student housing.

7 UNIVERSITY VILLAGE (apartments)

100 and 110 Bleecker Street, and 505 LaGuardia Place
1966, I. M. Pei & Partners

In a just world, the boundary between Greenwich Village and SoHo would somehow relate the two areas, pull them together, make them communicate. As it is, we have the superblock Washington Square Village, bounded by 3rd and Bleecker streets, LaGuardia Place, and Mercer Street, built from 1956 to 1958; the superblock University Village; and expressway-scaled Houston Street, one of the ugliest thoroughfares in the city. Pei's University Village, a trio of cast-in-place concrete apartment towers, is the best of these border elements, which is not saying much.

7 *University Village*

8 10TH STREET

From Sixth Avenue to Broadway

One of the most interesting streets in the Village. It has a little of everything, all harmoniously related and surpassingly urbane. Numbers 20 to 38, between Fifth and Sixth avenues, are know as **"The English Terrace Row."** Built in 1855-56 and attributed to James Renwick, Jr., architect of Grace Church (6.9) and St. Patrick's Cathedral (13.8), these ten severe Italianate façades are unified by a balcony that stretches continuously along the row above the ground story. This was also the first row of houses in the city to place its entrances at street level, abandoning the high Dutch stoop. The Italianate house at **14 West 10th Street,** also built in 1855-56 and once the home of Mark Twain, is a brick structure boldly ornamented with brownstone carvings. Note especially the large, arched first-floor windows framed by Corinthian pilasters, and the rusticated quoins. This is as handsome a house as its era produced. **Twelve West 10th Street,** built 1846, was renovated in 1895 by Bruce Price for his daughter, etiquette expert Emily Post.

At the northwest corner of Fifth Avenue and 10th Street stands the brownstone **Church of the Ascension** (Episcopal), a Gothic Revival church designed by Richard Upjohn and completed in 1841, just as he was starting his Trinity Church (1.17). It is a handsome building, but of interest chiefly as one of Upjohn's studies for Trinity Church. Note the shallow chancel, and you will see that Upjohn was unable to go as far in the direction of Pugin as he did with Trinity. Ascension's interior was remodeled in 1885-89 by McKim, Mead & White, at which time the altar mural and stained glass by John LaFarge and the altar relief by Augustus Saint-Gaudens were added. This interior, a monument of the American Renaissance, is well worth a visit. The Ascension Parish House at 12 West 11th Street was built in 1844 but renovated in 1889 by McKim, Mead & White.

At 7 East 10th Street between University Place and Fifth Avenue is the remarkable former **Lockwood De Forest house.** De Forest (1850–1932) was an artist who spent time in India attempting to revive ancient Indian woodcarving. His elaborately carved teakwood projecting bay and trim on this otherwise ordinary town house is one of this city's marvels, both for its intricate artistry and for its having so heartily survived the

9 *Jefferson Market Library*

elements all these years. Similar teakwood trim has been applied to the front of the apartment house next door at **number 9,** built a year later and designed by Renwick, Aspinwall & Russell.

Numbers 39 to 41, between University Place and Broadway, are an apartment house known as the **Lancaster,** also by Renwick, Aspinwall & Russell and built in 1887, around the time apartment living was first coming into vogue in the Village. This is my favorite block of 10th Street, even if it is the least historic. While the other blocks are small-scaled residential ones, this is a denser block, lined with high structures on both sides. There is a wonderful, warm feeling of enclosure. The buildings are old, not too high, and of traditional materials. There is great diversity here—this is one of the Village's true Jane Jacobs blocks. There are elegant antique stores, a chic restaurant that opens onto the sidewalk, apartment houses, warehouses. There is continuous commercial frontage, yet tranquillity as great as on the purely residential blocks of 10th Street. The city doesn't get any better than this.

9 JEFFERSON MARKET LIBRARY (formerly Jefferson Market Courthouse)

425 Sixth Avenue, southwest corner of 10th Street
1877, Vaux and Withers
Remodeled into library in 1967, Giorgio Cavaglieri

High Victorian gallimaufry, the Gothic Revival gone mad—and magnificent. The inspiration was Ruskin, for whom Withers and Vaux were New York's chief proselytizers. The idea is organic architecture—a building with the character of unpruned growth. Hence, the wildly varied skyline, polychromy, leaded glass, in-your-face asymmetry, gables, and pinnacles—an architecture of excrescences. Street's Law Courts in London is the masterpiece of the genre, but Jefferson Market is no slouch. It came close to being knocked down and was saved by local preservationists. It's recently been cleaned, the bell tower is working again, and the building looks better than at any time since it was built.

10 NEW SCHOOL FOR SOCIAL RESEARCH

66 West 12th Street, between Fifth and Sixth avenues
1930, Joseph Urban
Additions to the west and south in 1958, Mayer, Whittlesey & Glass

Urban's original New School building was one of the most startling modern structures in the city in 1930. It's one of those handsome buildings bridging Art Deco and International Style, a kind of kinder, gentler modernism than what was soon to emerge as the mainstream. But it may not have seemed thus in 1930. The brick striping and massive black doors have an in-your-face boldness that was a theatrical departure into the brave new world. Only sixty years later, and it's as quaint as a gaslit, cobblestoned street.

11 BUTTERFIELD HOUSE

37 West 12th Street, between Fifth and Sixth avenues
1962, Mayer, Whittlesey & Glass

Greenwich Village 1962: this building is the very emblem of its time and place. It works because it is the best design one could hope for from a mainstream firm at that time and in this place. The 12th Street elevation of this rather large apartment building is carefully tailored to fit into a

10 *The New School*

street of nineteenth-century town houses. The detailing is excellent, the brick warm, and the oriels lend a strong and appropriate rhythm to the façade. The building extends all the way to 13th Street, where it is higher and more massive, which is appropriate on that street of high, massive loft structures. Not many architects in 1962 were so conscientiously contextual, and few architects today seem capable of such utterly unfussy contextualism.

12 FIRST PRESBYTERIAN CHURCH

48 Fifth Avenue, between 11th and 12th streets
1846, Joseph C. Wells
South transept: 1893, McKim, Mead & White

CHURCH HOUSE

1960, Edgar Tafel

Completed in the same year as Trinity Church (1.17) and Grace Church (6.9), that banner year for the Gothic Revival in America, this is a handsome brownstone church modeled on Magdalen College, Oxford. Of particular note is Edgar Tafel's Church House, an even finer work of rare early sixties contextualism than Butterfield House (5.11). Tafel was an apprentice to Frank Lloyd Wright in the thirties, and served as project architect on Falling Water. It is interesting that a Wright acolyte should have chosen a career as an urban architect, but with this, as with other buildings, Tafel seems to have treated the built environment the way his mentor treated the natural environment: as the principal determinant of his design. The Church House uses continuous terra-cotta piers to echo the insistently vertical piers of the church; the Roman brick and earthy green-glazed terra-cotta blend well with the brownstone of the church and the green of the garden forecourt; and the quatrefoil balustrades, which are of course the really radical element of the design, sustain the church's quatrefoil motif. At the same time, there is a ground-hugging horizontality, respect for materials, and stylized lettering that mark this as a Wrightian building. Truly one of the best New York buildings of its period.

12 *Church House, First Presbyterian Church*

13 NORTHERN DISPENSARY

165 Waverly Place at Christopher Street
1831; third floor added in 1854

A noble neighborhood landmark, like the Jefferson Market Library. Yet the design could not be more different. This is a Federal building of mesmerizing simplicity—so utterly, mesmerizingly simple, in fact, that it has the power to rivet the attention as few buildings can.

14 5–16 ST. LUKE'S PLACE

Between Leroy and Hudson streets
1852–53

One of the city's most famous and truly loved rows of houses, and an outstanding exemplar of the Italianate style then taking over from Greek Revival in residential architecture. The heavy iron railings, the bold stoops, and the gingko trees make this my favorite New York street to walk down on a beautiful early autumn day.

15 MORTON STREET

From Hudson Street to Bedford Street

COMMERCE STREET

From Seventh Avenue South to Barrow Street

BEDFORD STREET

From Christopher Street to Morton Street

These three streets are the absolute epitome of picturesque, Hollywood back-lot Greenwich Village. People seeing these streets for the first time are amazed to discover that they are real-life counterparts to the old-time streets recreated at Disney World. Commerce is the most spectacular—an incredible jumble of buildings, lofts, tenements, elegant town houses, commercial structures, a famous off-Broadway theater, a neighborhood restaurant—making a jagged skyline and taking a *sharp* bend. Bedford contains several landmarks of West Village culture. The house at **number 75½,** said to be the narrowest in the city, once was home to Edna St. Vincent Millay, that captivating princess of the old bohemian Village. The house at **number** 77 is the oldest in the Village, dating from 1799. **Chumley's,** an unmarked bar and former speakeasy at number 86, is one of the city's famous literary watering holes, its walls festooned with dust jackets of books by Village authors. At number 102 is the **"Twin Peaks"** house (no relation to the short-lived TV series), an 1830 structure renovated in 1925 by Clifford Reed Daily, who felt Village architecture was too drab and in need of whimsy.

16 ST. LUKE-IN-THE-FIELDS CHURCH (Episcopal)

485 Hudson Street, between Barrow and Christopher streets
1822, James N. Wells
1986 expansion, Hardy Holzman Pfeiffer

The Federal twenties seemed to mass-produce beautiful, simple buildings, but every so often the simplicity—99 percent of the time soul stirring—resulted only in dull. This church, erected amid open fields, is a bit that way. There's a glorious garden, though, and some handsome 1820s town houses, and it all adds up to a civilized enclave.

17 ARCHIVES (apartments)

666 Greenwich Street, between Christopher and Barrow streets
1892–99, Willoughby J. Edbrooke

The most splendid Richardsonian Romanesque building in New York, and as wonderful an example as can be found anywhere of fine brickwork. The brickwork is so good it produces gooseflesh. Everything about this building is bold and authoritative—the arches, the rounded corners, the corbels. It was originally the U.S. Appraiser's Stores, then the Federal Archives Building, and is now luxury co-ops.

CHAPTER 6

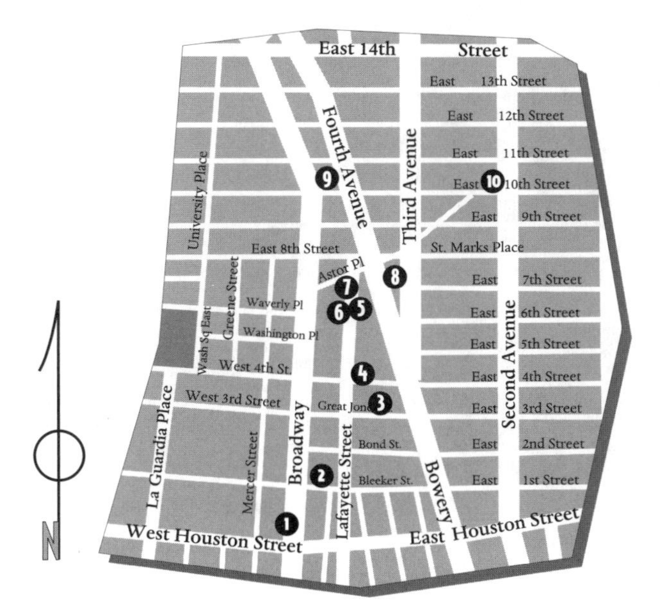

The East Village

2 *Bayard Building*

Chapter 6

The East Village

1 CABLE BUILDING

621 Broadway, northwest corner of Houston Street
1894, McKim, Mead & White

This building originally housed machinery for operating cable cars. It is like a big, ungainly, jeweled box. Of necessity it was made massive, and this massiveness is accentuated by the outsize arches. It is in certain details that this building glitters. Note especially the antefixes, or ornamental blocks running atop the edge of the cornice, and the beautifully sculpted figures touching hands over the wreath above the entrance on Broadway.

2 BAYARD BUILDING

65 Bleecker Street, between Broadway and Lafayette Street
1898, Louis Sullivan

There is only one way to approach this beautiful façade, and that is slightly off-axis up Crosby Street, one block east of Broadway. Starting at Houston, one is first vaguely aware of a fanciful façade closing the vista at Bleecker, two blocks away. As one draws nearer, the eye is led ineluctably upward by one of the most insistently, soaringly vertical façades anywhere. Lithe, non–load bearing, terra-cotta mullions complement heavy, load-bearing steel piers. The terra-cotta is emblazoned with Sullivan's exuberantly naturalistic ornament, and rising atop each of the structural piers is an angel with outspread wings, ready to take off and propel the building into flight. The Bayard soars to a climax. Sullivan is so often credited as a godfather to the Modern movement that his style is too little recognized as an original adaptation to peculiarly American technology of the meticulous classicism he learned as a student at the Ecole des Beaux-Arts in Paris. Sullivan was a Beaux-Arts architect, a figure as surely as, say, Stanford White in what is not too ridiculously termed the *American Renaissance.*

Given this, the setting of the building is startling. Originally intended to be an office building, the Bayard, for a number of reasons, took so long to complete that in the meantime its neighborhood changed into an industrial quarter, and it finally opened as a loft building. Amid its grimy warehouse setting, and especially since its recent steam cleaning, the Bayard hits you like a shaft of light from the heavens. Approaching it is one of the handful of truly fine architectural experiences in New York.

3 ENGINE COMPANY NO. 33

44 Great Jones Street, between the Bowery and Lafayette Street
1898, Flagg & Chambers

Once upon a time, firehouses were grand, proud structures, and none was ever grander or prouder than this one. It is a compact building made monumental by the placement of an enormous arch over a rusticated base. Particularly exciting is the very-French curved chamfering of the underside of the arch—an utterly graceful note bespeaking a philosophy of public service as noble gesture.

4 DEVINNE PRESS BUILDING

399 Lafayette Street, northeast corner of 4th Street
1885, Babb, Cook & Willard

As fine a specimen of the bricklayer's craft as you are ever likely to see. The bold, deeply incised, arched windows; the pitched roof, and the lack of ornament mark this as a utilitarian building in the classical Roman mode. If it has something of the feeling of the Chicago School, it is well to remember that the Chicago School, too, was essentially a classical style in the Roman utilitarian mode. The best thing here is the brick quoining, by itself enough to make this one of my favorite buildings in Manhattan.

5 NEW YORK PUBLIC THEATER

425 Lafayette Street, between 4th Street and Astor Place
South wing: 1853, Alexander Saeltzer
Central wing: 1859, Griffith Thomas
North wing: 1881, Thomas Stent
Conversion to theater in 1967–76, Giorgio Cavaglieri

Originally the Astor Library, forerunner of the New York Public Library. An excellent example of the Rundbogenstil, or round-arched style adapted from fifteenth-century models, that was at this time the most popular architectural style in Germany. This simple, forceful, neo-Renaissance style was well suited to a variety of modern building types, in this case the large public library. It is a style that works well with a tight approach, whereas the full-blown Beaux-Arts of the library at 42nd Street works best in a monumental setting. This is another example of the way America, far from being behind Europe in architectural fashion, was in fact quite

7 *Astor Place Subway Kiosk*

parallel to the mother continent. Note how beautifully this library was adapted to use as a theater—it is hard to believe it was not always one.

6 COLONNADE ROW

428–34 Lafayette Street, between 4th Street and Astor Place
1833, Seth Greer

Manhattan once had a number of such structures: rows of houses designed to look like single buildings, thus acquiring for the urban row house something of the grandeur of the country house. In this sense, such structures were precursors of the luxury apartment houses such as the Dakota (16.12)—grandeur achieved by a sort of architectural equivalent of the mutual fund. Originally there were nine houses behind the imposing Corinthian colonnade; now there are five, and they are like ruins. Back when this was in repair, it must have combined with the Astor Library across the street to make Lafayette one of the finest streets in New York.

7 ASTOR PLACE IRT SUBWAY STATION

Below Lafayette Street and Fourth Avenue at Astor Place
1904, Heins & LaFarge
Restored and kiosk replica in 1985, Prentice & Chan, Ohlhausen

It is hard to believe that when the IRT was built, its stations, designed by the prestigious firm of Heins & LaFarge (the original architects of the Cathedral of St. John the Divine), were very handsome spaces. Precious few have been restored. This is one that has, and it is a real treat. The fine beaver plaques, representing the roots of the Astor fortune in the fur trade (Philip Copp, the foremost historian of New York's subway stations, says, "Just mention *subway* and *art* in the same sentence, and nine out of ten ordinarily knowledgeable people will think of the beaver plaques at Astor Place"), have been cleaned up and combined with an abstract mural by Milton Glaser to create what has to be the most hospitable subway station in the city. Above on the street, the lovely cast-iron-and-glass entrance kiosk is not a restoration but a replica of the long-gone Heins & LaFarge original.

8 COOPER UNION

7th Street to Astor Place, from Fourth Avenue to the Bowery
1859, Frederick A. Peterson

Few buildings on the island are as conspicuously sited as this. The design is strong enough to hold the space. It is also the oldest existing steel-framed building in the country. Not much in the way of felicitous detail in the heavy, simple, Italianate, brownstone mass, a classical adaptation to modern function much in the spirit of the Rundbogenstil Astor Library around the corner on Lafayette Street. The front of the building is actually on the south side. Cooper Union forms an island at the point where the Bowery forks into Third and Fourth avenues between 6th and 7th streets. The open space in front of the main entrance is called Cooper Square, in which is located Augustus Saint-Gaudens's Peter Cooper monument (1894). The bronze figure is seated on a marble-and-granite base with canopy by Stanford White. There is a lovely contrast between White's

8A *Cooper Union*

8B *Statue outside Cooper Union*

feminine enveloping scheme and the manly, bearded, robust figure. This is one of New York's most exciting sculptures.

9 GRACE CHURCH and RECTORY

Broadway at 10th Street
1845–46, James Renwick, Jr.

Grace was completed in the same year as Trinity Church (1.17), and exhibits many of the same Gothic Revival design elements, but the spirit is altogether different. Renwick had none of Upjohn's philosophical commitment to the Gothic Revival and its associated liturgical movement. Renwick would have designed this church in any style that happened to be popular—and he would have done a good job of it. Like Upjohn, Renwick studied Pugin, but the result is an obvious forerunner of Renwick's flamboyant St. Patrick's (13.8). There is a laciness and lightness here which is completely absent from Trinity. In certain respects, Trinity and Grace, both Puginesque Gothic Revival designs, represent the twin poles of American architectural practice in the nineteenth century, poles later embodied by, respectively, Louis Sullivan and McKim, Mead & White. Grace occupies a bend in Broadway, making it visible for great distances. My favorite approach is from the loft canyon of 11th Street: as Grace looms into view, its scale seems far vaster than it is—downright cathedral-like.

9 *Grace Church*

There used to be a pizzeria on the southwest corner of Broadway and 10th, with a grand view of the church. It was like New York's Tour d'Argent overlooking Notre Dame.

10 ST. MARK'S-IN-THE-BOWERY CHURCH

Second Avenue, northwest corner of 10th Street
1799; steeple: 1828, Ithiel Town
Portico: 1854

RENWICK TRIANGLE

114–28 East 10th Street and 23–35 Stuyvesant Street, between Second and Third avenues
1861, attributed to James Renwick, Jr.

I include these together because they form one of the most civilized enclaves in Manhattan. The uniform Italianate brownstone fronts, with rusticated bases, of the houses create a fine sense of steep enclosure that breaks dramatically with the church and its spacious setting. The Federal body of St. Mark's is one of the all-too-few extant eighteenth-century structures left in Manhattan. The Greek portico is roughly contemporary with the houses attributed to Renwick. It was around the rear of the church that three apartment towers designed by Frank Lloyd Wright would have been built had not Depression intervened. Wright appropriated their design for his Price Tower in Bartlesville, Oklahoma.

CHAPTER 7

Chelsea

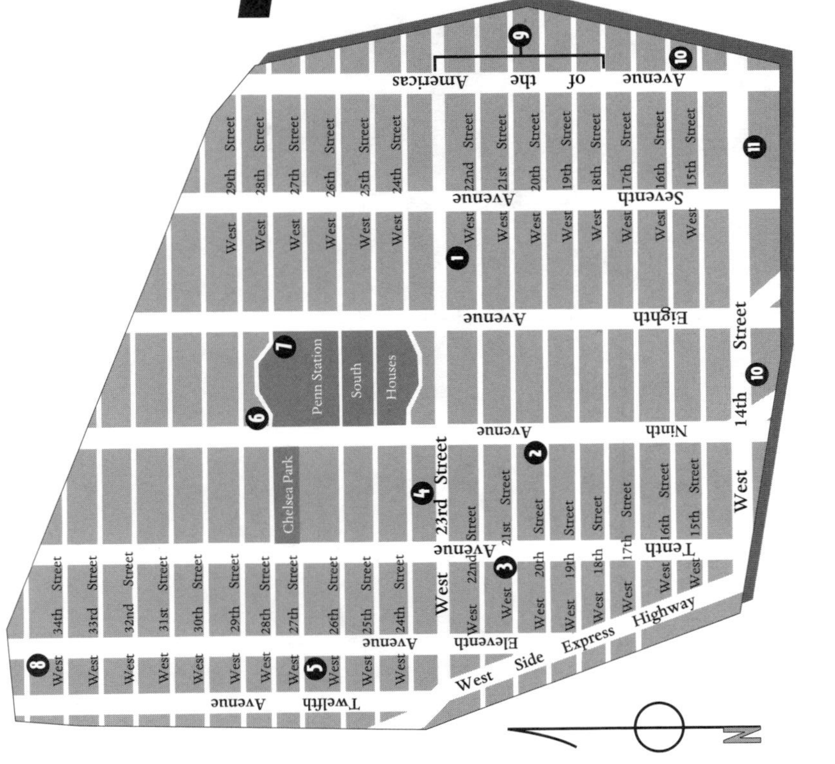

1 *Chelsea Hotel*

Chapter 7

Chelsea

1 CHELSEA HOTEL

222 West 23rd Street, between Seventh and Eighth avenues
1884, Hubert, Pirsson & Co.

A massive, twelve-story brick building with lacy, floral iron balconies. A Victorian pile that would have been right at home in London.

2 GENERAL THEOLOGICAL SEMINARY

Ninth Avenue, between 20th and 21st streets
Main buildings: 1883–1900, Charles C. Haight

406–18 WEST 20TH STREET

Between Ninth and Tenth avenues
1840

ST. PETER'S CHURCH

344 West 20th Street, between Eighth and Ninth avenues
1836–38, James W. Smith and Clement Clarke Moore
Rectory: 1832

Chelsea's charms are very spotty, but they are amply in evidence in this dignified enclave. The seminary campus is entered through the modern building (1960) on Ninth Avenue. The main brick-and-brownstone buildings are of the same Victorian cloth as the contemporary Chelsea Hotel. The open space surrounded by these buildings is accessible to the public, and serves as a neighborhood park. 20th Street between Ninth and Tenth avenues is one of the most pleasant areas in the city. The fine Greek

Revival row houses at numbers 406 to 418, built in 1840 (see Washington Square North, 5.3), form the southern wall, while the seminary buildings form the northern wall, just beyond which is the open space. The seminary's west building and St. Peter's, a block south and associated with the seminary, are among New York's first Gothic Revival buildings. St. Peter's Rectory, like the row houses, was designed in the still-prevalent Greek Revival.

3 GUARDIAN ANGEL CHURCH (Roman Catholic)

193 Tenth Avenue, northwest corner of 21st Street
1930, John Van Pelt

A wild and crazy Sicilian Romanesque building in which the limestone-framed façade is spread with an irregular brick pattern that resembles moss on a stone.

4 LONDON TERRACE

23rd Street to 24th Street, from Ninth Avenue to Tenth Avenue
1930, Farrar & Watmaugh

A massive apartment complex named after what it replaced: a landmark terrace of Greek Revival houses with a deep front yard, designed by Alexander Jackson Davis and built in 1840. The summer home of Clement Clarke Moore, Chelsea's principal early landowner and author of "A Visit from St. Nicholas," stood across 23rd Street from London Terrace until 1854. The apartment complex is actually fourteen connected buildings with a total of 1,670 apartments and a large interior garden. When it was built, it was supposedly the largest residential development in the world. Guided tours were given, and the doormen dressed as London bobbies—shades of Trump Tower, where the doormen originally dressed as beefeaters. This is one of a handful of buildings in New York that utterly dominates its surroundings. Here the effect seems to come from sheer brick mass, with just a hint of verticality in the Gothic detailing.

5 STARRETT-LEHIGH BUILDING

26th Street to 27th Street, from Eleventh Avenue to Twelfth Avenue
1931, Russell G. and Walter M. Cory and Yasuo Matsui

Of all Manhattan neighborhoods, Chelsea in the 1920s and '30s seemed

4 *London Terrace*

able to accommodate some outlandishly big buildings, whether residential, like London Terrace, or industrial, as here. This is a landmark of early modernism. There is a total absence of ornament or of revivalist detailing of any kind. There is nothing but continuous strip windows and brick spandrels. It is every bit the International-style building that Lescaze and Howe's Philadelphia Saving Fund Society is, and like that building, it has a dynamic curviness that gives a kind of kick that right-angled International Modernism could never quite manage. Starrett-Lehigh was built over railroad tracks to house small manufacturers which otherwise would be unable to afford facilities with proper rail and truck connections. It is technologically one of the noteworthy buildings of its time in the world. The central core of the nineteen-story structure included an elevator for trucks. Perhaps no single structure in the city says as much about the onetime industrial preeminence of New York, or about the broad-based commitment that once existed to the needs of small manufacturers.

6 CHURCH OF THE HOLY APOSTLES

300 Ninth Avenue, southeast corner of 28th Street
1848, Minard Lafever
Transepts: 1858, Richard Upjohn and Son

In the very heyday of the Gothic Revival (two years after Trinity Church, 1.17, and Grace Church, 6.9), Lafever created a church that boldly combined two styles that would not become popular until the next decade: Romanesque Revival and Italian Renaissance Revival (Italianate). Note particularly the splendid neo-Renaissance bronze-and-slate spire.

7 PENN STATION SOUTH

23rd Street to 29th Street, from Eighth Avenue to Ninth Avenue
1962, Herman Jessor

Chelsea is a large area of Manhattan that is on the whole rather characterless. It has, of course, its splendid enclaves, such as 20th Street between Ninth and Tenth avenues (7.2); its architectural wonders, such as the Starrett-Lehigh Building (7.5); and a handful of vital mixed-use streets walled by robust loft buildings (e.g., 18th Street between Fifth and Sixth avenues). On the whole, however, Chelsea presents to the walker rather a bleak townscape: parking lots and in general far too much open space of the type inadequately enclosed by appropriately scaled buildings; dilapidated commercial strips dominated by cheap "taxpayers" (one- to two-story buildings); ugly modern institutional and residential buildings; and side streets with long blocks and little diversity. The development that dominates a walk through Chelsea is this giant housing project. Built as middle-income subsidized housing for members of the International Ladies Garment Workers Union, who toil in the nearby Garment District, it contains 2,820 units. It is designed in the standard Corbusian superblock style, in which spartan apartment towers are scattered about a large parklike setting with minimal reference to preexisting street patterns. Part of the intent in a project of this kind is to create open space, which is of course a laudable aim. In practice, however, urban open space becomes extremely problematical when it is amorphous and irregularly enclosed, as here. Cities, like houses, work physically only when they provide the comfort of appropriate enclosure. Better a small space walled by modestly scaled buildings than a large space scattered with towers. A project such as Penn Station South, which is very typical of the many housing projects throughout New York City, is disorienting and exhausting. Because it dominates Chelsea, it is a major reason that Chelsea itself is disorienting and exhausting.

8 JACOB K. JAVITS CONVENTION CENTER

Eleventh Avenue to Twelfth Avenue, from 34th Street to 37th Street
1986, James I. Freed of I. M. Pei & Partners

It is almost impossible for a convention center, however desperately it may be needed for the sake of the city's economy, to be anything but a blight on the cityscape. The best a city can do with a convention center is to put it off to the side, where it is not going to be a nuisance. That's what New York has done with its new convention center. In fact, it's *so* off to the side that it seems like it's in the hinterland. There are probably twenty locations in the outer boroughs where this center would be more accessible than here, even though technically it's located in mid-Manhattan. Subways don't stop anywhere near it, and the streets leading to it from the closest station—the IND at Eighth Avenue and 34th Street—are rather desolate and uninviting. It's a shame that conventioneers in New York are forced to get to the convention center from their hotels—there are also, strangely, no hotels near it—by bus or taxicab, just as they would in Dallas or Las Vegas.

Still, I'm not complaining. This building is gigantic, and no matter how well designed such a huge structure may be, to have located it practically anywhere else in Manhattan would surely have meant greater disruption and destruction than here at the western extremity of 34th Street. In its rather there-less setting, the Javits Center is a handsome modern object—not nearly as bloody awful as the vast majority of convention halls in this great land of ours. The vast scale of the place is beautifully modulated by the space-frame-and-truss structural system of steel tubes and spherical nodes. In a classical building, enormous size can be offset by the breakdown of parts according to a hierarchical organization of ornament. In a modern building, such breakdowns are far more difficult, and vastness more than ever becomes a problem. Freed's attempted solution—partly successful—is to set up a basic tube-and-node unit and replicate it a million times. The best time, by far, to view the Javits Center is at night, when it is lit from within and glows like the most outsized lantern on earth.

9 SIXTH AVENUE

From 18th Street to 23rd Street

This is part of what was once known as "Ladies Mile": the shopping district, the "downtown" of turn-of-the-century Manhattan. This stretch of Sixth Avenue is remarkable because it is lined with edifices that once were among the city's grandest department stores. The department store is what lent the central business districts of American cities their peculiar urbanity in the nineteenth century. The expansion of the metropolitan economy stirred a mass desire for a life of solid comfort, involving the buying, if not of luxury goods, at least of goods beyond necessities. As the century progressed, lower and lower social classes endeavored to stock their lives with home furnishings, ready-made clothing, and children's toys. What is commonplace today—the extension beyond necessity of the desire for goods, and the opportunity at all social levels to acquire these goods—was once a revolutionary social change. With the nineteenth century's mass extension of the market for goods of all kinds, great emporiums that came to be called department stores emerged in the central business districts of American cities.

Why was it called "Ladies' Mile"? I'm glad you asked.

Women—"ladies"—became the family purchasing agents and flocked to the new emporiums. Before the department store, central business districts were the rough-hewn domains of men in which women were largely unwelcome. The department store brought elegance to these districts, and led to the modern downtown as the beautiful heart of the city. The parade of women into and out of the stores, the stores' maintenance of their sidewalks, and the store buildings with their beautiful displays behind large plate-glass windows gave a whole new look and feel to the central business district. The great European dry-goods merchants were mainly concerned with the carriage trade. Not so their American counterparts; in the socially mobile city without the rigid class stratifications common in Europe, the American department store evolved as an institution for the masses, serving women of all segments of society. An Italian visitor to Boston around the turn of the century remarked: "The public is here a common noun of the feminine gender." America offered to the world

9[A] *Sixth Avenue with former Siegel-Cooper Dry Goods Store on right*

the spectacle of a feminine public. In their zeal to appeal to women of all classes, the department stores strictly observed the principle of "first come, first served"—a sentiment worthy of the Founding Fathers. *Miss Leslie's Behaviour Book* counseled the well-bred woman of the 1850s to "testify no impatience if a servant-girl, making a sixpenny purchase, is served before you." This would have been inconceivable as counsel to the grand ladies of Europe in the 1850s. Gordon Selfridge, the Chicagoan who in 1906 opened London's largest department store, said of its appeal to women: "It's so much brighter than their homes. This is not a shop—it's a community center."

Women emerged as what the historian Gunther Barth terms "directors of family consumption." Shopping came into being as a way of getting out from under family and domestic confinement and drudgery. In the 1860s and 1870s, shopping functioned as a means of female emancipation. Feminists such as Elizabeth Cady Stanton exhorted women to go out and shop. Because of their female clientele, department stores reformed their seedy neighborhoods. Women who would never visit one another's homes or even neighborhoods mingled freely in the new downtown.

Prices were clearly marked on all goods so shoppers need not risk the embarrassment of asking how much something cost. Haggling became passé. As shoppers began to spend hours at a stretch in the stores, special facilities were introduced, from restaurants to rest rooms, post offices, nurseries, even writing rooms. The great merchants extolled good service as the most important element of business. Salesclerks were encouraged to think of themselves not as slaves but as public servants, ready with advice or a flattering comment. The clerks typically worked a ten-hour day and earned six dollars a week in the 1890s. As the economy expanded and well-paid jobs opened up for men, women came to dominate the clerk jobs in the big stores. This was another emancipating phenomenon: unlike other jobs open to women—sweatshop work, say, or domestic service—a job in a depart-

9[B] *Former B. Altman Dry Goods Store*

ment store smacked of the great world, a far remove from domesticity and traditional roles.

Styles became obsolete well before the goods themselves. The fashion cycle became ever more rapid as customers, egged on by advertisements in the metropolitan press, clamored for the new, greeting each change with a binge of buying. Shopping became a great game, refuting the theories of the eighteenth-century "science" of economics, based on the idea of "rational choice." Before scoffing at the idea of the fashion cycle, remember that in the seventeenth century, for example, not only did such perpetual change not occur, it was often actually barred by law from occurring; in the Free Imperial City of Frankfurt, it was as natural that there be a civic dress code as that there be laws regulating the design of buildings. In Boston in 1676, a servant girl was publicly admonished for excess in her apparel. And so on. The expansion of the metropolitan economy, both spawning and sustained by the fashion cycle, went hand in hand with an unprecedented opening of horizons in the lives of ordinary men and women.

In the American city, areas such as Sixth Avenue were monuments to the new freedoms based on consumption. "Ultimately," writes Gunther Barth, "the department store gave urban life a downtown focus, not only bestowing charm and civility but also evoking democratic qualities that enriched the urbanity of the modern city and reaffirmed its egalitarian nature."

There are six former major department stores on this stretch of Sixth Avenue. The former Siegel-Cooper Dry Goods Store, on the east side of the avenue between 18th and 19th streets, was built in 1896 and designed by DeLemos and Cordes (who also designed Macy's at Herald Square). It was the grandest of all New York's department stores, and its building is one of the most imposing in the city. The dominant note is one of sheer sumptuousness, of ceaseless accretion of decorative details, many of which are fine in isolation but do not even begin to add up to a coherent whole. The incoherence does not indicate lack of skill among the architects. It must be remembered what Sixth Avenue was like when the building was erected. The Sixth Avenue elevated railway—the "El"—made impossible any clear, unobstructed view of these façades, so it was isolated detail, not the whole composition, that made its appeal to the viewer.

Siegel-Cooper advertised itself as "The Big Store—A City in Itself." One entered between towering bronze columns onto a main floor dominated by a huge fountain. "Meet me at the fountain" was a stock phrase of turn-of-the-century New York. Siegel-Cooper's fountain was the city's most popular point of rendezvous, whether of shoppers, businessmen, lovers, or tourists. From the second floor, one looked down from behind a mahogany balustrade into the fountain well, with its replica of Daniel Chester French's *Republic* (now in Forest Lawn Cemetery in Los Angeles). The quintessential New York experience was to buy a five-cent ice-cream soda and sit beside the fountain, taking in the pageant of fashionably attired women making their shopping rounds. Today the building is a glitzy shopping mall, but if you look hard, you can still make out some original detail in the interior.

Across Sixth Avenue from Siegel-Cooper was B. Altman and Company, built in 1877 and designed by D. and J. Jardine. "The Palace of Trade," as it was called, is a neo-Renaissance cast-iron palazzo. Altman's served its *Age of Innocence* clientele from this store before moving to Fifth Avenue and 34th Street in 1906.

On the west side of the avenue between 19th and 20th streets is the former Simpson Crawford Simpson Store, designed by William H. Hume and Son and built in 1900. This was the most "carriage trade" of the Ladies' Mile department stores, comparable, I suppose, to Bergdorf-Goodman in our day.

The west side between 20th and 21st is taken up by the splendid cast-iron hulk of the former Hugh O'Neill Dry Goods Store, designed by Mortimer C. Merritt and built in 1875. O'Neill's was, in contrast to Simpson Crawford Simpson, for the hoi polloi. (Siegel-Cooper was for both the carriage trade and the hoi polloi.)

The former Adams Dry Goods Store on the west side between 21st and 22nd is in full-blown Beaux-Arts style, designed, like Siegel-Cooper, by DeLemos and Cordes; it was built in 1900. This was another elegant emporium and has recently been sparklingly renovated to include a large Barnes and Noble bookstore. Separating Barnes and Noble's book and music departments is the building's original light well, fully restored and affording a fine sense of what the old store was like.

Between 22nd and 23rd on the west side is the former Ehrich Brothers Store, which evolved into Ohrbach's of 34th Street. Designed by William Schickel, it was built in 1889. At this writing, the Sixth Avenue façade of this splendid cast-iron structure has been fully restored and looks as good as new; the 23rd Street façade, on the other hand, has not yet been restored and looks like what it is—a heap of rusted metal. One almost wishes it could be kept this way as an object lesson in restoration. Ehrich Brothers is built around another cast-iron building, the former Riker's Drug Store on the corner of 23rd Street.

Unrelated to Ladies' Mile, except for being on the northeast corner of Sixth Avenue and 21st Street, is one of Richard Upjohn's finest works—Church of the Holy Communion, a picturesque Gothic Revival church from 1846, the year of the same architect's Trinity Church (1.17). Alas, in the 1970s it was converted into the Limelight Discotheque, the church fittings removed, ravaged, or otherwise profaned.

9C *Former Hugh O'Neill Dry Goods Store*

10 CHURCH OF ST. BERNARD (Roman Catholic)

330 West 14th Street, between Eighth and Ninth avenues
1875, P. C. Keely

CHURCH OF ST. FRANCIS XAVIER (Roman Catholic)

30 West 16th Street, between Fifth and Sixth avenues
1882, P. C. Keely

The Irish-born Keely was something like the in-house architect of the Roman Catholic church in New York during the church's period of greatest expansion, and examples of his work abound in the city. Like his contemporary, Renwick, Keely was wildly eclectic, as can be seen by comparing these two churches that are separated by only a few years and a few blocks. St. Bernard's is mainstream Ruskinian Gothic, vastly different from, and vastly more conventional than, Renwick's flamboyant French Gothic St. Patrick's Cathedral (13.8), which was built at around the same time. St. Francis Xavier, by contrast, is ornate neo-Baroque, and another of the many Manhattan instances of a monumental building squeezed into a side-street lot: here a gigantic Baroque porch virtually swallows the sidewalk. Though it is far from the best church in Manhattan, few others have so pleasantly startling an impact on the walker.

11 SALVATION ARMY CENTENNIAL MEMORIAL TEMPLE

120 West 14th Street, between Sixth and Seventh avenues
1930, Voorhees, Gmelin & Walker

Hum tunes from *Guys and Dolls* when you look at this building. Another classic Art Deco tower from Ralph Walker, who virtually invented the Art Deco skyscraper. This is one of the most sculptured buildings in town, looking very much as though it has been carved from a single mass of bricks.

CHAPTER 8

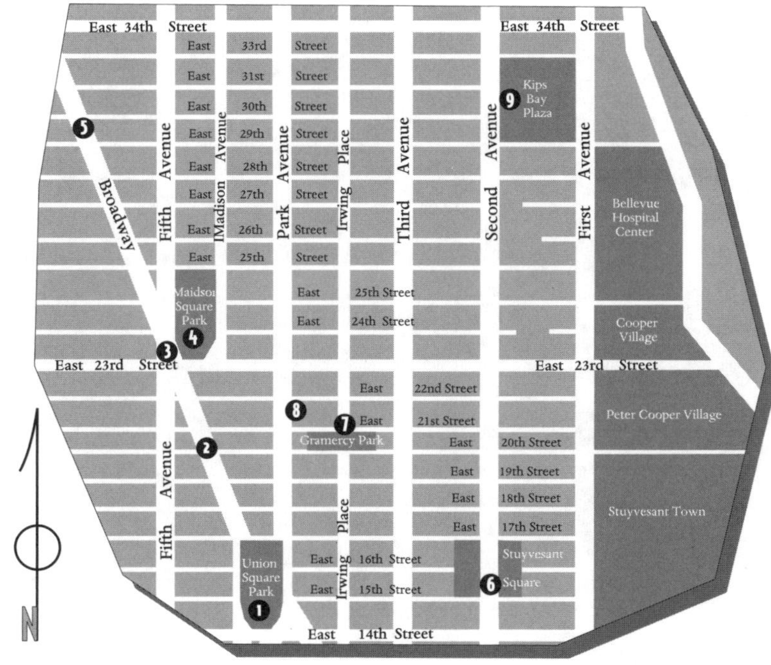

From Union Square to Kips Bay

1A *Zeckendorf Towers*

Chapter 8
From Union Square to Kips Bay

1 UNION SQUARE PARK

14th Street to 17th Street, from Broadway to Park Avenue South
Laid out in 1830, opened in 1839
Rebuilt in 1986

Although in recent years Union Square Park has been rebuilt and the surrounding neighborhood has become a high-rent district, nonetheless there is probably no way short of scorched-earth makeover that this area can ever be made to seem other than tawdry. It has its admirers, of course: this is as good a place as any to note the dismaying fact that part of the reason so much of Manhattan has a tawdry and threatening appearance is that there is in this city a large and active contingent of *champions* of the tawdry and threatening. In this era of such cultural phenomena as deconstruction and performance art, there are many who profess to admire the jarring, the disordered, the discontinuous. This is New York as stage set for the dominant intellectual and cultural inclinations of our time. If you doubt what I say, I ask only that you look at a recent book, *The Conscience of the Eye: The Design and Social Life of Cities,* by the distinguished sociologist Richard Sennett, who argues the merits of precisely the area covered in this entry.

Tawdry though it may be, like just about any section of Manhattan, the Union Square Park area is not without its virtues. There are some good buildings here. Most conspicuous among those that are *not* good is the **Zeckendorf Towers** development at One Irving Place between

14th and 15th streets. Designed by Davis, Brody & Associates and built in 1987, this massive apartment and office complex represents the most strenuous effort to date to gentrify the neighborhood. The basic ungentrifiability of Union Square, however, is verified by the fact that Zeckendorf Towers turns its back on the square and places its main entrance around the block on the relatively tranquil and attractive Irving Place. The quartet of illuminated pyramids that top Zeckendorf Towers have become a conspicuous skyline feature, and sadly block the uptown view of the lighted clock face of the **Consolidated Edison Building** across the street at Four Irving Place, an ill-proportioned, but finely detailed, neoclassical base (1915, Henry J. Hardenbergh), surmounted by an ill-proportioned, but finely detailed, neoclassical tower (1926, Warren and Wetmore) which bears the clock.

At 20 Union Square East (Park Avenue South), at the northeast corner of 15th Street, is the **American Savings Bank,** designed by Henry Bacon and built in 1907. This is a compact building with an incredibly stately porch with four massive Corinthian columns. It is the only major building in New York by Bacon, who designed the Lincoln Memorial (1922) in Washington, D.C., and who was one of America's finest classical architects. At 201 Park Avenue South, at the northeast corner of 17th Street, is the **Guardian Life Insurance Building** of 1911, by D'Oench & Yost. It is a brooding, mansarded affair, exactly the kind of building that should be constructed to wall a square such as Union. Appended to it, at **105 East 17th Street** between Park Avenue South and Irving Place, is a Miesian modern annex dating from 1961 and designed by Skidmore, Owings & Merrill.

The Century Building, former headquarters of one of the most popular magazines of the nineteenth century, stands at 33 East 17th Street between Park Avenue South and Broadway. Built in 1881 and designed by William Schickel, this red-brick-and-limestone Queen Anne pile comes straight out of Victorian London. It is one of the few extant major Queen Anne buildings in Manhattan; see also the Gramercy apartments (1883, G. W. da Cunha, 8.7) at Gramercy Park, and the former Mercantile Exchange (1884, Thomas R. Jackson, 3.12) in TriBeCa. The former **Bank of the Metropolis,** designed by Bruce Price, at 31 Union Square West, at the northwest corner of 16th Street, was built in 1903 and is another gem from the perhaps underrated father of Emily Post. Its Union Square

1B *American Savings Bank*

front is extremely narrow. Between an Ionic portico and a heavy cornice is a sleek, tastefully ornamented shaft; as with other Price buildings, it is a forerunner of the stripped classicism later practiced by such architects as Paul Philippe Cret.

The best thing about Union Square, however, is none of the buildings that surround it, but the splendid Greenmarket that regularly occupies much of the park itself. Farmers come from nearby outlying areas to sell, from the backs of trucks, their fresh produce as well as various homemade foodstuffs. Although there are many other Greenmarkets in the city, all of them worthy, this is the best, the biggest, the most diverse, the most colorful, the most fragrant, and the most popular. It is a joy to the senses, and the single best source for produce in the city, since the goods are modestly priced and everything is regionally produced and minimally handled. The market is the one compelling reason to visit Union Square.

2 Former GOELET BUILDING

900 Broadway, southeast corner of 20th Street
1887, McKim, Mead & White

This is one of the most unjustly neglected buildings in Manhattan. McKim, Mead & White were in the full bloom of the first phase of their work, embodying the fashionable ideas of the Richardsonian Romanesque, when they designed the Goelet Building. Nine bold arches wrap around the corner of 20th Street, as elegant and exhilarating a corner turning (despite banal modernization) as can be found in the city. The arches form a base for a marvelous curved mass of polychromatic brickwork. There is no applied ornament here—at least since the removal of the jewel-like cornice—save for the Ionic capitals of the columns flanking the front entrance. The Richardsonian and Ruskinian ideas here embodied have perhaps never been expressed in so stately and elegant a form. There is nothing picturesque about this building. It is a very classical handling of romantic ideas.

3 FLATIRON BUILDING

175 Fifth Avenue, between 22nd and 23rd streets
1902, D. H. Burnham & Company

One of the most famous and photographed buildings in America. Many of those who like it so much—and it is a truly well-liked building—probably think the reason is some combination of its famous shape (it was originally called the Fuller Building, but was nicknamed "Flatiron" by a bemused public), and its status as a conspicuous relic of Manhattan's fabled turn of the century, when the Madison Square area was where the action was. These Flatiron admirers may be surprised to learn that these two factors alone cannot account for this building's peculiar power. There is a third factor that has made this a Manhattan icon: it is a completely successful work of architecture. "Burnham Baroque" it has been called—the style perfected in the first two decades of the twentieth century by Chicago's Daniel H. Burnham, who was perhaps the single most successful architect in the country at that time. Burnham began, with his partner John Wellborn Root, as one of the pioneers of the Chicago school of architecture, considered a protomodern movement that not only invented the skyscraper, but evolved a new aesthetic of the tall building,

3 *Flatiron Building*

emphasizing forthright expression of internal structure and, under the influence of Henry Hobson Richardson and John Ruskin, limiting use of applied ornament, in order to accentuate the unique features of the new building type. After Root's death, Burnham, in charge of design at the Columbian Exposition in Chicago in 1893, reverted to a rich hyperclassicizing style, and became the leading exponent of the City Beautiful movement. The Burnham Baroque exemplifies the integration of the Chicago school with the City Beautiful, in which classical ornament is slathered all over the building, but never in such a way as to conceal structure—indeed, the ornament is applied so as to accentuate structure, and in this sense the Burnham Baroque has more than a little in common with the work of the Beaux-Arts–trained master of the Chicago school, Louis Sullivan. (See Sullivan's Bayard Building of 1898 on Bleecker Street, 6.2).

I think the best approach to the Flatiron Building is not head-on, in the manner of most photographers, but from the rear. This is the clearest way to see how the ornament energizes the form of the building. The façade along 22nd Street, viewed straight on, makes this look like a conventional, if extravagantly ornamented, foursquare building. Move around to one of the sides, however, and the projecting ornament begins positively to undulate as the sides of the building seem to become detached, floating planes. It is then clear how the design of the façades is responsible for the power of the triangular shape of the building. Finally, at the front, the side planes are reattached in the sharp prow pointed up Fifth Avenue.

4 MADISON SQUARE PARK

Fifth Avenue to Madison Avenue, from 23rd Street to 26th Street
Opened in 1847

There is a lot more coherence here than at Union Square. By day, the streets around Madison Square throb with business—of countless wholesale import shops, of the wholesale toy market, of the giant insurance companies, and, beginning in recent years, of publishing, advertising, design, and architectural firms. By night, the area is rather dead: long gone are its days as a residential area or the site of grand hotels. Visit on a weekday, and the workaday bustle is as appealing and diverse as you will find anywhere in town. There are also a lot of worthy works of architecture in these parts.

From the time of the opening of Madison Square Park until the 1870s, this was a high-toned residential area. An excellent sense of the kind of life lived here then can be had from visiting the **Theodore Roosevelt Birthplace Museum** at 28 East 20th Street between Broadway and Park Avenue South. This building is a 1923 exact replica, by Theodate Pope Riddle, of the original Roosevelt house, built in 1848 (a year after the opening of Madison Square Park) and demolished in 1910. Theodore Roosevelt was born in that house in 1858, and his family remained there until 1873. The current four-story brownstone is a museum of Rooseveltiana, including numerous period furnishings, many of which were originally in the Roosevelt house.

From the 1870s to the turn of the century, this area was Manhattan's "downtown," where the major hotels were located and also near to the Sixth Avenue department stores. Around the turn of the century, this became Manhattan's megaoffice district, and the volume of office development continued through the boom of the 1920s. After World War II, the area became dominated by warehouse and light-manufacturing enterprises, and in the 1980s, many businesses relocated here to escape the hyperinflated midtown real-estate market. The pivotal event marking the transition of the area from retailing mecca to megaoffice district was the completion, in 1902, of the Flatiron Building.

Such is the landmark status of that great building that as the area experienced changes in the 1980s, it came popularly to be known as the "Flatiron District." Twelve years prior to the Flatiron, Stanford White's Madison Square Garden had opened, occupying the entire block bounded by Madison and Fourth avenues and 26th and 27th streets, on the site of the Union Depot of the New York and Harlem Railroad, which had stood from 1845 to 1871 and the need for which had been obviated by the new Grand Central Terminal at 42nd Street. (The old Union Depot remained standing for almost twenty more years, serving as the first Madison Square Garden.)

4A *Metropolitan Life Tower*

Almost as soon as the Garden opened, it became identified worldwide with New York. With the Brooklyn Bridge (2.13), completed in 1883, and the Statue of Liberty, completed in 1886, the Garden was, in the last decade of the nineteenth century, one of the three most famous New York landmarks. Though the Garden was easily the most spectacular place of its kind in the world, it did not in fact fare very well financially. It was demolished in 1925. A new building erected to serve similar functions on Eighth Avenue and 49th Street was also christened Madison Square Garden, as was *its* successor, on the site of McKim, Mead & White's Pennsylvania Station, for even though neither of these was located anywhere near Madison Square, the association of the name *Madison Square* with spectacular entertainments had become so strong that it has led to a bit of an identity crisis for the *real* Madison Square. Say "Madison Square" and people are bound to think of the Knicks and the Rangers, which may be one reason they have taken to calling this the Flatiron District.

The building now on the site of Madison Square Garden is Cass Gilbert's **New York Life Insurance Company Headquarters** (51 Madison Avenue) of 1928. At forty-nine stories, over 1.1 million square feet, and an entire block in size, this is surely the biggest classical skyscraper in town. It is limestone neo-Renaissance: its base, wrapped around with arches, supports a bulky shaft made more graceful by the vertical accent of continuous limestone mullions, complementing the heavy, blocky piers, and culminating, like Gilbert's United States Courthouse (2.15), in a gold pyramidal crown, which is lit up at night, a skyline beacon for this part of town. There is also one of those splendid through-block lobbies. This building has been criticized for its somewhat ungainly proportions and for what by 1928 was considered its old-fashioned style. Still, it seems to me an excellent, urbanistically appropriate building for its off-square site.

At 35 East 25th Street, at the northeast corner of Madison Avenue, is James Brown Lord's **Appellate Division of the Supreme Court of the State of New York** (1900), an exceptionally beautiful Beaux-Arts courthouse; with the Surrogate's Court (2.11), it is one of the two most beautiful courthouses in Manhattan. In the words of Henry Hope Reed, it represents "the epitome of the academic tradition in the arts at the turn of the century." This compact and exceedingly elegant structure features a 25th Street porch, where six massive, fluted Corinthian columns support a broad pediment bearing elaborate reliefs by Charles

4B *New York Life Insurance Building*

Henry Niehaus; there are few such pediments in New York. Flanking the porch are seated figures by Frederick Wellington Ruckstull. The building's narrow side on Madison Avenue is dominated by four fluted Corinthian columns of the same scale as the porch ones. These columns support an entablature and cornice surmounted by four beautiful caryatids, representing the four seasons, by Thomas Shields Clarke. The most notable feature of the building is the phalanx of statues along the top of the façades. These statues were carved by some of the most noteworthy academic sculptors of the day, and are:

From west to east along 25th Street:
Zoroaster by Edward Clark Potter
Alfred the Great by Jonathan Scott Hartley
Lycurgus by George Edwin Bissell
Solon by Herbert Adams
Justice by Daniel Chester French

St. Louis of France by John Donoghue
Manu by Henry Augustus Lukeman
Justinian by Henry Kirke Bush-Brown
From north to south along Madison Avenue:
Confucius by Philip Martiny
Peace by Karl Bitter
Moses by William Cowper

In these days of political correctness, it is interesting to note what a multicultural group these statues represent!

At the northeast corner of Madison Avenue and 23rd Street is the twelve-story **Main Building of the Metropolitan Life Insurance Company,** built in 1964 and designed by Lloyd Morgan, replacing the great 1893 original. At the turn of the century, Metropolitan Life was the largest insurance company in the world. It is therefore not surprising that in 1909 they added to their headquarters the **Metropolitan Life Tower,** at the southeast corner of Madison Avenue and 24th Street, modeled on the campanile in St. Mark's Square in Venice. At seven hundred feet high (fifty-one stories), the tower was the tallest building in the world, and was designed by Napoleon LeBrun & Sons. Here is yet another solution to the problem of skyscraper style. Just as St. Mark's Square has its campanile, so, too, does Madison Square Park. The shaft of the Metropolitan Life Tower was originally richly ornamented, but in an utterly ill-conceived attempt to make it look more modern, the ornament was stripped in 1964.

Just across 24th Street from the tower is still another addition to the Metropolitan Life complex. **The North Building of the Metropolitan Life Insurance Company** was designed by Harvey Wiley Corbett and D. Everett Waid and built in 1932. This is one of the most sculptured Art Deco piles in the city. It was originally intended to be an eighty- to one hundred-story tower, which would have made it the tallest building in the world, and it would have surpassed Ralph Walker's One Wall Street (1.16) as the New York skyscraper that looked most like a Hugh Ferriss drawing. The Depression, however, intervened to limit Corbett and Waid's plans, and the building that emerged represents only the base of the proposed tower. It occupies the full block bounded by Madison Avenue and Park Avenue South and 24th and 25th streets. At each of its four corners is a monumentally scaled, arcaded entrance—scaled for the original eighty- to one hundred-story tower. For the pedestrian, there is a dreamlike quality in happening upon these superscaled and majestic monumental entrances on bustling Park Avenue South or Madison Avenue.

Within Madison Square Park itself is a wealth of statuary. At the southern end of the square is Randolph Rogers's 1876 bronze statue of William Henry Seward (1801–72), New York governor, U.S. senator, secretary of state, and antislavery crusader. Opposite Seward, at the northern end of the square, is Augustus Saint-Gaudens's magnificent 1880 bronze statue of Admiral David Glasgow Farragut (1801–70), atop a black granite base by Stanford White. The wind-blown visage of the Civil War admiral, with the most courageous eyes one is ever likely to see, is the very image of heroism. It is often the case with Saint-Gaudens's statues that strong, masculine figures are paired with delicate, feminine settings, e.g., Peter Cooper seated beneath a columned canopy, or General Sherman and his horse being led by Winged Victory. Here there is a marvelous contrast between the heroic Farragut and Stanford White's delicate, willowy, almost Art Nouveau base. At the southeast corner of the park is John Quincy Adams Ward's 1893 bronze statue of Roscoe Conkling (1829–88), U.S. senator. In the northeast corner of the park is George Edwin Bissell's 1898 bronze statue of Chester A. Arthur (1830–86), twenty-first president

5 *1880 Statue of Admiral David Glasgow Farragut*

of the United States. Just outside the park, on a traffic island between Broadway and Fifth Avenue, is a granite obelisk marking the burial place of General William Jenkins Worth, designed by James Goodwin Batterson and built in 1857. Between the statues in the park and those at the Appellate Courthouse, Madison Square may be America's greatest outdoor museum of nineteenth-century academic sculpture.

5 GILSEY HOUSE

1200 Broadway, northeast corner of 29th Street
1871, Stephen D. Hatch

This is one of those buildings that has to be included in an architectural guide because no one passes it without wondering, *What's that?* What it is is cast-iron French Second Empire, as that style could be rendered only in the profligate, vulgar America of President Ulysses S. Grant. Built as a luxury hotel (it closed in 1904), it had a bar with a floor embedded with silver dollars. This may be the most riotously eclectic building in Manhattan. Name a classical element, and chances are it can be found on this building. One design element is just heaped on another. The façades, especially the one along 29th Street, are deeply modeled—these may be the most deeply modeled cast-iron façades in the city. Note that when it opened, it was painted a gleaming white.

6 STUYVESANT SQUARE PARK

Second Avenue, from 15th Street to 17th Street
1836; renovated in 1936

The west side of Stuyvesant Square Park is as urbane an enclave as you will find in Manhattan. **St. George's Episcopal Church** fronts on a two-block-long street called Rutherford Place that runs from 15th to 17th streets between Second and Third avenues to form the western boundary of Stuyvesant Square. One of the most notable things about St. George's is the way its somber-faced, looming form acts as a wall, giving exactly the right amount of enclosure to the open space of the square. It is New York's nearest equivalent to such gems of European urbanism as the Place Saint-Sulpice in Paris.

St. George's, at the northwest corner of 16th Street, was designed by Leopold Eidlitz and Otto Blesch and completed in 1848, two years

6 *St. George's Church*

after Trinity Church (1.17) and Grace Church (6.9). Spires were added in 1856, but were removed in 1889 after a fire. Eidlitz, nearly all of whose works have been demolished, was one of New York's most prominent Victorian architects. Perhaps his most famous building was the old Temple Emanu-El, which stood at the northeast corner of Fifth Avenue and 43rd Street. Completed in 1868 in an outrageously picturesque "Moorish" style, it was demolished in 1927 when the congregation moved to its present home on Fifth Avenue and 65th Street.

Both Blesch the Bavarian and Eidlitz the Bohemian were fired by an enthusiasm for the south German Romanesque. This was in sharp contrast to the prevailing Anglican Gothic of Trinity Church and Grace Church. St. George's has a German "hall-church" plan, with aisles equal in height to the nave, as opposed to the basilican and Gothic high nave flanked by low aisles. There is a German tradition of churches with an open-hall appearance. This idea of the church as an open hall is as "unpopish" as you can get, and the hall church omits the articulated chancel. Representing the soon-to-burgeon Romanesque Revival amid the high tide of the Anglican "counter-reformation" and the ecclesiological movement, St. George's proved that American Episcopalians were hardly convinced by the moral claims made on behalf of the Gothic style. While in the 1840s English taste was still prevalent in America, it was being given a real run for its money by the immigration, not only of Germans, but of German ideas, German tastes, German customs. Many things that are "typically American," such as picnics, parades, marching bands, apple pie, kindergarten, the preference for lager over ale, and much of our popular music, are in fact imports from Germany. While hardly all Romanesque Revival designs in America were based on German precedents, nonetheless the style caught on, at least in part because the Romanesque was enjoying a contemporaneous, and considerable, revival in Germany. And there was no Romanesque Revival to speak of at the time in England.

The hall church was an invention of the German Romanesque. The inspiration for this type of church seems to have derived from the Cistercians, and later the Dominicans and Franciscans, for whom the church was less the setting for intricate pageantry than a place in which to gather to hear sermons. The hall church was as suited to the aims of St. George's rector at the time it was built, the Reverend Dr. Stephen Tyng, as the English medieval parish church was to the aims of the ecclesiologists. Tyng (1800–85) was an evangelical Episcopalian, opposed to the "popery" of some of his colleagues, and demanded an evangelican church, a kind of meeting hall in which to preach and be preached to. He was one of the most famous orators of his day, and for him the main point of the church service was not the enactment of complex sacramental rituals but preaching and oratory. For Tyng, the design of Trinity Church reeked of Catholicism. He gave explicit instructions to Eidlitz that the "communion table" should not be mistakable for an "altar." An evangelical touch is exhibited on the west wall, where the Lord's Prayer is plainly printed in large, easy-to-read letters.

The exterior of St. George's exudes solidity and propriety. There is nothing even remotely lyrical or elevating about it. It is a handsome wall for Stuyvesant Square. The church is on the corner, so there is an unobstructed view of two full sides. It is faced in earthy, smooth brownstone that blends beautifully with the green of Stuyvesant Square. The now-spireless towers flank a triple portal, with an arcade running above the three round-arched entrances. Above the arcade and below the lushly ornamented and corbeled gable is a very fine rose window, framed by a broad expanse of unadorned brownstone. The corbeling, or decorative, round-arched, arcaded molding, continues along the tops of the bases of the two towers, and from there along the roof lines of the sides. The south side, along 16th Street, is marked by high buttresses placed between the nave windows.

Montgomery Schuyler was critical of Blesch and Eidlitz's failure to reflect the interior gallery in their treatment of the south side, and suggested that the windows should have been subdivided to indicate the interior placement of the gallery, and also to relieve a "monotony which seems to have been entirely unavoidable." I wonder, though, if the architects of St. George's purposely eschewed any unnecessary functional indications as smacking of ecclesiology. Despite his reservations, Schuyler nonetheless felt that St. George's was "one of our most seemly and dignified New York churches, inside and out."

The Gothic parish house, designed by Leopold Eidlitz, though often wrongly ascribed to his son, Cyrus L. W. Eidlitz, is at **207 East 16th Street** between Rutherford Place and Third Avenue. It was built in 1888 of that most romantic of materials, rockfaced brownstone. The church presents a staid and proper face to Stuyvesant Square, concealing the little devil of a parish house, one of those real no-holds-barred high-Victorian picturesque monstrosities that are impossible not to love. The former rectory, now the **Henry Hill Pierce House** of St. George's Church, between the parish house and the church on 16th Street, dates from the 1850s and was also designed by Eidlitz. The chapel, at **4 Rutherford Place,** directly north of the church and fronting on the square, is a perhaps overlabored combination of Romanesque and Byzantine elements, designed by Matthew and Henry Emery and built in 1911.

On the northwest corner of Rutherford Place and 15th Street is the **Friends Meeting House and Seminary,** designed by Charles T. Bunting and built in 1860. The Quakers went even further than Tyng's evangelical Episcopalians in the direction of the house of worship as meeting hall. The Friends Meeting House is red brick with brownstone quoins, and as austere as anything in modern architecture.

Stuyvesant Square Park is bisected by Second Avenue. On the south side of the western half of the square, at 246 East 15th Street, at the southwest corner of Second Avenue, is one of the few modern church buildings in Manhattan. **St. Mary's Catholic Church of the Byzantine Rite** was designed by Brother Cajetan J. B. Baumann and built in 1964. Concrete with large stained-glass expanses, it seems designed less to flood its sanctuary with filtered light than to radiate light at night when the sanctuary is lit from within. In this, its aesthetic differs from that of traditional church architecture in much the same way that modern glass office buildings differ from the solid masonry ones of the past.

The eastern side of Stuyvesant Square is fronted on Nathan D. Perlman Place (the eastern two-block-long counterpart to Rutherford Place) by the large institutional buildings of **Beth Israel Hospital,** and so lacks the tranquillity and urbanity of the western half. Readers of Saul Bellow will recall that Beth Israel is where Artur Sammler in *Mr. Sammler's Planet* (1970) goes to visit the dying Elya Gruner. Here is Sammler leaving the hospital:

> On Second Avenue the springtime scraping of roller skates was heard on hollow, brittle sidewalks, a soothing harshness. Turning from the new New York of massed apartments into the older New York of brownstone and wrought-iron, Sammler saw through large black circles in a fence daffodils and tulips, the mouths of these flowers open and glowing, but on the pure yellow the fallout of soot already was sprinkled. You might in this city become a flower-washer. . . . Red brick, the Friends Seminary, and ruddy coarse warm stone, broad, clumsy, solid, the Episcopal church, St. George's. Sammler had heard that the original J. Pierpont Morgan had been an usher there. . . . At St. George's, Sundays, the god of stockbrokers could breathe easy awhile in the riotous city. In thought, Mr. Sammler was testy with White Protestant America for not keeping better order.

The "new New York of massed apartments": One block east of Stuyvesant Square are the vast **Stuyvesant Town** and **Peter Cooper Village** housing projects, extending from 14th Street on the south to 23rd Street on the north, and from First Avenue on the west to the F.D.R. Drive on the east. These projects, designed by Irwin Clavan and Gilmore Clarke, were built in 1947 by the Metropolitan Life Insurance Company as middle-income housing for returning servicemen. At the time they were constructed, urban critics such as Jane Jacobs and Lewis Mumford harshly criticized the regimentation and gigantism of these projects, which followed Corbusian superblock principles by placing tall, plain towers in a park without reference to preexisting street patterns. Today the weathering process and the growth of trees has softened the brutality of these projects, and they are regarded as a highly desirable, secure, insulated place to live.

7 GRAMERCY PARK

From 20th Street to 21st Street, on axis with Lexington Avenue to the north and Irving Place to the south
1831, Samuel Ruggles

One of the most celebrated places in New York is this proper London square. As is traditional in London, the park is open only to residents of the surrounding buildings, who are supplied with keys. Though the walker, unless he or she knows someone who lives on the square, cannot enjoy the park's benches and shade, nonetheless this is a delightful area in which to walk, for there are some very good buildings to be seen. From the south up Irving Place is my favorite approach to Gramercy Park. Irving Place is the extension of Lexington Avenue which runs south of Gramercy Park from 14th Street to 20th Street. Irving Place is one of those occasional Manhattan streets—like 18th Street between Fifth and Sixth avenues, 10th Street between Broadway and University Place (5.8), and 38th Street between Park and Lexington avenues (9.11)—where the scale is just right to create the sensation that the street is cradling you in its arms, and the sense of enclosure is warm and comforting. Irving Place is lined mostly with large loft structures, very different from what bursts on the senses when one reaches Gramercy Park. This is exactly how cities are supposed to work, and you can search the world over and not find anything that works better than this. Take a right at the park.

At 28 Gramercy Park South (20th Street) between Irving Place and Third Avenue is the **Brotherhood Synagogue.** This was originally a Friends Meeting House, similar in feel to the Friends Meeting House on Stuyvesant Square (8.6), but, though completed a year earlier than that late-Georgian meeting house, it was designed in a more fashionable Italianate style. It was created by Gamaliel King and John Kellum, who only two years earlier had designed the cast-iron Cary Building on Chambers Street (2.11), also Italianate with a peaked roof. In 1975, the Friends Meeting House was sensitively remodeled by James Stewart Polshek and Partners into the Brotherhood Synagogue.

At 34 Gramercy Park East, at the northeast corner of 20th Street, is the **Gramercy apartments,** designed by George W. da Cunha and built in 1883, a red-brick Queen Anne pile of looming, evocative majesty. Its high Victorian brethren include Thomas R. Jackson's Mercantile Exchange (3.12) of 1884 and William Schickel's Century Building (8.1) of 1881. **Thirty-six Gramercy Park East,** between 20th and 21st streets, is a fanciful apartment house faced in gleaming white terra-cotta Gothic ornament, with a pair of white-stone armored knights standing guard outside. The architect was James Riely Gordon, and it was built in 1910. On the other side of the park, at **3 and 4 Gramercy Park West,** between 20th and 21st streets, are a pair of red-brick Greek Revival town houses, similar to those on Washington Square North (5.3), except that here they have elaborate, lacy, wrought-iron porches that look like they belong in New Orleans. These houses date from 1846 (the year of Trinity Church, 1.17) and were designed by Alexander Jackson Davis, perhaps the country's most prestigious architect at the time.

On the south side of the park at 15 Gramercy Park South (20th Street), between Park Avenue South and Irving Place, is the **National Arts Club,** a private club that was originally the home of Samuel J. Tilden, who came as close to being president of the United States as you can without actually making it. Search the city and you will not find a more robust brownstone than this looming Ruskinian Gothic town house, built in 1845 but redone by Calvert Vaux in 1884—a year after the Gramercy apartments, marking the early 1880s as the pinnacle of romantic New York. Next door, at 16 Gramercy Park South is **the Players,** a private club for theater people. It was originally a town house, built in 1845, but the famous actor Edwin Booth bought it and hired Stanford White to remodel it into a clubhouse. White's main contribution to the exterior was the impressive classical porch. Both the National Arts Club and the Players Club are superb street-wall buildings for the open space they front.

8 FORMER CHURCH MISSIONS HOUSE

281 Park Avenue South, southeast corner of 22nd Street
1894, R. W. Gibson and E. J. N. Stent

A glassy block with a boldly articulated frame, cousin to Louis Sullivan's Bayard Building (6.2) of four years later. Gibson's and Stent's design sense told them that they could achieve this result while simultaneously inflating an ornate, gabled Romanesque Dutch guildhall. This is a remarkable example of progressive ideas linked to traditional forms.

9 KIPS BAY PLAZA

30th Street to 33rd Street, from First Avenue to Second Avenue
North building in 1960, south building in 1965: I. M. Pei & Partners and S. J. Kessler

Honeycombs yesterday and today: compare this with the Church Missions House (8.8). A pair of apartment giants, the first exposed reinforced-concrete buildings in Manhattan. With their narrow ends to Second Avenue, on which there is a feeble stab at continuous street activity, they are oriented toward a large park: for architectural detail and planning concept, the purest Corbusian work in New York.

gs Bank

CHAPTER 9

From Herald Square to Murray Hill

Empire State Building

Chapter 9 From Herald Square to Murray Hill

1 MACY'S

34th Street to 35th Street, from Broadway to Seventh Avenue
1902, DeLemos & Cordes
Additions in 1924, 1928, 1931, Robert D. Kohn

The world's largest store. The original portion, on Broadway, was designed by DeLemos & Cordes, who six years earlier had designed an earlier "world's largest store," Siegel-Cooper (7.9). The Broadway portion of Macy's is in the Beaux-Arts vein of all the large stores of its period. The later additions to the west, extending to Seventh Avenue, are by Robert D. Kohn, architect of the Art Nouveau Evening Post Building (2.7), and are Art Deco. Macy's is a stimulus to all the senses. On the main floor, the scents of countless perfumes from the cosmetics counters waft through the air. The eye is dazzled by the gleam of glass, by mirrors, and by artful displays of merchandise. The ear rings with hushed waves of voices, keys jangling glass, cases sliding closed, music in the air. The tactile sense is aroused by the caress of fine fabrics, just there for the fingering. In the Cellar, the tongue is rewarded by an extensive selection of foods, including imported chocolates. Great department stores are empires of the senses.

2 GENERAL POST OFFICE

Eighth Avenue, from 31st Street to 33rd Street
1913, McKim, Mead & White

Two blocks of fifty-three-foot-high Corinthian columns. Even in this age of megastructures, the sheer scale of this place continues to astound. McKim, Mead & White undoubtedly selected this Imperial Roman style to accentuate the sheer scale, to leave the impression that if nothing else (alas, in 1913 it was much more), the U.S. Post Office is one *big* operation. It is jarringly juxtaposed with Madison Square Garden across the street. I did not live in New York when McKim, Mead & White's great Penn Station still stood. What a sight these two buildings, right across Eighth Avenue from each other, must have made! At this writing, Amtrak is talking about moving its passenger operations across Eighth Avenue into the post office building. Amtrak feels a grander passenger facility makes marketing sense.

In 1962, architects rose to protest the demolition of the old Penn Station. Yet those were modern architects, the very ones who had wrought the aesthetic transformation that made it conceivable for a developer to tear down something like Penn Station and replace it with something like the current Madison Square Garden. The developers did not invent their own bad taste. The new Penn Station is one of the most squalid places in Manhattan. Its recent renovation has ameliorated this squalor only a little. Madison Square Garden, however, is a sports arena, and sports arenas, alas, are defined less by their architecture than by the collective memories they contain. It was only a year after the current Madison Square Garden opened that the Knicks created wonderful memories, undiminished as local legend even a quarter century later. The Knicks added to this legend four years later. These great Red Holzman–coached basketball teams of enormous character included players Willis Reed, Walt Frazier, Dave DeBusschere, Bill Bradley, Earl Monroe, Phil Jackson. Names that resonate in the psyches of New Yorkers. When they decide to tear down this Madison Square Garden, there will be placard-wielding Knicks fans decrying the desecration of their fondest memories.

3 MANHATTAN MALL

1275 Broadway, between 32nd and 33rd streets
1912, D. H. Burnham & Company
Conversion to mall in 1988, RTKL Associates

The yuppie eighties brought chic to every nook and cranny of Manhattan south of Harlem, so much so that the island began to seem largely divested of working-class amusements. Manhattan Mall gave midtown a jolt of much-needed proletarian glitz. The former Gimbels department store was gutted and turned into a mass-cult shopping mall, anchored by a sizable branch of Brooklyn's venerable Abraham & Straus department store. The mall is bright and clangy, with escalators and glass elevators, fast-food outlets, and ubiquitous chain clothing stores. No chic. Nothing upscale. Nothing you wouldn't find in Milwaukee. There's of course a bit more of a buzz in the air than you'd find in Milwaukee, for after all Broadway is right outside with its welfare hotels and flier people and Senegalese merchants and kamikaze bicyclists. Manhattan Mall is New York playing at being Milwaukee, perhaps not getting it exactly right, but nonetheless providing a much-needed corrective to tiresome chic.

4 EMPIRE STATE BUILDING

350 Fifth Avenue, between 33rd and 34th streets
1931, Shreve, Lamb & Harmon

This is the proof that office towers of awesome size can be humane. The setback massing diminishes the building's impact on the street—so much so that many a casual pedestrian is hardly aware that he or she is walking past the world's fourth-tallest building. Maintaining the street wall has a lot to do with this. In the 1960s and 1970s, tall office buildings rose sheer behind plazas. Some plazas work, others don't, but no pedestrian ever in the least doubts the size of the building fronting the plaza. The continuous street wall creates the sense of a row of modestly scaled commercial buildings, while the tower lives on the skyline, not the street. For your information: the Empire State Building is 102 stories high, with outdoor observation decks at the 86th and 102nd floors. It is 1,250 feet high and 1,472 feet to the top of its television antenna, which was built in 1951. It includes a whopping 2.8 million square feet of space.

5 *22 West 34th Street*

5 22 WEST 34TH STREET

Between Fifth Avenue and Sixth avenues
1934, De Young & Moscowitz

Five years before Edward Durell Stone and Philip Goodwin's Museum of Modern Art (13.12) came this equally startling (for New York) modern retail building, originally a store specializing in popular knockoffs of modern furniture styles. It is reminiscent not only of the Museum of Modern Art, but also of Fellheimer & Wagner's CBS Studio Building of 1940 on 52nd Street between Madison and Park avenues; and of Shreve, Lamb & Harmon, and Harrison & Fouilhoux's Hunter College building, also of 1940, on Park Avenue between 68th and 69th streets. The 1930s were an astonishing period in American architecture, the only decade in which every conceivable style, from Beaux-Arts to International Style, could boast committed clients. This building was until recently almost completely covered by a billboard advertising jeans.

6 Former B. ALTMAN & COMPANY

361 Fifth Avenue, between 34th and 35th streets
1906; extended in 1914, Trowbridge & Livingston

Former GORHAM BUILDING

390 Fifth Avenue, southwest corner of 36th Street
1906, McKim, Mead & White

Former TIFFANY BUILDING

409 Fifth Avenue, southeast corner of 37th Street
1906, McKim, Mead & White

Manhattan 1906: the birth of midtown Fifth Avenue as the retail center it remains today, although the kind of elegant stores once housed in these sumptuous edifices has moved twenty-or-so blocks uptown. Theodore Roosevelt was president. New York was the second-largest city in the world, after London, and closing in. England ruled a fifth of the globe. It was the year of the great San Francisco earthquake. It was also the year in which, after designing the Gorham and Tiffany buildings, Stanford White was shot dead in the roof restaurant of his own Madison Square Garden by Harry K. Thaw, the husband of White's lover, the actress Evelyn Nesbit. These buildings were, then, the swan song of one of the greatest American architects, and among his greatest achievements.

The Gorham Building is a stolid neo-Renaissance palazzo, enlivened by a smooth, rounded corner turning (see McKim, Mead & White's Judge Building of 1889 on Fifth Avenue and 16th Street) and especially by the biggest, boldest cornice in town. The ground-floor Ionic arcade has been brutally "modernized." The ground floor of the Tiffany Building has been even more brutally "modernized," and both buildings, once such proud exemplars of American elegance, are now ghostly relics. The Tiffany is a true masterpiece, and maybe Fifth Avenue's most beautiful building. White based his design on the Venetian Renaissance Palazzo Grimani of the second half of the sixteenth century, designed by Michele Sanmichele. Note also the similarity between the Tiffany Building and J. P. Gaynor's great cast-iron Haughwout Building (4.3) of 1857. The superimposed Corinthian columns framing high, arched windows give this marble jewel box a powerful stateliness. What is most impressive about it, however, is how White used the Venetian prototype, which

6 *Tiffany Building*

featured larger window openings than other forms of Renaissance architecture, to follow unmistakably the rhythm of the steel frame. White even simplified the decorative scheme of the Palazzo Grimani by stripping the fluting from the columns and toning down the Corinthian capitals. There is a phenomenal lightness to this building that is an almost perfect amalgam of the Beaux-Arts and the Modern; the Tiffany Building is a truly underappreciated work that makes one wonder what wonders White might have produced had he not died so tragically young.

The B. Altman building was the first department store on midtown Fifth Avenue, and its stately Renaissance style was meant to be a tasteful neighbor to the avenue's mansions. Altman's closed a few years ago. It was by all odds the most splendid department store in New York in my time, the epitome—in its architecture, in its merchandise, in its standard of service—of a kind of utterly unostentatious bourgeois life that flourished in, indeed was the very backbone of, New York in its years of greatest glory, and which has now virtually disappeared.

7 Former KNOX HAT BUILDING

452 Fifth Avenue, southwest corner of 40th Street
1902, John H. Duncan

REPUBLIC BANK TOWER

452 Fifth Avenue, between 39th and 40th streets
1986, Attia & Perkins

The Knox Hat, by the architect of Grant's Tomb, is another in Fifth Avenue's impressive row of elegant classical retail structures. Once the most renowned men's hat store in the city, it later became the headquarters of the Republic National Bank, complete with "modernized" ground floor. When the bank outgrew the modestly scaled structure, Attia & Perkins's enormous tower was wrapped around it. The old building was splendidly restored in the process, and now looks good as new. The new building is crisply detailed and has been given a contextual multiple orientation: it hugs the old building on Fifth Avenue, standing very much on its own when viewed from the west. Alas, the old Knox Hat is too rich a building to be made to cower beneath a modern office tower, and the new twenty-seven-story tower utterly cuts off the view of the Empire State Building from farther up Fifth Avenue.

8 BRYANT PARK

Sixth Avenue, from 40th Street to 42nd Street
1871; renovated in 1934; renovated again in 1992

Once a festering sore on the face of midtown. Nine million dollars later, it is one of the best things in New York. When I first moved to New York in the late seventies, Bryant Park was known for only one thing: drug dealers. It was an officially tolerated, open-air drug market. In part we have Robert Moses to thank for that, for it was under him that the park was renovated during the depression and given those design elements that contributed mightily to its attractiveness to nefarious types. Moses's park was the antiurban ideal, as cut off as possible from its surrounding city. To this end, huge plantings around the perimeter of the park obscured views into or out of it, and so tens of thousands of

8 *Bryant Park*

office workers and tourists would walk past it every day oblivious to the activities within. Oblivious, that is, unless some poor soul should enter it in search of a park's tranquillity, which, alas, seldom happened, for the design that makes a park appealing to villains also makes it uninviting to ordinary passersby.

In the latest, glorious renovation by landscape architects Hannah/Olin, Moses's huge plantings have been removed, and the park has been much opened up to the street. Instead of Moses's high hedges, there are now borders of perennials. The original Beaux-Arts formality of the space has been properly retained. Entering from Sixth Avenue, one encounters a large plaza with trees and movable chairs, and the large, splendid, Italian Renaissance-style Josephine Shaw Lowell Memorial Fountain, designed by Charles Adams Platt and built in 1912. Beyond the plaza is a vast, unadorned *lawn,* perhaps the only lawn in midtown. The fine, protomodern rear façade of the New York Public Library butts right up to the rear of the park, making a superb wall. Another superb wall is formed by the buildings of 40th Street between Sixth and Fifth avenues. The most notable of these buildings are the **Bryant Park Studios,** a lovely, large-windowed Beaux-Arts building dating from 1901, designed by Lamb & Rich and built as artists' studios, with exceptional north light from across the park; and the twenty-three-story former **American Radiator Building,** a neo-Gothic tower in the 1920s setback mode: a dark, craggy, looming, and altogether fine building by Hood & Fouilhoux from 1924, hot on the heels of Hood & Howells's famous competition-winning neo-Gothic Tribune Tower in Chicago.

9 461 FIFTH AVENUE

Northeast corner of 40th Street
1988, Skidmore, Owings & Merrill

This building seems to me to be representative of the postmodern work Skidmore, Owings and Merrill did around the country through the 1980s. The exposed trusses are an overtly decorative bow to the spirit of Viollet-le-Duc. It's not nearly as fussy as a Kohn Pedersen Fox building, and it's not a tin can like a Helmut Jahn building, and the corner store is very striking.

10 2 PARK AVENUE

Between 32nd and 33rd streets
1927, Ely Jacques Kahn

One of New York's most famous Art Deco buildings. In 1928, Lewis Mumford wrote that this "building strikes the boldest and clearest note among all our recent achievements in skyscraper architecture." Mumford praised "its unique synthesis of the constructive and the feeling elements"—i.e., of the cold structuralism of European modernism and the overdecorated Beaux-Arts and Art Deco styles. Kahn's solution to the problem of architectural expression in skyscraper design in a dense urban setting, in which programs are set not by architects, but by developers and engineers, was to outline the very boxy structure in a vigorously rhythmical brick-and-terra-cotta polychromy that does not alter its course as it is continued into the elevator lobby. This is a dense urban equivalent of the organic architecture of Frank Lloyd Wright, in which interior and exterior are unified through decoration to render a total artistic experience of site and structure.

11 PIERPONT MORGAN LIBRARY

33 East 36th Street, between Madison and Park avenues
1906, McKim, Mead & White
Addition at 29 East 36th Street in 1928, Benjamin Wistar Morris
Addition on Madison Avenue in 1991, Voorsanger & Mills

231 MADISON AVENUE

Southeast corner of 37th Street
1853

In the former Tiffany Building (9.6), we see the work of Stanford White at his best. In the Morgan Library, we see the work of White's partner, Charles Follen McKim, at *his* best. McKim's is a much more severe Renaissance style, sharp edged and with finely etched details. The model here was Baldassare Peruzzi's Palazzo Pietro Massimi (completed in 1536) in Rome. McKim's main change is his use of the arched Palladian entrance with Ionic columns. The severity of Peruzzi's façade recalls the purity of Greek architecture. McKim's façade uses solid marble blocks without mortar, and it is interesting to note that the only other Manhattan building that does this is the Greek Revival Federal Hall National Memorial (1.12) on Wall Street. The smooth mortarless façade also puts one in mind of the "God is in the details" aesthetic of such high-modern works as Mies van der Rohe's Seagram Building (10.11), in which joints are slickly concealed to create façades of bold, stark, classical rhythms. In this respect, the Morgan Library may be cited with the work of the German Karl Friedrich Schinkel as an example of a kind of proto-Miesian neoclassical architecture.

The unusual freestanding, pre-Civil War brownstone house at **231 Madison Avenue** was formerly the home of J. P. Morgan, Jr., and was for many years the headquarters of the Lutheran Church in America. It is now part of the Morgan Library, connected to it by Voorsanger & Mills's rather jarring glass atrium along Madison Avenue. Voorsanger & Mills went the modern route in recognition of the basic irreconcilability of the very different Renaissance approaches of the Morgan Library and

11 *Pierpont Morgan Library*

231 Madison. Where the former is hard-edged marble, the latter is pliant brownstone, where the general, inevitably romantic, effect is more important than the details.

12 233 MADISON AVENUE

Northeast corner of 37th Street
1905, C. P. H. Gilbert

A parvenu's mansion, a *patissier's* confection, now the Polish Consulate. This is a massive French Second Empire pile of a house, with rampant rustication, exuberant chamfering, and a real top-hat mansard. My favorite part of this utterly delightful building is the central portion of the 37th Street façade, with its elegant French window, topped by a fancy bracketed balcony.

13 38TH STREET

From Park Avenue to Third Avenue

Murray Hill is basically a solid, stolid bourgeois precinct, unassuming and unostentatious, punctuated by the occasional parvenu's pile, such as 233 Madison. Thirty-eighth Street seems to me to evoke as well as any street the sturdy comforts of what strikes the casual observer as one of the most livable neighborhoods in Manhattan. None of the buildings here is a barn burner, but there is a great deal of variety in scale, function, and style, and it all has the feeling of a discreet enclave—I believe Jane Jacobs would approve. Paul W. Reilly's Roman Catholic **Church of Our Saviour,** on the southeast corner of Park Avenue and 38th Street, was built in 1959, and its reputation has never recovered from its universal denunciation as a Gothic *retardataire*. From my own perspective, though, it is an exceptionally handsome church indeed, well detailed and beautifully maintained, and well worth a look inside. It is quite a rebuke to those who, circa 1959, said that one of the reasons we should no longer build in traditional styles was that the expense was too great and the quality of workmanship unobtainable. At 108 East 38th Street is Bowden & Russell's Art Deco **Town House apartments,** built in 1930. It is a high setback structure in brick with a dazzling crown of glazed terra-cotta. It is only fitting that in its base should be a sturdy neighborhood Italian restaurant. At **149 East 38th Street** is a Dutch Renaissance-style, steep-gabled carriage house, converted, in a manner common in Murray Hill, into a residence. It dates from 1902. Elsewhere along the street are row houses and apartments, some fine, some plain, all combining to create the kind of street designed for living.

CHAPTER 10

Grand Central

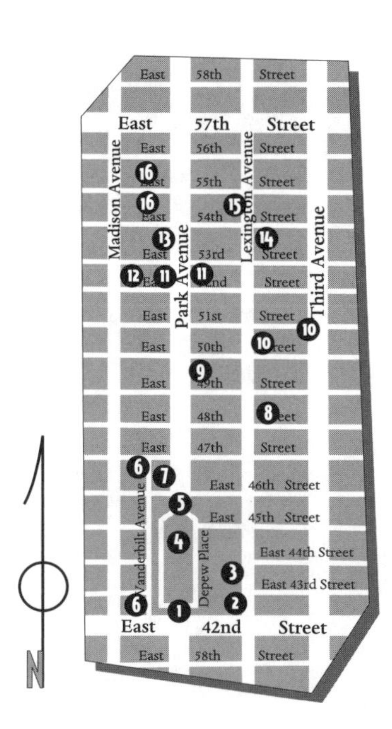

1 *Grand Central Terminal*

Chapter 10

Grand Central

1 GRAND CENTRAL TERMINAL

42nd Street and Park Avenue
1903–13, Reed & Stem and Warren & Wetmore

André Malraux said that the defining concept of modern times was that of *access.* In the 1850s and '60s, Baron Haussmann cut broad boulevards through the pestilential maze of twisting, dead-end *rues* that had prevented the vast majority of Parisians from, among many other things, ever setting eyes on the Louvre. Today ordinary American homes are furnished with computers that convey the world's knowledge at the touch of a key. Somewhere between Haussmann's boulevards and CD-ROM came Grand Central Terminal. Cities are information-access systems. Haussmann opened new worlds of knowledge to the cloistered denizens of working-class Paris. Grand Central Terminal combined this urban ideal of congestion (information) with movement (access). Cognitive scientists may err in attempting to explicate the human brain by comparing it to computer circuitry. The computer is not like a brain: it is like a city. It is congestion with movement: vast stores of information with the means of rapid retrieval. Grand Central—the terminal together with the planned development of its trackage air rights—is almost a conceptual prototype of the computer. "Access tree" is the name Rai Okamoto and Frank Williams of the Regional Plan Association have given to the organic interrelation of all forms of urban movement. They view all the episodes of, say, the morning commute to work—subway, station platform, stairs or escalator, sidewalks, elevator, building corridors—as parts of a single transportation system, or system of access. The points of change in mode of transport they call "mixing chambers." Grand Central is the grandest mixing chamber of them all, tying together twenty-one buildings, regional interurban railroads, subways, automobile viaducts, escalators, elevators, and pedestrian ramps.

The New York & Harlem and New York Central & Hudson River railroads began operating from the first Grand Central on this site in 1871. The immense danger and occasional disasters of the steam tunnels led to a public demand to convert the rail operations to electricity. The New York Central's chief engineer, William J. Wilgus, and the St. Paul, Minnesota–based architectural firm of Reed & Stem were the original designers of the electrified Grand Central that began construction in 1903. About two hundred buildings housing an established community were demolished to make way for the new terminal, and all the blocks bounded by 42nd and 50th streets and Madison and Lexington avenues, and on Park Avenue from 50th to 57th streets were excavated with one million pounds of dynamite. The new Grand Central opened on February 2, 1913. It cost eighty million dollars. Its replacement cost today would be over two billion dollars. At the height of its activity, in the years just after the Second World War, Grand Central served about the same number of passengers as the world's busiest airport does today, even though Grand Central uses only *1 percent* as much land as the airport does.

After Reed & Stem planned the terminal, Warren & Wetmore were called in to dress it up, and they did so in the style that had always been associated with urban access. From the Athenian agora to Haussmann's boulevards, Classicism had been the garb of urbanity. The principal, or 42nd Street, façade—of Stony Creek granite from Connecticut and Bedford limestone from Indiana—is best viewed from a couple of blocks down Park Avenue. Pairs of fluted Doric columns flank each of three large arched windows. Jules-Alexis Coutan's pediment sculpture of Mercury, god of transportation, and his companions is fifteen hundred tons of Bedford limestone. Henry Hope Reed calls it the "best piece of monumental sculpture in America."

It is inside, though, that Grand Central comes true. The concourse floor is of Tennessee marble; the staircases, balconies, and wainscoting are of Botticino marble; and the walls are of Caen stone. Reed & Stem originally called for a skylighted concourse, but Whitney Warren opted to commission Paul Helleu to create the zodiac ceiling, which contains twenty-five hundred painted stars and crests at the equivalent of nine stories high. Lewis Mumford wrote, almost four decades ago, of Grand Central and the now-demolished Pennsylvania Station:

> The major quality of each station, one that too few buildings in this city today possess, is space—space generously even nobly handled. These two large gifts of space . . . still give the tired traveler a lift when he leaves the comparatively cramped quarters of a train after a long trip. The combination of mass and volume is one of the special blessings of monumental architecture, and people journey thousands of miles to behold it in the remains of the Baths of Caracalla and the Colosseum.

When you descend the ramp from 42nd and Vanderbilt on a weekday morning, it is warm and stuffy with musty, then frying, smells till the concourse, and in the clearing the lungs fill again with breathable air as broad streamers of white light fall from the east, and amid the muffled mass of footfalls and voices, all is steady, unagitated activity. If ever there were an apotheosis of New York, this is it. There is another kind of urban movement: the soaring spirit.

2 GRAND HYATT HOTEL

125 East 42nd Street, northwest corner of Lexington Avenue
1980, Gruzen & Partners and Der Scutt

Like Manhattan Mall (9.3), this is New York playing at being some other city. Donald Trump took the grand old Commodore Hotel and refaced it in mirror glass and gave it a glitzy lobby complete with chrome and waterfall. The Commodore was opened in 1919, six years after the present Grand Central Terminal, and was designed, like the terminal, by Warren & Wetmore. When built, it may have been the largest hotel in the world, and it claimed to have the most spacious hotel lobby ever. The lobby is still enormous, exceeded in size among New York hotels only by the Waldorf-Astoria (10.9). It is the kind of hotel lobby one expects to find in Houston or Atlanta, not in New York. Like Manhattan Mall, which seems to belong in Milwaukee, the Grand Hyatt's cavernous lobby works splendidly in midtown Manhattan: it manages to be both a bustling and a relaxing space. There are constant motion and reflective surfaces, but there are also plenty of seating, excellent sound absorption, waterfall and tinkling piano sounds, accessible toilets, and a policy of being open to the public. Somehow this is a space that does not lose its middle-class glitz even if a couple of homeless people happen in. There is no question that it is garish, but it is extremely welcome at a time when big hotel lobbies are increasingly inaccessible. See the Marriott Marquis (12.5).

The exterior of the Grand Hyatt, on the other hand, is a mirror box, and an utter and inexcusable outrage to the cityscape of East 42nd Street, situated as it is between two masterpieces, Grand Central Terminal (10.1) and the Chrysler Building (11.4). The old Commodore was a brick and masonry structure of appropriately modest and deferential design. The Grand Hyatt imposes its garish vacuity with a painful lack of concern about the way it relates to one of the architecturally most-significant streets in America.

3 GRAYBAR BUILDING

420 Lexington Avenue, between 43rd and 44th streets
1926, Sloan & Robertson

For some reason, among classic New York skyscrapers, the Graybar seems, despite its immense size, to be the one most likely to slip from the mind. It is, astonishingly, not even included in the encyclopedic, indispensable *AIA Guide to New York City.* Very odd for a building exceeding 1.2 million square feet of space. I submit that this very invisibility is a tribute to this building. The Graybar is fit so snugly into the complex of buildings that includes Grand Central Terminal and the Grand Hyatt Hotel that this complex seems to be a single megastructure. The Graybar opens onto the broad corridor that leads from Lexington Avenue, directly north of the Grand Hyatt, to the Grand Central concourse. A commuter who lives in Westchester County and takes the train to work, or who lives in Brooklyn and takes the subway, and who works in the Graybar Building or in the Pan Am Building, need never set foot onto Manhattan pavement, for all services essential to his or her daily needs are contained within this complex. The Graybar is one of the city's earliest Art Deco skyscrapers. Its twenty-six stories are symmetrically disposed along Lexington Avenue, with two setback projecting wings flanking a deep setback and recessed central section. This is an urbanistically superb building, with its bulk concealed and with its link to the Grand Central concourse. It also has a great entrance on Lexington. The cables supporting the canopy depict rats climbing ships' cables and being halted by cones placed by sailors to keep the rats off the ship. Notice also the rats' heads peering down from the tops of the cables.

4 Former PAN AM BUILDING

200 Park Avenue, from 43rd Street to 45th Street
1963, Emery Roth & Sons with Walter Gropius and Pietro Belluschi

The architectural historian Carl W. Condit has described this building as "one of the supreme acts of folly in the history of the city's real estate operations." The 2.4 million square feet packed into its fifty-five stories made it the largest office building in the world when it was built. The New York Central Railroad announced in 1958 that Erwin S. Wolfson would develop the area directly north of the Grand Central Terminal head house, and directly across 45th Street from the New York Central Building. The original development of the Grand Central trackage air rights in the 1910s and '20s had yielded what Condit calls "one of the most urbane groups of commercial buildings in the world." Park Avenue north of Grand Central was lined with modestly scaled, neo-Renaissance apartment houses, hotels, and office buildings. The view south on Park Avenue from above 46th Street was capped by the majestic New York Central, now Helmsley, Building (10.5). The New York Central tower did not plug the vista, but served as punctuation, allowing sky to penetrate 'round its sides. Park Avenue, then, with its planted center strip, fine buildings all built out to the street line, and superb closure in the form of the New York Central Building, was one of the most beautiful streets in the world. It all too obviously no longer is. What happened?

The Pan Am Building, for one thing. Rising sheer behind the New York Central Building, it completely obliterated the graceful punctuation of Park Avenue. Now the view down Park from above 46th or up Park from below 42nd is totally consumed by the looming hulk of the Pan Am Building. If for no reason other than its bulk, this is a loathsome building. Alas, there are other reasons besides. Everything that is good about modern architecture is here absent: fine proportions, elegant detailing, volumetric expression—none are present in the Pan Am Building.

The precast concrete curtain wall, fine technological achievement though it undoubtedly is, combines with sheer unsculptured mass to make it seem as if the architects did everything in their power to emphasize the bulk and speculative soullessness of this building—a far cry indeed from the Empire State Building, where pains were taken to soften the impact of such bulk on the street below.

The Pan Am has a vast through-block lobby, leading via escalators to the concourse of Grand Central Terminal. A more jarring juxtaposition of spaces is scarcely imaginable—it is like a living example of one of those two-page spreads in Henry Hope Reed's *The Golden City,* in which the poverty of modernism is highlighted by direct comparisons between modern and premodern buildings. Banal as the Pan Am lobby always was, in 1987 Warren Platner was brought in to postmodernize it a bit, and, amazingly, he made it even worse—much worse. Platner gave it all the character of a suburban banquet hall. It only goes to prove the point traditional conservative thinkers have been making for two centuries: there is nothing so bad it cannot be made even worse.

Pan Am, long the principal tenant, has, as you probably know, recently gone belly-up, and so obviously no longer has any connection with the building bearing its name. When it was recently proposed that the gigantic Pan Am sign be removed from the top of the building, there was actually a preservationist uproar. It only goes to prove that no matter how reviled a building may be when it is first built, there is probably nothing in the city that someone won't try to preserve when it is threatened with demolition.

5 HELMSLEY BUILDING (former New York Central Building)

230 Park Avenue, between 45th and 46th streets
1929, Warren & Wetmore

Like the Municipal Building (2.12) downtown, this is high Beaux-Arts wedded to the most advanced building technology of its time. It is thirty-four stories, and contains over 1.2 million square feet of space, which means it is a very, very large building. Yet it is a building that takes every one of its urbanistic responsibilities with the utmost seriousness—the antithesis of the Pan Am Building. It takes seriously its role as a vista

5 *New York Central (Helmsley) Building*

closer, with its tower set between much shorter projecting wings, punctuating the vista while allowing sky to seep around the sides. It takes seriously its role in traffic circulation, with vehicular tunnels carrying automotive traffic onto the ramps around Grand Central Terminal to continue the journey down Park Avenue. It takes seriously its role in pedestrian circulation, with its splendid through-block lobby and its pedestrian tunnels. It takes seriously its role as the symbol of Park Avenue, with its unabashedly rich profusion of classical detail, an appropriate step up from the more restrained neo-Renaissance style of the buildings that lined Park Avenue in 1928. Few things in New York compare with glimpsing the tower of the New York Central Building from Fifth or Madison avenues in midtown. From such a vantage point, what one sees is a veritable palace, with three-story-high Corinthian columns, a pyramidal roof, and a magnificent lantern, floating above the city. As Henry Hope Reed has often pointed out, one of the great contributions America has made to the classical tradition is this way of building palaces in the air. The Helmsley is an utterly dreamlike vision, a symbol for this utterly dreamlike city.

6 VANDERBILT AVENUE

From 43rd Street to 48th Street

270 Park Avenue at the northwest corner of 47th Street is a fifty-three story, sheer-rise, glass tower that used to be the Union Carbide Building until that company's much publicized defection to Danbury Connecticut in the 1970s. It is now the headquarters for Chemical Bank. Designed by Skidmore, Owings & Merrill, it was built in 1960. At that time the city was not yet swarmed with glass skyscrapers and the Union Carbide Building was much admired. Today it would be hard to find people who would prefer it to what it replaced: the graceful stone twelve-story neo-Renaissance Hotel Marguery built in 1917, demolished in 1957 and a typical Park Avenue building of the glory days of Park Avenue. Note that the arcade between the east and west wings of 270 Park Avenue is on axis with Vanderbilt Avenue as is the similar arcade of the Banker's Trust Building (east wing 1963, west wing 1971, both by Emery Roth & Sons) between 48th and 49th streets. Between 43rd and 44th on the west side of Vanderbilt is a hideous building called Bank of America Plaza, a re-facing of the skeleton of the grand old Biltmore Hotel, built in 1914 and designed by Warren & Wetmore and a place richly present in the memories of countless New Yorkers who used its lobby as a meeting place.

7 Former POSTUM BUILDING

250 Park Avenue, between 46th and 47th streets
1925, Cross & Cross

This is the last building on Park Avenue between 46th and 54th streets that gives a sense of the type, scale, and style of the buildings that lined both sides of the avenue in its years of greatest glory. It is twenty stories, very simply designed with a central recess and a slight setback, and decorated in a restrained Renaissance style. It is a modest and utterly dignified street-wall building of the kind which makes great cities.

8 Former SHELTON TOWERS HOTEL (now New York Marriott East Side)

525 Lexington Avenue, between 48th and 49th streets
1924, Arthur Loomis Harmon

When the Equitable Building (2.4) at 120 Broadway, the Pan Am Building of its day, was built in 1915, its 1.7 million-square-foot bulk on a 50,000-square-foot lot caused such alarm at the prospect of a sunless city that a year later New York City enacted the nation's first zoning ordinance, mandating that high buildings be set back at certain intervals to diminish the street impact of their bulk and allow penetration of sunlight. The first tall building to be designed in accordance with the new zoning regulations was the Shelton Towers Hotel. Its gracefully stepped-back form was an entirely new vision on the cityscape, as new as the first skyscraper or the first steel-and-glass curtain wall. It so captured the imagination of artists that Alfred Stieglitz photographed it, Georgia O'Keeffe painted it, and the two of them went so far as to move into it. Harmon did not merely create a stepped-back ziggurat form, but carefully, ingeniously molded his façades with setbacks and deep and shallow recesses, making the changing play of light and shadow an integral element of his composition. Harmon can be said to have invented the modern, sculptured, masonry skyscraper façade, which he lightly adorned with Romanesque ornament. Later architects would wed Harmon's sculpturing to the new, insistently vertical Art Deco ornament to create the great skyscraper classics of the twenties and thirties.

9 WALDORF-ASTORIA HOTEL

301 Park Avenue, between 49th and 50th streets
1931, Schultze & Weaver

This is New York's grandest hotel by far. It massively fills the entire block bounded by Park and Lexington avenues and 49th and 50th streets. New

York, strangely, is not rich in the kind of grand hotel lobbies that serve as public common rooms. Chicago, for example, is much richer in this respect than New York. The Waldorf is an exception. Though it is a floor above street level, there is nothing uninviting about this vast through-block lobby, which was restored in the 1980s to its original Art Deco appearance after some twenty years in which it had been made to look "Edwardian." The exterior is a soft Deco, limestone with a pair of familiar copper-clad towers, reaching forty-seven stories in the air. Every building on this stretch of Park Avenue is extremely impressive from a purely technological standpoint, built as it is over railroad tracks. The Waldorf is no exception. The site had been occupied by the steam-generating plant of Grand Central Terminal, a facility that became redundant when a new, underground plant was built on Lexington and 43rd.

10 ST. BARTHOLOMEW'S CHURCH (Episcopal)

Park Avenue, between 50th and 51st streets
1919, Bertram Grosvenor Goodhue
Portal: 1904, McKim, Mead & White
Community house at 109 East 50th Street: 1927, Bertram G. Goodhue Associates and Mayers, Murray & Philip

GENERAL ELECTRIC BUILDING

570 Lexington Avenue, southwest corner of 51st Street
1931, Cross & Cross

560 LEXINGTON AVENUE

Northwest corner of 50th Street
1981, Eggers Group

The Episcopal congregation of St. Bartholomew's dates to 1835 and a church at Lafayette and Great Jones Street, when that was the most fashionable neighborhood in Manhattan. (Some of its congregation undoubtedly lived in Colonnade Row, 6.6) As fashionable Manhattan moved uptown, so did St. Bartholomew's. The second St. Bartholomew's Church was designed by Renwick & Sands and built in 1876 on Madison Avenue and 44th Street. In 1903, the family of the second Cornelius Vanderbilt provided the church with the money to add a new portal designed by Stanford White. White modeled his design on the triple portal of the Romanesque church of Saint-Gilles-du-Gard (circa 1135–95)

10^A GE Building

near Arles in the south of France. White believed Saint Gilles-du-Gard to be the most beautiful work of architecture in France. (The portal of Trinity Church, Boston, added to H. H. Richardson's masterpiece in 1897 by Shepley, Rutan & Coolidge, was also modeled on the portal of Saint-Gilles-du-Gard.) White worked out the basic scheme, but left the specific design of the figures to the sculptors: Herbert Adams (left portal), Daniel Chester French and Andrew O'Connor (central portal), and Philip Martiny (right portal). The French and O'Connor portal, with its tympanum depicting *Christ in Glory*, is the finest of the three. The frieze connecting the three portal arches was designed by O'Connor and strongly influenced by the contemporary sculpture of Auguste Rodin.

In 1914, the congregation purchased its present site from the Schaefer Brewing Company, which had been making beer there for fifty-four years. Fourth Avenue had been rechristened Park Avenue as early as 1875, although the street did not begin to take on its exalted character until the

10[B] *St. Bartholomew's Church*

New York Central Railroad covered over its depressed tracks in 1913 as part of the Grand Central Terminal electrification project. Bertram Grosvenor Goodhue, hot off the success of St. Thomas Church (13.13) on Fifth Avenue and 53rd Street, was chosen to be the architect of the new church. Part of the plan was to incorporate the Stanford White portal from the old St. Bartholomew's. In the old church, the front of the portal had been flush with the front of the main body of the church. Goodhue decided to have the portal project from the main body of the new church, just as the portal of Saint-Gilles-du-Gard does. This gave Goodhue greater freedom in designing the main body at the same time that it gave greater prominence to the magnificent portal. In his choice of the Byzantine style, Goodhue was unquestionably influenced by John Francis Bentley's Westminster Roman Catholic Cathedral, completed in 1902 in London.

St. Bartholomew's is one of the vanishing breed of churches to observe an open-door policy, and it is well worthwhile to devote some time to exploring the decorative riches of the interior. The narthex, just inside the portal, has ceiling mosaics by Hildreth Meiere, depicting the story of creation. The narthex opens onto a three-aisle nave. The plan is cruciform, with the crossing space bounded by four arches resting on four large square piers. Radiating from the crossing are a fairly short three-bay nave, a chancel with choir and apse, and two stubby transepts. The nave, chancel, and transepts are all barrel vaulted in tile. Along the north and south sides of the nave are gallery-surmounted aisles. Among the columns marking off the aisles, no two capitals are alike. The north and south walls are surfaced in rough-textured Guastavino tile with stone trim. The chancel wall surfacing is marble, and other surfaces are marble and stone. The apse ceiling, like the narthex ceiling, bears a Hildreth Meiere mosaic, this one depicting, in glass and gold leaf, the transfiguration of Christ.

The clerestory windows were produced by the Rambusch Studios and designed by Hildreth Meiere in the Art Deco style, with heavy, geometrical leading that recalls mechanical grillwork. The brilliantly colored figures in these windows are set off by sizable surrounding expanses of clear glass, with a lot of natural light consequently finding unimpeded entry into the nave. These dazzling windows were not completed and installed until the mid-1950s, although they were conceived and begun in the 1930s. The aisle windows, with their lush, fantastic illustration and foliate grisaille, were designed by J. Gordon Guthrie and date from about 1925. The 1918 rose window in the south transept, by Reynolds, Francis & Rohnestock, uses bold, almost Art Deco forms to express a medieval content, and is completely successful. There is no rose window in the north transept because Goodhue had intended to site the church midblock, in expectation that it would one day want to erect an income-producing office building on the north side, with the north transept wall serving as a common one. When it was decided to relocate the church, Goodhue was involved in other projects and was unable to change his design, not anticipating that the church might one day choose to erect an office building on the *south* side.

The Baptistery, in the east wall of the north transept, has a font, depicting a kneeling angel holding a shell, by the Danish sculptor Bertel Thorwaldsen (1770–1844), considered with John Flaxman and Antonio Canova one of the three most important neoclassical sculptors. In the chapel, which is entered through a door in the south aisle wall, Goodhue used marble column shafts from the old St. Bartholomew's, adding new capitals. The chapel's painted and gilded ceiling is done in the manner of the Romanesque San Miniato al Monte (1018–62) in Florence.

On the exterior, Goodhue used a facing of salmon brick, offset by Indiana-limestone bands. The bricks were handmade, resulting in varied sizes and tones of color. According to Goodhue, "we too often forget that New York is blessed with the brilliant skies of Italy." The exterior brick and stone were meant "to keep the building in harmony with the atmospheric effects of New York." Goodhue died in 1924. The community house was added in 1927 and the low, tiled, polychromatic dome in 1930 by Goodhue's successor firm, Mayers, Murray & Philip.

The year after St. Bartholomew's dome was installed, the R.C.A. Victor Building (later known as the General Electric Building) by Cross & Cross was completed on the southwest corner of Lexington Avenue and 51st Street, immediately behind the main church building, almost serving as a campanile. This is one of the most remarkable skyscrapers in New York. At fifty stories, it manages to be both an archetypically romantic Manhattan tower and a completely friendly, unaggressive neighbor to St. Bartholomew's. There may be no other building in New York that strikes such a perfect balance. In certain respects, the General Electric was the Woolworth Building up to date (2.9). The basic forms are Gothic, but here they are streamlined and wedded to the post-1916 tapered silhouette, resulting in what may be the most insistently vertical tower in town. The tower is faced, like St. Bartholomew's, in salmon brick. Cross & Cross did everything they could to make the shaft slender and soaring, including chamfering its corners and creating a crown of open tracery, illuminated from within to evoke radio waves—one of the most distinctive skyscraper crowns in the world. If the Woolworth was, with its Gothic forms, the "Cathedral of Commerce," then the General Electric might be implying that the religion of modern times is broadcasting. This is my favorite New York skyscraper.

Exactly fifty years after the completion of the General Electric, **560 Lexington Avenue,** a speculative office building by the Eggers Group, was completed on the northwest corner of Lexington Avenue and 50th Street, directly behind St. Bartholomew's community house. This is a little-noticed, but extremely successful, building. Indeed, a major measure of its success is in how little noticed it is. This twenty-two-story building attempts to be nothing more than a responsible neighbor to both St. Bartholomew's and

General Electric. In materials and scale, it does nothing to divert attention from its illustrious neighbors. It is also urbanistically first-rate on its Lexington Avenue side, where it has a corner arcade with a subway entrance and a nice brick bas-relief by Alexandra Kasuba.

Together, these buildings are one of the great twentieth-century architectural and urbanistic ensembles, diverse in their intermixture of traditional and modern forms, yet the very model of humane urban scale and the sensitive interrelationship of forms and materials. Here is one block where New York succeeds completely.

11 SEAGRAM BUILDING

375 Park Avenue, between 52nd and 53rd streets
1958, Mies van der Rohe and Philip Johnson

RACQUET AND TENNIS CLUB

370 Park Avenue, between 52nd and 53rd streets
1918, McKim, Mead & White

With its elegant plaza, its rigorous symmetry, its ultrarefined detailing, and its rich, somber presence, the Seagram Building strikes me as squarely within the tradition of New York neoclassicism. Indeed, I would go so far as to say that the Seagram has more in common with such works as McKim, Mead and White's Racquet and Tennis Club across the street or the Pierpont Morgan Library (9.11) than with such modern monuments as the catercorner Lever House (10.13). The 1916 zoning regulations mandated that tall buildings be set back at certain intervals to prevent streets from being shrouded in shadow. The Seagram initiated a new mode of skyscraper design in New York and the world. Instead of using setbacks, the Seagram rises sheer behind a generous open plaza. The plaza, flanked by twin fountains, is paved in pink granite with green marble benches along the fountains, open to sitters and a popular spot for eating lunch or people watching. The lobby walls, clearly visible behind the glass façade, are sheathed in travertine. The exterior of the building is bronze and smoked glass. Never before had a high-modern structure been executed in such rich materials, and the effect is to accentuate the neoclassical roots of this strand of modernism. Mies goes for effects here. The structural frame only *looks* exposed. In fact, the bronze I-beams have been pasted onto the exterior. They reveal the frame while

11 *Seagram Building*

imparting to the façade a refined rhythmic verticality. The columns at the base are of course continued through to the top of the building, but unlike his earlier works, Mies recesses these columns above the base behind his curtain wall, so as not to upset the rhythm of his slender mullions. At their base, then, these columns evoke a classical colonnade.

Across Park Avenue is McKim, Mead & White's Racquet and Tennis Club, a stately neo-Renaissance private clubhouse. This is late McKim, Mead & White, and was designed by William Symmes Richardson. The form is basically that of a Florentine palazzo, with vigorous wraparound rustication at the base, incised with a sequence of bold Tuscan arches; a deep, balustraded cornice; and three massive two-story Tuscan arches, behind which is an open porch above the main entrance. This arched porch is directly on axis with the Seagram plaza. Perhaps the most interesting thing is the sequence of blind arches across the top third of the building. These arches are positioned to indicate the interior placement of the tennis courts. Thus McKim, Mead & White slightly alter their neoclassical forms for modernist reasons, while Mies slightly alters his modernist forms for neoclassical reasons, making for one of the most felicitous juxtapositions of buildings in the city.

12 PARK AVENUE PLAZA

52nd Street to 53rd Street, from Madison Avenue to Park Avenue
1981, Skidmore, Owings & Merrill

It is interesting to compare this with Skidmore, Owings & Merrill's Tower Forty-nine on 49th Street between Fifth and Madison avenues. The ordinary pedestrian often confuses these two buildings, which are similarly scaled, shaped, and clad. Both are hulking midblock megastructures, representatives of the kind of overdevelopment that has destroyed most of the once-wonderful side streets of midtown Manhattan. What Skidmore, Owings & Merrill is to other firms that traffic in speculative hulks is evident in Park Avenue Plaza's undeniably beautiful skin. The flush reflective glass panels, bordered by pencil-stripe mullions with no visible joints and with plumb-perfect construction, are trademark Skidmore, Owings & Merrill. Built using the air rights of the designated-landmark Racquet and Tennis Club (10.11), Park Avenue Plaza is forty-four stories and contains over a million square feet of space. While the nearby Seagram Building (10.11) broke with the setback mode in favor of a sheer-rise tower behind an open plaza, Park Avenue Plaza eschews the open plaza in favor of a large indoor public atrium space. The scale of this atrium is impressive, the detailing is more trademark Skidmore, Owings & Merrill, and the corridor of shops is designed to evoke an elegant London arcade. Still, this atrium allowed greater density to the building, and does not compensate for its rude intrusion on a side street. Indeed, there is very little Skidmore, Owings & Merrill's skilled skinsmanship can do to mitigate the impact of such brutal midblock gigantism.

13 LEVER HOUSE

390 Park Avenue, between 53rd and 54th streets
1952, Gordon Bunshaft for Skidmore, Owings & Merrill

Catercorner to each other are the Seagram Building (10.11) and Lever House, New York's, and the country's, two most influential high-modern

13 *Lever House*

office buildings. These two buildings do everything in the power of the high-modern mode to be good works of urban architecture. Lever House, the headquarters of the Lever Brothers soap company, was the first steel-and-glass building on neo-Renaissance Park Avenue. Today we rightly decry the wanton destruction of that elegant parkway, but when Lever House was built, it seemed a marvelous apparition. Lewis Mumford, for example, virtually proclaimed Lever House the greatest office building ever built. It is much more than just a glistening aquamarine glass-and-stainless-steel slab. What is even more notable in its design is the way it makes use of its site by opening up so much of it. In this, it is the polar opposite of Park Avenue Plaza (10.12) across 53rd Street, a work by the same firm twenty-nine years later.

Gordon Bunshaft made the tower a slab, with its narrow side on Park Avenue and the broad sides exposed to north and south. The slab is placed atop the north end of a one-story rectangular pavilion, set on one-story stainless-steel columns. The pavilion is a ring of offices around a hollow core, and is open to the sky. The resulting plaza is landscaped, as is the roof area along the perimeter of the pavilion. The effect of this disposition of masses is to make the slab seem to hover over its base, creating a marvelous apparition: a glistening slab floating ethereally above the solid masonry of Park Avenue.

No one had ever seen or imagined such a building. It was like something from a fairy tale. Many buildings, including later ones on Park Avenue, imitated Lever House's skin, or its slab form, but none, due to real-estate economics, was ever able to imitate its disposition of masses. Perhaps it is just as well. This is the ideal architecture of Le Corbusier's *ville radieuse,* and its replication might have had an even more deadening effect on our cities than did the countless knockoffs of Mies van der Rohe. Cities can take only so much ethereality. Better that Lever House remain the lone landmark that it is.

14 CITICORP CENTER

Lexington Avenue, from 53rd Street to 54th Street
1978, Hugh Stubbins & Associates

ST. PETER'S CHURCH (Lutheran)

Lexington Avenue, southeast of 54th Street
Hugh Stubbins & Associates

Citicorp Center, occupying the entire block bounded by Lexington and Third avenues and 53rd and 54th streets, is fifty-seven stories of smooth, blinding, silver-colored aluminum and reflective glass, housing nearly 1.8 million square feet of space. Described this way, it hardly sounds as though it could be one of the city's most successful modern tall buildings, but it is. Here we have an open plaza as at the Seagram Building (10.11), *and* an indoor public atrium, as at Park Avenue Plaza (10.12). Unlike those other buildings, Citicorp Center also has a subway station and a *church.* The plaza, atrium, subway station, and church are all fitted neatly under the office tower, which is raised on four massive 114-foot aluminum columns that succeed more than anything else in Manhattan in looking like a set from a futuristic fantasy movie about the dehumanized twenty-first century. The columns are located not at the corners of the tower, but at the centers of the sides. The corners are thus cantilevered.

14^A *Citicorp Center, left, and "Lipstick Building"*

The church, which sits in the northwest corner of the site, loomed over by the 914-foot-high tower, was the reason Stubbins developed this unusual cantilevered design. **St. Peter's Lutheran Church** was founded in 1861 by twenty-three German immigrants. In 1904, the congregation built a Gothic Revival church on the site of the present St. Peter's. Seventy-three years later, a new St. Peter's was built in a marriage of religion and commerce on a scale which those twenty-three immigrants could scarcely have imagined. The church agreed to sell its property to Citicorp only on the condition that the company devise an acceptable way to incorporate a new church into the development. St. Peter's was very concerned that the church not be swallowed up by the rest of the project, that it somehow retain a distinct individual presence. It was thus to accommodate the new church that Stubbins came up with the idea of cantilevering the tower over the corners of the site, thus creating a prominent corner niche for St. Peter's.

The other corner niche on Lexington Avenue is taken up by a nine thousand-square-foot sunken plaza with subway and atrium entrances. Under the other half of the tower, along Third Avenue, is a seven-story skylit atrium, with three stories of shops and restaurants, four stories of offices, and the elevator banks for the tower. This atrium is Citicorp's most important gift to the city. It is a spectacularly successful public space. Through-access from all sides combines with broad walkways, stairways, escalators, and elevators to make pedestrian movement easy, even during periods of peak use. There is ample public seating, and of the best kind, with movable chairs and tables. There are frequent free musical performances. There are several restaurants and shops, catering to a broad range of tastes and incomes. There are public rest rooms and several public telephones.

And there is a *church,* which in this context can be considered another amenity. The main entrance to St. Peter's is located just inside the Lexington Avenue street-level entrance to the atrium. One enters the church through what can only be called its lobby, for in addition to its sanctuary and chapel, St. Peter's houses a 250-seat theater, a music room,

14[B] *St. Peter's Church, Citicorp Center*

and a studio. This is one of the culturally most active congregations in the city, and can be said to be to the arts what Riverside Church (19.8) is to social programs. To the left of the "lobby" is the entrance to the Erol Beker Chapel of the Good Shepherd. This chapel is a tiny room, open daily for prayer and meditation. Each of the chapel's five wall surfaces is covered by a sculptural work created especially for the chapel by the famous sculptor, Louise Nevelson. In her characteristic fashion, these wall sculptures are white-painted assemblages of found wooden objects.

To the left of the chapel entrance is a door leading to a balcony overlooking the sanctuary. The sanctuary is below street level, and is acoustically isolated from the noise of the subway below it. The interior design of the sanctuary is by Vignelli Associates, and is in an idiom that can only be called Danish modern. The tall window above the altar, with a view out to 54th Street, like the large Palladian window behind the altar of St. Paul's Chapel (2.6) downtown, distracts the eye and unfocuses the concentration. This window, however, affords a view of the sanctuary from the street. The sanctuary walls are of ivory-colored stucco, the floors of gray granite, and the pews and chancel floor of blonde wood. It all adds up to Fairfield County, circa 1966. The most impressive thing here is the 2,150-pipe organ built by Hans Gerd Klais of Bonn. In addition to being a superb instrument in the great German organ-building tradition, it is a stunning piece of modern sculpture.

On the exterior, St. Peter's has an expressionistic form: the chamfered granite cube is explicitly intended to evoke a rock, a popular symbol for St. Peter based on the New Testament; so far as I can tell, it is the only explicitly *religious* symbol in the architecture of this church.

15 CENTRAL SYNAGOGUE (Congregation Ahavat Chesed Shaarey Hashomayim)

652 Lexington Avenue, southwest corner of 55th Street
1872, Henry Fernbach

The style is called Moorish, but it actually perfectly reflects high Victorian Gothic. The synagogue's cousins among Manhattan buildings are the Jefferson Market Courthouse (5.9) and the parish house of St. George's Church (8.6). Like these others, it is a polychrome extravaganza, its façades festooned with numerous window arches composed of alternating light and dark stone blocks, and its dark stone surfaces liberally crisscrossed with light stone bands. The choice of style seems peculiarly apt for the incorporation of Jewish symbols, as in the interlaced Stars of David in the rose and clerestory windows. The "organic" ornament marks this style as a way station en route from the Early Gothic Revival of Trinity Church (1.17), via John Ruskin, to the functional and structural expressionism of the Modern movement. Unlike other examples of this style, however, there is a rigorous symmetry, and the net result is that the Central Synagogue is a stately presence on an otherwise drab stretch of Lexington Avenue.

16 HERON TOWER

70 East 55th Street, between Madison and Park avenues
1987 Kohn Pedersen Fox

PARK AVENUE TOWER

65 East 55th Street, between Madison and Park avenues
1987, Murphy/Jahn

Erected simultaneously right across the street from each other, these two office buildings, by what may be the two most successful firms of the 1980s, make for an interesting comparison. The Kohn Pedersen Fox building is an overtly retro setback tower with a gray granite surface punctuated with rough-hewn stone blocks. A continuous vertical strip of glass occupies the central bay of the tower, a vertical foil to the punched stone façade. The setbacks and vertical emphasis make this about as skillful a side-street skyscraper as can be found. The detailing, however, has the appliquéd delicacy so unfortunately characteristic of Kohn Pedersen Fox's work. A much greater problem is the way any skyscraper, no matter how skillful, kills a midtown side street.

The Jahn building takes a very different and generally less skillful tack. While Heron Tower properly maintains the street line, Park Avenue Tower is set behind a small plaza that is nonetheless large enough to destroy the street wall. In typical Jahn fashion, a peculiar stasis is achieved by the omnidirectionality of the façade—here vertical, there horizontal—and with as many diagonals as the guy can work in. The building is also a riot of varicolored glass and stone. Park Avenue Tower is a work of manic nervous energy, where the Heron Tower merely suffers from some irritating tics.

CHAPTER 11

Turtle Bay

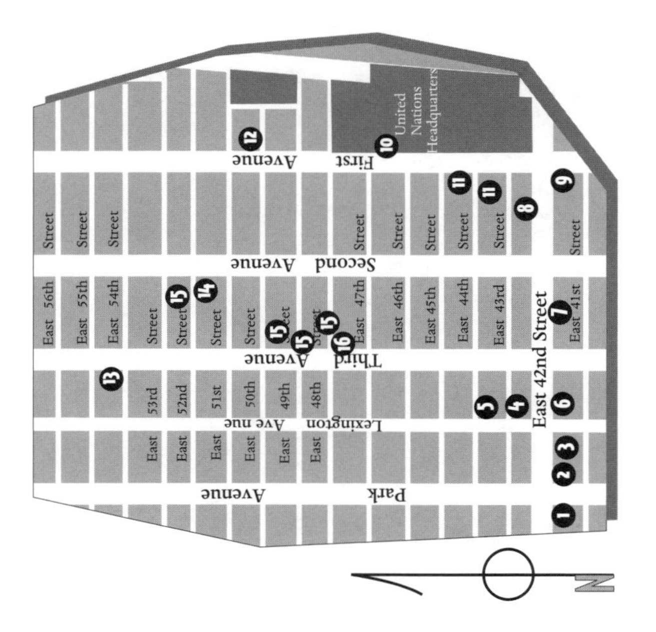

1 *Philip Morris Building*

Chapter 11

Turtle Bay

1 PHILIP MORRIS HEADQUARTERS

120 Park Avenue, southwest corner of 42nd Street
1982, Ulrich Franzen & Associates

A twenty-six-story, six hundred-thousand-square-foot granite box that makes contextual and urbanistic bows. The 42nd Street façade is flat with horizontal strip windows, an apparent attempt to acknowledge the generally horizontal north side of 42nd Street, in particular Grand Central Terminal. The Park Avenue façade, on the other hand, is three-dimensional and vertical, to fit in with the tall office buildings on this part of Park Avenue. The urbanistic bow is in the arcaded base, with subway entrance, along 42nd Street, and especially in the public space inside the base, with its seating, espresso counter, and branch of the Whitney Museum of American Art. God knows this part of midtown can use as many public spaces like this as it can get, and this one is intensively used, but there is something rather dank and unappealing about it, a feeling not unlike that at the base of the Sony Building (14.11). Mostly it is the total absence of natural light, a condition not suffered by more successful public spaces inside skyscraper bases, e.g., the IBM Building (14.10) and Citicorp Center (10.14), which have skylights. All those ghastly sculptures from the Whitney's collection hardly help. At the base of the Philip Morris, as at the base of the Sony, it is always a rain-gray day.

2 BOWERY SAVINGS BANK (now Home Savings of America)

110 East 42nd Street between Park and Lexington avenues
1923, York & Sawyer

The most spectacular banking room in New York. The Bowery Savings Bank had a splendid headquarters on the Bowery (hence the bank's name) and Grand Street, designed by McKim, Mead & White and built in 1894 (2.19). After World War I, the bank built this new headquarters across the street from the new Grand Central Terminal, in a location convenient to the middle-class midtown workers who compose savings banks' main clientele. For these not-rich patrons, the Bowery erected a structure of stupendous grandeur, a commercial, yes, but also a civic gesture intended to ennoble the daily rounds of ordinary people, precisely in the

2 *Home (formerly Bowery) Savings Bank*

spirit of Grand Central Terminal. The Bowery's exterior on 42nd Street is dominated by one of the grandest arches in New York, leading into the banking room. What rises above the arch is a conventional limestone office building, eighteen stories of somewhat dour neo-Romanesque. It is the banking hall, though, that is the Bowery's glory. It is New York's Hagia Sophia, a space of Byzantine ecclesiastical splendor. Indeed, the lighting fixtures hanging from the ceiling are directly modeled on those in the Hagia Sophia. The hall is 75 feet wide and 200 feet long (the Grand Central concourse, by comparison, is 125 feet wide and 300 feet long). The side walls each bear five huge arches resting on varicolored marble columns. Within the niches created by the arches are mosaic panels. The coffered ceiling, with stained-glass panels framed by painted wooden beams, is 70 feet high (Grand Central crests at 125 feet). The floor, as beautiful as any in New York, is inlaid with varicolored marble mosaics. Stylistically the most similar thing in Manhattan is the Romanesque chapel of St. Bartholomew's Church (10.10), which only serves to underscore how ecclesiastical the Bowery Savings Bank feels. One does not talk loudly in this room. One walks around it on light feet, carefully and silently examining its every detail, just as one looks at a church. Perhaps York and Sawyer's message is something about the worship of money. Be that as it may, time spent conducting pecuniary transactions in a space like this is time well spent.

3 CHANIN BUILDING

122 East 42nd Street, southwest corner of Lexington Avenue
1929, Sloan & Robertson

Fifty-six stories of brick, with the most distinctive slab tower in the city. The narrow end of the slab faces 42nd Street; the wide end, Lexington Avenue. In the developer Irwin Chanin's promotional brochure for the building bearing his name, it is called the "*mise-en-scène* for the romantic drama of American business." The base is richly decorated according to a scheme worked out by Rene Chambellan and Jacques Delamarre.

Shop windows are framed in black marble and bronze. Above them is a bronze relief depicting the story of evolution. Above this are terracotta relief panels displaying abstract floral forms. The lobby is one of the city's Art Deco shrines, an efflorescence of bronze grillwork.

4 *Chrysler Building*

4 CHRYSLER BUILDING

405 Lexington Avenue, northeast corner of 42nd Street
1930, William Van Alen

I find it slightly unsettling that nowadays architects and critics regard the Chrysler Building as one of the very greatest buildings in America. I'm sure an architects' poll would rate it as the single greatest building in New York. Yet not so long ago, architects and critics regarded it as at best an amusing folly; at worst, meretricious kitsch. Such is the fickleness of fashion. What I find unsettling, however, is not this professional fickleness, but the present lack of any critical distance on this building. That is, it may well be a great building, but it is not a kind of greatness that should be taken for granted. For there is indeed a hearty dose of kitsch in the Chrysler Building, and it is a measure of our present cultural confusion that it should be so instantly admired. I want to defend this building. The only problem is that there is no one to defend it to. Let me say, then, what everyone already takes for granted: nothing in the Manhattan cityscape has such power to elicit a smile as the Chrysler spire with the sun glinting off it. No other skyscraper audaciously adapted itself to the setback zoning regulations by rising in a series of receding parabolic arches. No other skyscraper, even in that period of fantastic tops, was so conspicuously and self-dramatically crowned. No other skyscraper had such a thoroughly worked-out iconographic program, resulting in blatant self-advertisement.

Most notable of all about this building is its unusual triangular lobby, an Art Deco 1930s movie set that one can easily imagine Fred and Ginger gliding across, with a liberal dash of *The Cabinet of Dr. Caligari.* Red and blue marble, yellow sienna, amber onyx, Edward Trumbull's ceiling mural (*Energy, Result, Workmanship, and Transportation*), and a painting of the Chrysler Building itself are indirectly illuminated by Van Alen's dramatic custom lighting. The elevator doors and the interiors of the cabs are veneered in exotic wood marquetry which forms abstract floral patterns. No two cab interiors are identical. These are the most famous elevators in the city. Lewis Mumford derided the Chrysler for its "inane romanticism," "meaningless voluptuousness," and "void symbolism." As for the symbolism, the self-advertising iconography, one can only say that there is indeed something ironic in such a brazen monument to the automotive age towering over Grand Central Terminal, the greatest monument to the golden age of railroads.

6 *Mobil Building (center)*

5 425 LEXINGTON AVENUE

Between 43rd and 44th streets
1988, Murphy/Jahn

There are two Helmut Jahns. There is the modern architect of fecund imagination whose dramatic, expressive forms may be a harbinger of a new, plastic skyscraper aesthetic. Then there is the incorrigible postmodernizer who tacks doodads all over his buildings. Four twenty-five Lexington is a thirty-one-story, six hundred thousand-square-foot, outward-rising, top-heavy tower clearly inspired by the Florentine Palazzo Vecchio (completed in 1314) and perhaps also by the Milanese Torre Velasca (1958), by Ernesto Rogers and Enrico Peressutti. Jahn gussies up the basic form with tacky details, especially that hideous mock corbeling. Very Disneyland.

6 MOBIL BUILDING

150 East 42nd Street, between Lexington and Third avenues
1955, Harrison & Abramovitz

A forty-two-story, nearly 1.6 million-square-foot behemoth, made all the more conspicuous by its embossed, "self-cleaning," stainless-steel cladding. This massive tin can rests atop a blue-glass base. The Mobil is one of the most ridiculed buildings in Manhattan, but I cannot help believing that anything that is as evocative a piece of period tack as this will not one day be admired as camp. As such, it will take its place beside the lobbies of the U.N. General Assembly Building and the Time-Life Building.

7 DAILY NEWS BUILDING

220 East 42nd Street, between Second and Third avenues
1930, Howells & Hood
Addition, southwest corner of Second Avenue: 1958, Harrison & Abramovitz

Thirty-seven stories. Raymond Hood, working with John Mead Howells, had used Gothic forms in the Chicago Tribune Tower to achieve an effect of soaring verticality, and, working with J. Andre Fouilhoux, had also used them in the American Radiator Building on Bryant Park (9.8). Working once again with Howells in the Daily News Building, Hood finally took a step beyond Gothic and created purely modern, bold, vertical striping by projecting limestone piers beyond the window wall. This is the Gothic skyscraper stripped of its Gothic ornament, and the first Manhattan skyscraper with an unornamented top. The decorative impulse was reserved for the lobby, which has been altered, but many of its original features remain. In particular, there is a gigantic revolving globe set into a well in the center of the lobby floor beneath a faceted black glass ceiling. Also note the weather instruments set into the lobby walls. When opened, this lobby was an enormous tourist attraction, though it is virtually unknown today.

8 FORD FOUNDATION BUILDING

321 East 42nd Street, between First and Second avenues
1967, Kevin Roche John Dinkeloo & Associates

Hands down the best modern building in New York, and clearly a building

7A *Daily News Building*

7B *Interior of Daily News Building*

8 *Ford Foundation*

that only a fabulously rich nonprofit organization could build. By far the major portion of the building's volume is a twelve-story skylighted atrium. The offices occupy the perimeter of the building, and every office opens onto the atrium. The office floors front the atrium with exposed steel beams in the strictest Miesian idiom, and the broad expanses of glass afford office workers glorious views of what the atrium contains: an improbably lush assemblage of flora—not a few trees and tasteful plantings, but a romantic garden strewn with paths leading to a central fountain overhung by trees. It is a bit like the Ramble in Central Park. It is an amazing juxtaposition of romantic garden with the rigorous rationalism of Miesian architecture. There is nothing like this anywhere in the country. Both the architecture and the garden are executed at the highest levels of detailing and proportion. On the exterior, massive brick piers form a cubical framework holding a downward-receding, Palazzo Vecchia-like, glass-and-steel curtain wall.

9 TUDOR CITY

40th Street to 43rd Street, from First Avenue to Second Avenue
1925–28, H. Douglas Ives for the Fred F. French Company

Up a sidewalk stairway from the Ford Foundation, raised over First Avenue, is Tudor City Place, along which are arrayed twelve mock-Tudor apartment high-rises. These are nice-enough 1920s apartment houses, obviously preferable to their post–World War II counterparts. It is not the architecture of individual buildings here, however, that is of interest, but the development as a whole, forming a residential enclave that in its entirety evokes the romantic age of skyscraper living. This is the neighborhood equivalent of the great cocktail music of the 1920s and '30s. It is also one of the models for the residential portion of Battery Park City (3.2). Though these buildings are right on the East River, they are oriented inward, toward the private Tudor City Park and midtown Manhattan. This is because when they were built, the riverfront was lined with slaughterhouses.

10 UNITED NATIONS HEADQUARTERS

First Avenue, from 42nd Street to 48th Street
1947–53, Wallace K. Harrison and others

William Zeckendorf assembled the site, and John D. Rockefeller, Jr., donated it to the international organization thought at the time of its inception to be the great hope of world peace. The tall one is the Secretariat Building, a thirty-nine-story glass, marble, and aluminum slab. The north and south ends are windowless expanses of white marble; the east and west façades are aluminum and green glass. All the façades are completely flat and smooth. The great, green glass wall on the river is a gigantic mirror, and made quite a splash when it was first built: New Yorkers had never before seen the constantly shifting patterns changing light could play on vast, freestanding glass planes.

The General Assembly Building is the low one with concave walls and roof. Lewis Mumford said when it was built that at best it was suited to be a modern movie palace, down to its Fernand Leger murals. Mumford also noted that the best view of the United Nations was from the north on First Avenue, with the curved roof of the General Assembly intersecting the tall slab of the Secretariat, making a pleasant abstract composition, the quality of which is unfortunately not repeated from any other vantage point. The

10 *United Nations Headquarters*

vast lobby of the General Assembly is a real kick: a piece of period camp with its parabolic-arch-supported ramp; jutting, curved balconies; "marbleized" glass panels; and everywhere blue, screaming 1950s. Symbolically, it is a commentary on our time—and quite disturbing at that—that the Secretariat, the bureaucratic component of the United Nations, dominates the composition, while the General Assembly cowers at its feet.

11 ONE UNITED NATIONS PLAZA

First Avenue, northwest corner of 44th Street
1976, Kevin Roche John Dinkeloo & Associates

TWO UNITED NATIONS PLAZA

44th Street, north side, between First and Second avenues
1983, Kevin Roche John Dinkeloo & Associates

THREE UNITED NATIONS PLAZA

44th Street, south side, between First and Second avenues
1987, Kevin Roche John Dinkeloo & Associates

Eleven years of Roche Dinkeloo. One and Two are pure prismatic volumes; mirror-glass surfaces with arbitrary bulges and buckles that express nothing. They represent the stage beyond the United Nations Secretariat Building in the evolution of the freestanding glass skyscraper as reflecting screen. It is hard to believe that the same architects responsible for the Ford Foundation (11.8) were also responsible for these. Three United Nations Plaza is postmodern Roche Dinkeloo, featuring their patented Egyptoid forms—see their Morgan Bank Headquarters (1.6) and 31 West 52nd Street (13.11).

11 *One and Two United Nations Plaza*

12 BEEKMAN PLACE

49th Street to 51st Street, from First Avenue to the F.D.R. Drive

One of the toniest residential enclaves in Manhattan. 49th Street between First Avenue and the F.D.R. Drive is called Mitchell Place. At 3 Mitchell Place, on the northeast corner of First Avenue, is the twenty-three-story **Beekman Tower,** formerly the Panhellenic Tower, designed by John Mead Howells and built in 1928. Perhaps no other building in Manhattan looks so much like it was carved from a single block of stone. The windows of this somber sculptured mass are so deeply recessed that the building appears to be windowless. Howells was Raymond Hood's partner in the design of the Chicago Tribune Tower completed in 1925. Howells and Hood used Gothic forms as a means of unifying the various elements of the setback tower and creating a single soaring mass. In the 1922 international competition for the design of the Tribune Tower, second place was awarded to the design submitted by the Finnish architect, Eliel Saarinen. Saarinen's design is in many ways similar to Howells and Hood's, in that it eschews the traditional approach of designing a tall building in tripartite fashion—with a distinct base, shaft, and crown, as though it were a classical column. Saarinen diverged from Howells and Hood, however, in also eschewing eclectic ornament. Saarinen instead used a carefully modeled façade of receding and projecting planes to achieve the unity and verticality Howells and Hood had thought only Gothic forms could provide. Many architects were deeply impressed by Saarinen's "astylar" design. One of those architects was John Mead Howells himself, and the Beekman Tower is the fruit of his conversion. In the evolution of the New York skyscraper, it was the next step beyond Arthur Loomis Harmon's Shelton Towers Hotel (now the New York Marriott East Side, 10.8). One of the best observation decks in Manhattan is the Top of the Tower cocktail lounge atop the Beekman Tower. This movie set–like Art Deco room affords marvelous views, which, because they are from only 23 stories up, and not, as at the Empire State Building, 86 or 102 stories up, allow one actually to perceive details—all while a piano tinkles in the background.

Around the corner at **23 Beekman Place,** between 50th and 51st streets, is the town house designed by Paul Rudolph for himself. It was completed in 1987. Rudolph is one of the foremost figures in the history of twentieth-century American architecture. Perhaps his most famous effort is the ill-starred Art and Architecture Building at Yale University, a work that for young postmodernists became a symbol of everything they were rejecting. It is interesting, and perhaps ironic, that Rudolph should desire to live in the eclectic, cozy, low-key environment of Beekman Place.

Continuing northward, at 435 East 52nd Street at the F.D.R. Drive, is one of Manhattan's most exclusive and fabled apartment buildings. The twenty-six-story **River House** was designed by Bottomley, Wagner & White and built in 1931. In my opinion, it is one of the finest works of architecture in New York. Its architect, William Lawrence Bottomley, is best known for his neo-Georgian mansions in verdant Virginia. For his only Manhattan high-rise, Bottomley chose a stripped-down version of his trademark eclectic Georgian style. There is almost an Art Deco feeling to the details of this utterly graceful mass, the very epitome of the fabled Manhattan of Cole Porter, the dry martini, and witty repartee. For anyone who has seen Vincente Minnelli's *Bells Are Ringing,* it is impossible to look into the courtyard of this building and not imagine Judy Holliday and Dean Martin dancing across it. Perhaps nowhere has the peculiar, beguiling urbanity of Manhattan been better expressed than by this Virginian.

13 900 THIRD AVENUE

Northwest corner of 54th Street
1983, Cesar Pelli and Rafael Vinoly with Emery Roth & Sons

885 THIRD AVENUE

Between 53rd and 54th streets
1986, John Burgee with Philip Johnson

Nine hundred Third Avenue is a sleek, straightforward, thirty-six-story, speculative office building that does not shout for attention. Its most notable feature is the four-story downward-curving "greenhouse" atop the northern half of the building—an element reminiscent of Pelli's famous Pacific Design Center in Los Angeles. Eight eighty-five Third Avenue, on the other hand, is about as attention grabbing as you can get, which is what we have come to expect from Philip Johnson. This three-tiered, thirty-four-story, glass-and-red-granite ellipse is known locally as the "Lipstick Building." There is a feeling of sweeping openness at its base. Johnson has attempted to introduce into the bleak Third Avenue grid a touch of the drama one finds in the bulgy rounded façades of the Financial District, such as Delmonico's (1.6) and the Banca Commerciale Italiana (1.5).

14 GREENACRE PARK

217–221 East 51st Street, from Second Avenue to Third Avenue
1971, Sasaki, Dawson, DeMay Associates

William H. Whyte, a former editor at *Fortune* and author of the 1950s bestseller *The Organization Man,* has in recent years given himself to the close study of urban open spaces. Influenced by Jane Jacobs, Whyte has used the results of his studies to urge new approaches to the design and preservation of aspects of the public environment in New York. For example, a number of Whyte's prescriptions have been taken in the recent redesign of Bryant Park (9.8), such as the use of movable, rather than fixed, seating, Whyte having observed that open spaces with movable seating attract more sitters. As head of the private nonprofit New York Landmarks Conservancy, Whyte petitioned the Internal Revenue Service to broaden

14 *Greenacre Park*

its definition of scenic easements to include inner cities. Thus, property owners can now be granted significant tax breaks in exchange for not impinging on the sunlight in nearby open spaces. In the very first test of the new easement regulation, Seymour Durst, a famous Manhattan developer, was provided an easement on his four-story property directly across the street from what became Greenacre Park. Durst agreed not to exceed the four-story height of his structure, thus ensuring that the "vest-pocket" park would forever remain in light. This is an utterly heartwarming example of enlightened cooperation where every party benefits and the public receives an amenity of inestimable value. Greenacre Park is a splendid, if tiny, oasis, and one of the most intensively used public open spaces in Manhattan. Trees and flowers and sun and water are all packed into this compact space, with a refreshment stand and movable seating. All people are welcome, and all kinds of people use the space, including messengers and corporate executives, small children and old people, tourists and people who have lived in the neighborhood for twenty years. If our public environment is to be revitalized, this is how it will have to be done.

15 211 EAST 48TH STREET

Between Second and Third avenues
1934, William Lescaze

212 EAST 49TH STREET

Between Second and Third avenues
1986, Mitchell/Giurgola

219 EAST 49TH STREET

Between Second and Third avenues
1935, Morris Sanders

242 EAST 52ND STREET

Between Second and Third avenues
1950, Philip Johnson

Turtle Bay is a museum of the modern town house. Two Eleven East 48th Street, between Second and Third avenues, was designed by William Lescaze as his own residence and office, and is said to be the first modern town house in New York. The way the second-floor bay curves beside the "stoop" is distinctly reminiscent of the sleek curve of the base of the pioneering Philadelphia Saving Fund Society skyscraper, completed two years earlier, that Lescaze codesigned with George Howe. The curving bay of the house also uses a strip window similar to that of the base of that Philadelphia building, and, like the same base, the house's curved bay is surmounted by a slightly cantilevered, right-angled structure. House designs have been blown up to skyscraper proportions, but the Lescaze house may be the first time a skyscraper design was ever scaled down to fit a house. The first floor and the portion surmounting the curved bay are faced in glass block, and the house glows when it is lit from within at night.

Two Twelve East 49th Street, between Second and Third avenues, is by the firm of Mitchell/Giurgola, famous for their contextualized modernist designs influenced by Louis Kahn. Here is a very sleek, ritzy, neo-Deco town house of marble, granite, and limestone, with a large, round, oceanliner-porthole window and thick tubular railings lending a strong nautical feeling. Two Nineteen East 49th Street between Second and Third avenues, designed by Morris Sanders and built in 1935, seems more like the work of Mitchell/Giurgola than their own house does. The Sanders house is reminiscent of Mitchell/Giurgola's Fairchild Center for the Life Sciences at Columbia University (19.3), and I would not be surprised to learn that the Columbia building was influenced by the Sanders house. Sanders renovated a conventional brownstone by placing a screen of glazed brick and glass block in front of it. Mitchell/Giurgola would later become well known for their use of projecting screens as an urbanistic gesture, which is rather the opposite effect desired by Sanders, who wanted his house to stick out on 49th Street like the proverbial sore thumb.

Last but not least, Philip Johnson's 242 East 52nd Street, between Second and Third avenues, is regarded as one of the classic urban houses of the Modern movement. It was originally built in 1950 as a guest house for the Rockefeller family, who later donated it to the Museum of Modern Art for use as *their* guest house. The lower portion of the façade is an expanse of Roman brick, broken only in its middle by a simple wooden door. The upper portion is skyscraper-style tripartite glass-and-steel bays. The composition is severely geometrical and very simple, its entire kick coming from the sensuous contrast between the soft, traditional materials of the lower portion and the hard-edged, glassy upper portion. It is

16 *767 Third Avenue*

actually a remodeled stable, and at stable scale, as opposed to skyscraper scale, such an aesthetic can work, so long as it's not overused.

16 767 THIRD AVENUE

Southeast corner of 48th Street
1980, Fox & Fowle

This forty-story speculative office building was the first major Manhattan project by the later-ubiquitous Fox & Fowle. It is a thoroughly modernist building that nonetheless thoroughly eschews the Miesian idiom without resorting to gimmickry. There are no visible steel beams. The recessed lobby has medium-sized panes of glass, framed by wood. The five-story base and thirty-four-story tower are faced in alternating horizontal bands of brick and glass and round 48th Street in graceful curves that seem inspired by Wright's Johnson Wax headquarters in Racine, Wisconsin, and, even more, Howe and Lescaze's Philadelphia Saving Fund Society Building. It is thus interesting to compare 767 Third Avenue with Lescaze's town house nearby at 211 East 48th Street between Second and Third avenues (11.15).

CHAPTER 12

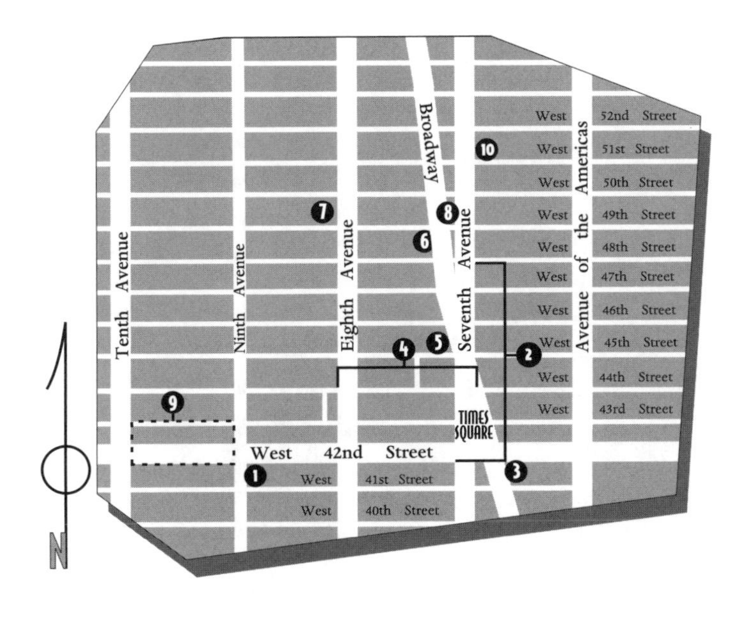

Times Square

1 *McGraw Hill Building*

Chapter 12

Times Square

1 Former MCGRAW-HILL BUILDING

330 West 42nd Street, between Eighth and Ninth avenues
1931, Raymond Hood, Godley & Fouilhoux

Wishful thinking: when the giant publishing firm of McGraw-Hill decided to locate its headquarters so far west on 42nd Street, the company was sure it was leading the way for others to follow. Part of what has always made this building so distinctive is its isolation. Few Manhattan skyscrapers stand so free. Along with Hood and Howells's Daily News Building (11.7), the McGraw-Hill was one of the first tall buildings in New York with a completely unornamented exterior—unless, of course, one counts the intersecting planes at the top as ornament, as Vincent Scully does when he describes this building's style as "jukebox modern." This was the *only* New York building included by Henry-Russell Hitchcock and Philip Johnson in their famous *Modern Architecture: International Exhibition* at the Museum of Modern Art in 1932. The Daily News Building uses bold vertical stripes in lieu of any ornament; the McGraw-Hill uses alternating continuous bands of windows and green terra-cotta. The original praise heaped on this building had to do with its role in the genealogy of modernism. Later, when that genealogy was thrown out the window, the McGraw-Hill was praised as an Art Deco classic.

2 TIMES SQUARE and DUFFY SQUARE

Broadway to Seventh Avenue, from 42nd Street to 48th Street

Only recently it was the tawdry crossroads of the world. At night, the tall, raucous signs remained a sight to behold. As for the rest, it had sunk to a level of seediness no other downtown area in a major Western city could match. The frying odors, the litter, the vacant-eyed drifters, the prostitutes, the pornography, the sensation-seeking tourists have led to a major public and private joint effort to clean up the streets and restore something resembling civility. Many intelligent and sensitive people, who wouldn't be caught dead in a dirty bookstore, oppose these efforts. Why? They fear another Avenue of the Americas. They fear a center of lower-class amusements will be "gentrified." But isn't there something patronizing in the notion, held mostly by well-off, college-educated people, that working-class amusements need be tawdry and obscene? Okay, Walt Disney may not be the answer. But are drug pushers and transvestite hookers? The transformation of Times Square is one of the most startling things in New York—and to all but the jaded, one of the most welcome things in New York. And the big electric signs have been preserved.

During the 1980s real-estate boom, a number of nefarious uses were displaced by gargantuan new office buildings and hotels. The forty-six-story **Holiday Inn Crowne Plaza,** the biggest, most luxurious, and most expensive Holiday Inn on earth, at 1603-07 Broadway between 48th and 49th streets, opened in 1989. It was designed by Alan Lapidus, son of Morris Lapidus, who designed Miami Beach's most flamboyant hotels. The twelve stories of illuminated signs above the hundred-foot-high arched entrance are the result of special zoning legislation, intended to preserve the character of Times Square, which mandates that all new buildings on the square incorporate garish, pulsating electric signs on their façades. Lapidus, truly his father's son, goes the zoners one better: not only did he incorporate the signage, but he designed the whole burgundy-glass and pink-granite building to look like a Wurlitzer jukebox. It's surprising there's no music piping out of it onto the square.

Fox & Fowle's **Embassy Suites Hotel** at 1564-66 Broadway between 46th and 47th streets opened in 1990. Huge steel trusses lift the thirty-eight-story hotel above the landmark five-story, seventeen hundred-seat Palace Theatre (Kirchoff & Rose, 1913). Fox & Fowle, whose work is nothing if not tasteful, turned to a kind of colorized industrial aesthetic to create an appropriate carriage for the required 125-foot-high illuminated sign.

David Childs of Skidmore, Owings & Merrill was the architect of the forty-four-story **1540 Broadway,** completed in 1990 at the "bow tie" where Broadway and Seventh Avenue cross at 45th Street. The façade of superimposed grids and the hundred-foot-high steel-framework spire impart a distinctly De Stijl feeling to this building. It is interesting to see what Fox & Fowle and David Childs are doing here. When Times Square, during the "Wurlitzer era" in the first couple of decades of this century, first became the forest of electric billboards it remains to this day, the architectural styles (e.g., Bauhaus and De Stijl) that emerged, partly in celebration of the flashy new electric technology, were hardly what developers were going to commission in the business crossroads of Manhattan. Fox & Fowle and David Childs reveal a remarkable historical sense when, in an effort to preserve the character of Times Square, they turn to the celebratory styles that could not be built then, but can now. Lapidus, in contrast, goes for an abstracted version of Wurlitzer-era conventions, and ends not with history but with Disneyland. Embassy Suites and 1540 Broadway are buildings I probably would not like if they were anywhere else in the city, but being where they are, I can only respect the hard thought their architects have put into the solution of some daunting aesthetic problems.

3 Former KNICKERBOCKER HOTEL

1466 Broadway, southwest corner of 42nd Street
1907, Trowbridge & Livingston and Marvin & Davis with Bruce Price

Fifteen stories. John Jacob Astor's grand Knickerbocker Hotel lasted only fourteen years, a victim of Prohibition. From 1940 to 1959, the building was the headquarters of *Newsweek.* Today it is an office building. This is very jazzy, Wurlitzer Beaux-Arts. The architects took the same elements that might have been used to create a stately Upper East Side town house, and used them to create the building that more than any other says *Times Square.* The red-brick and limestone-trim façades have a frenetic rhythm, with dense, varied fenestration, ornate balconies, and bold quoining. It is all topped by a three-story copper-dormered mansard that, with its high chimneys, balustrades, and urns, may be the most dynamic one in the city.

4 44TH STREET

From Broadway to Eighth Avenue

This block seems to me characteristic of the several fine side streets that compose the heart of the theater district. From the east, it starts at the **Paramount Building,** completed in 1927, at 1505 Broadway between 43rd and 44th streets. This building was designed by C. W. and George L. Rapp, architects famous for their spectacular movie palaces (e.g., the Chicago Theater, 1928). The thirty-three-story buff-brick skyscraper is stepped back eight times, and has one of the most distinctive tops in town: a huge clock surmounted by a once-illuminated globe. There was originally a glass-enclosed observation deck on the thirty-second-floor setback, and the Rapp and Rapp–designed Paramount Theater in the base. In the north side of the base of the Paramount Building are two very large, very popular, very inexpensive, and very *designed* restaurants: **Ollie's Noodle Shop** (Chinese, in a take on kitschy 1950s' Chinese restaurant design), and **Carmine's** (southern Italian, modeled after big Little Italy restaurants). In décor, prices, and cuisine, these restaurants, under the same ownership, answer to a popular hankering after the 1950s and early '60s, when today's baby boomers were kids, and the world was a less sophisticated and less cynical place than it is now.

Across 44th Street at 1515 Broadway, between 44th and 45th streets, is the fifty-two-story, nearly 1.8 million-square-foot office building known as **One Astor Plaza,** having appropriated the name of the grand Astor Hotel (1904, Clinton and Russell) that it replaced. Completed in 1970, 1515 Broadway was designed by Kahn and Jacobs (as in Robert Jacobs, husband of Jane). Under the provisions of the special zoning for the theater district, extra bulk was allowed by the incorporation of a legitimate theater—the 1,620-seat Minskoff (1973, Robert Jacobs)—into the building. The things that are wrong here are obvious. The big blank south wall of the huge projecting base saps vitality from 44th Street. On Broadway, however, that projecting base has a glass curtain wall revealing the three-story foyer of the Minskoff, a touch of Lincoln Center in Times Square. The building also has a distinctive top, with four huge fins emerging from the clean lines of the limestone-and-smoked-glass tower.

At 225 West 44th Street, just west of 1515 Broadway, is the fifteen hundred-seat **Shubert Theatre** (1913, Henry B. Herts). *A Chorus Line* ran here for fifteen years. This is also where Katharine Hepburn starred in 1939

4 *Paramount Building*

in Philip Barry's *The Philadelphia Story.* At this writing, the well-received Gershwin pastiche, *Crazy for You,* is a big hit at the Shubert. At number 240 is the neo-Colonial five hundred-seat **Helen Hayes Theater** (1912, Ingalls & Hoffman). This was originally called the Little Theater, but the name was changed in 1982 when the original Helen Hayes Theater on West 46th Street was demolished to make way for the Marriott Marquis Hotel (12.5). It is where Joseph Kesselring's *Arsenic and Old Lace* premiered in 1941. At number 246 is the neo-Georgian sixteen hundred-seat **St. James Theater** (1927, Warren & Wetmore), called the Erlanger when it was opened by George M. Cohan. This is the theater where in 1943 Rodgers and Hammerstein's *Oklahoma!* premiered; their *The King and I* also premiered here in 1951. At number 245 is the seventeen hundred-seat **Majestic Theater** (1927, Herbert J. Krapp). Rodgers and Hammerstein's *Carousel* (1945) and *South Pacific* (1949) premiered here, and at this writing, the Majestic is home to the megablockbuster, *The Phantom of the Opera.* At number 235 is the twelve hundred-seat **Broadhurst Theater**

(1917, Herbert J. Krapp), where in 1935 Humphrey Bogart starred in Robert E. Sherwood's *The Petrified Forest*. And at number 234 is **Sardi's,** a theatrical hangout and an awfully nice-looking old-style restaurant, its walls festooned with caricatures of famous theater people. My favorite restaurant critic, Seymour Britchky, proves that these caricatures are not everyone's cup of tea: "There is no pleasure in being surrounded by hundreds of grotesque heads, some of them up close. Lucille Ball at five feet, gaudily grinning at you in primary colors, is actually frightening."

5 MARRIOTT MARQUIS HOTEL

1535–1547 Broadway, between 45th and 46th streets
1985, John Portman

Developer-architect Portman is the king of the glitzy atrium hotel, having pioneered the form in numerous Hyatt Regency jobs across the country. The look is quintessential 1970s. The Marriott Marquis was conceived in the seventies, though it was not completed until 1985. In characteristic Portman fashion, the fifty-four-story, nineteen hundred-room hotel presents an enormous blank face to the streets around it. Everything is oriented inward, toward the vast glass-and-chrome atrium, which, it is said, is the highest atrium in the world, beginning on the eighth floor (another antipedestrian gesture) and rising to the top of the building. It comes complete with tubular glass elevators. This place even has a revolving rooftop restaurant, such as one might find in a Holiday Inn in Indianapolis, though, to be sure, the views are stunning. Such a design may make sense in Los Angeles or near an airport, but in the middle of an intensively trafficked pedestrian area like Times Square, the effect is deadening. On the third floor is the sixteen hundred-seat Marquis Theatre.

6 1585 BROADWAY

Southwest corner of 48th Street
1990, Gwathmey Siegel & Associates

This forty-two-story office building is Gwathmey Siegel's first high-rise, and one of the better 1980s skyscrapers in town. Its forerunners are 140 Broadway (1967, Skidmore, Owings & Merrill, 2.3E) and Museum Tower (1983, Cesar Pelli, 13.12). These buildings are attempts to carry the high-modern idiom into a new era of building technology in which the relatively robust Corbusian and Miesian ideal of structural clarity has been dealt a blow by the emergence of the ultrasmooth, flush-panel, reflective, energy-efficient curtain wall. Gwathmey Siegel's aquamarine, white, and reflective-glass-and-aluminum-grid skin ekes maximum expressiveness from its rigorously modern idiom. In their attempt to make it fresh, the architects have even borrowed from a classic Beaux-Arts skyscraper, Carrère & Hastings's 26 Broadway (1922, 1.2). Like 26 Broadway, Gwathmey Siegel's building has a curved base relating to the Broadway diagonal, while the tower is oriented to the orthogonal grid.

7 WORLDWIDE PLAZA

Eighth Avenue to Ninth Avenue, from 49th Street to 50th Street
Office building: 1989, David Childs for Skidmore, Owings & Merrill
Apartment buildings: 1989, Frank Williams

Built on the site of the third Madison Square Garden, which stood from 1925 to 1966, Worldwide Plaza became nationally famous when its construction was chronicled in great and arresting detail in the public-television series "Skyscraper." It comprises a forty-nine-story, 1.6 million-square-foot office tower, two apartment high-rises, a generously scaled public plaza, and an immense, labyrinthine, underground multiplex cinema. As Gertrude Stein might say, there is now definitely a "there" in this previously dingy part of Clinton. Indeed, no 1980s development, save Battery Park City, so thoroughly transformed its setting as did Worldwide Plaza. David Childs's office building is self-consciously indebted to the tradition of classic skyscraper design that flourished in New York from the 1890s to the 1930s, and I think it is the best of the retro high-rises built in New York in the 1980s. The setback massing and, especially, the illuminated copper pyramidal top have made this building a conspicuous skyline element, and most people who see it assume it is a grand old skyscraper.

At street level, Childs's solution to the clients' demands is striking. The four principal tenants—the advertising firms of Ogilvy & Mather and N. W. Ayer, the law firm of Cravath, Swaine & Moore, and Polygram Records—each wanted a separate entrance to the building. Rather than merely sticking an entrance on each of the four sides, Childs created a wraparound arcade at the base in the manner of a London arcade or an Italian galleria, in effect creating a new pedestrian street and the illusion that each of the entrances goes to a different building along a row of uniform façades. Along the arcade wall opposite the building are subway entrances and openings onto Eighth Avenue, 49th and 50th streets, and the large plaza that separates the office tower from the apartment houses. Childs's arcade is a splendid gesture. Williams's apartment buildings are fine, cleanly designed, red-brick background structures with polychrome trim; they do not upstage Childs's tower.

8 750 SEVENTH AVENUE

Between 49th and 50th streets
1989, Kevin Roche John Dinkeloo & Associates

Roche and Dinkeloo seem finally to be getting that Egyptoid monkey off their backs, but they are still into arcane symbolism, here exemplified by the obelisk sticking out of the top of the building. Seven fifty Seventh Avenue is a thirty-four-story stepped ziggurat made classy by its fine skin, a flush gray and silver-reflective and ceramic-coated glass grid that puts this building into the same genre as Gwathmey Siegel's 1585 Broadway down the street. This is Roche and Dinkeloo's best New York building since the Ford Foundation (1967, 11.8).

9 MANHATTAN PLAZA

42nd Street to 43rd Street, from Ninth Avenue to Tenth Avenue
1977, David Todd & Associates

THEATER ROW

South side of 42nd Street, from Ninth Avenue to Tenth Avenue

Here is the proof that high-quality design is not always necessary to make a civilized place. The two forty-five-story towers of Manhattan Plaza contain almost seventeen hundred apartments, of which the majority are government-subsidized housing for performing artists, who pay 30 percent of their gross income in rent. Manhattan Plaza was conceived in 1973 as a megaluxury development intended to upgrade the depressed Clinton neighborhood, but the 1975 real-estate crash led to a change in plans, resulting in one of those *only in New York* phenomena. The towers themselves are hulking brick behemoths, hardly what any planner worth his salt would think might set off a wave of imaginative small-scale development on its periphery. Yet, in large part because of the vast concentration of performing-arts people living in the towers, the late 1970s and early '80s saw the transformation of the south side of 42nd Street between Ninth and Tenth avenues, a notorious strip of porn parlors, into what is called Theater Row: a long block of small, off-off-Broadway, experimental and workshop theaters, interspersed with lively restaurants, the **Theatre Arts Bookshop,** and a Richard Haas mural. The first theater to move here was **Playwrights Horizons,** at 416 West 42nd Street, in 1976. A joint public and private redevelopment effort began in 1978, and there are now about a dozen theaters. (Playwrights Horizons has premiered *Driving Miss Daisy, Sunday in the Park with George,* and *The Heidi Chronicles.*)

On the north side of Manhattan Plaza, on the south side of 43rd Street between Ninth and Tenth avenues, is a pleasant tree-lined strip plaza, fronted by two noteworthy take-out food shops: **Good & Plenty to Go,** designed by Milton Glaser, serves some of the best take-out meals in the city and sets up tables and chairs outside in good weather; and the **Little Pie Company** is a purveyor of delicious pies by the slice. Across 43rd Street are more theaters and restaurants.

10 EQUITABLE CENTER

787 Seventh Avenue, between 51st and 52nd streets
1986, Edward Larrabee Barnes Associates

The Equitable is one of the great muffed opportunities in the history of New York architecture. Seldom is an architect given such an opportunity to create a major public space. If ever there was an occasion to create the kind of space people would gravitate to from all over, this was it. But this space does not even draw you in when you're next to it. The fifty-four-story, 1.7 million-square-foot tower is sheathed in smooth beige limestone and orange granite, and has a gigantic arched entrance on seedy Seventh Avenue. Inside the arch is an eighty-foot-high atrium, comparable in scale to the atrium at Citicorp Center (10.14). Barnes and Equitable decided that rather than filling their atrium with shops and restaurants, they would devote it to the exhibition of works of art.

This is a laudable aim, but the space is designed like a vastly, numbingly overblown, boxlike art gallery. And the works of art on permanent display unfortunately do absolutely nothing to energize the space. The focal point of the atrium, opposite the front entrance, is an immense, hideous *Mural with Blue Brushstroke* by Roy Lichtenstein. On the floor in front of it is a semicircular marble bench/sculpture, *Atrium Furnishment,* by Scott Burton. In the north corridor beyond the atrium is Thomas Hart Benton's mural, *America Today,* completed in 1931 for the New School for Social Research, where years of neglect led to its purchase and restoration by Equitable. Benton's folksy social realism probably has more admirers today than at any time since the 1930s, but I believe it pales in comparison with the truly fine work that was being done at that time. The atrium also includes two large galleries that were originally a branch of the Whitney Museum of American Art; as of this writing, however, the Whitney has vacated, and Equitable will presumably operate the galleries on its own. Outside, along the east side of the building, is the through-block Galleria, at either end of which are Barry Flanagan's bronze sculptures, *Young Elephant* (1985) and *Hare on Bell* (1983), surely among the most ludicrous public sculptures ever erected in an American city.

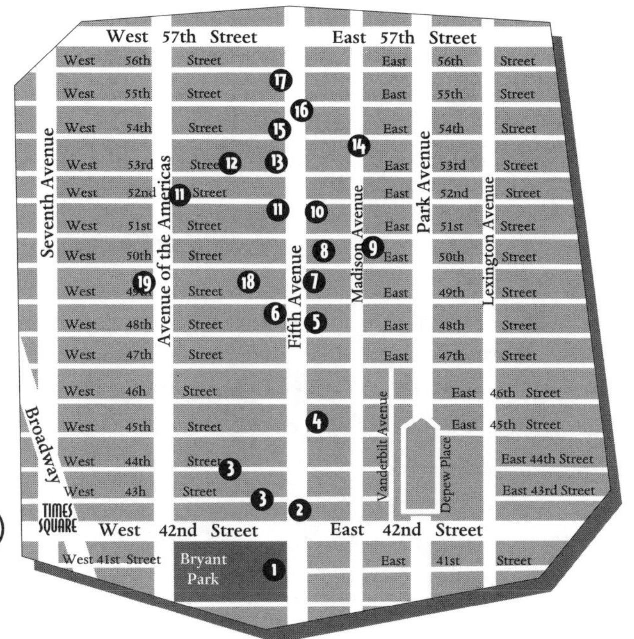

Fifth Avenue

5 *Scribner Bookstore*

Chapter 13

Fifth Avenue

1 NEW YORK PUBLIC LIBRARY

Fifth Avenue, from 40th Street to 42nd Street
1911, Carrère & Hastings

More than to any other institution, New York owes its status as an intellectual center to the New York Public Library, perhaps the most accessible repository of knowledge in the world. Such a collection may be appropriately housed only in a structure that glorifies the common man, and no building performs that task like Carrère & Hastings's palace of the people on Fifth Avenue. It is astoundingly just that this building should be located a mere two blocks from Grand Central Terminal (10.1), for it seems to me the very apotheosis of the modern city that the greatest transportational nexus ever built should directly lead to the stores of knowledge gathered within the New York Public Library. Cities, said Aristotle, exist to fulfill human nature, which is to say that cities satisfy the distinctively human capacity for learning. Never in human history was a city so built for learning. It is so easy for us to take midtown Manhattan for granted, to decry the congestion, the overdevelopment, the 42nd Street sleaze, and we are right to decry them. We must never lose sight, however, of the glory in our midst. Grand Central Terminal and the New York Public Library are emblems and exemplars of the essential justness of big-city life.

The New York Public Library was formed by the consolidation of the Astor Library, the Lenox Library, and the Tilden Trust in 1895. The Astor Library, founded by John Jacob Astor, was a privately owned reference library on Lafayette Street between Fourth Street and Astor Place, in the building, completed in 1881, that is now the Public Theater (6.5). Until the 42nd Street library was opened, the Astor Library was for all intents and purposes New York's public library. The Lenox Library was the vast collection of James Lenox, and was housed in an 1875 building on Fifth Avenue between 70th and 71st streets on the present site of the Frick Collection (17.11). In contrast to the Astor Library, the Lenox Library was not open to the general public. The two-million-dollar Tilden Trust was incorporated in 1887, the bequest of former New York Governor Samuel J. Tilden for the purpose of establishing a public library. (Tilden lived in the house that is now the National Arts Club on Gramercy Park, 8.7). The obvious location for the erection of a new public library was the site, abandoned in 1900, of the Croton Distributing Reservoir, which had been erected in 1837 (sixteen years before the Astor Library opened on Lafayette Street) on the west side of Fifth Avenue between 40th and 42nd streets.

Carrère & Hastings's monumental Beaux-Arts design incorporated numerous modern elements inspired by the contemporary work of such French architects as Henri Labrouste, whose Bibliothèques Nationale and Sainte-Genevieve in Paris had set a new standard in library design. The New York Public Library's façades were designed to reveal internal functions, with pediments marking the internal placement of reading rooms, large Fifth Avenue windows indicating offices, and, most notably, narrow vertical strips of windows pointing out book stacks. It is the glass-ceilinged Celeste Bartos Forum inside, formerly the circulating library and one of the best rooms in New York, that most invokes Labrouste's protomodern iron style. At the same time, the library's design clearly owes a great deal to the Beaux-Arts tradition growing out of the eighteenth century and the work of such men as Jacques-Ange Gabriel. The Corinthian-columned, tripartite, Fifth Avenue façade, based on the east front of the Louvre, with its statuary, sculptural niches, grand staircase, and sculpture-filled pediments, is one of the grandest Beaux-Arts façades in America, an effusion of superbly detailed white Vermont marble, and a bravura landmark presence plugging the westward vista on 41st Street from east of Fifth Avenue.

Throughout the interior, there is scarcely an inch that is not beautifully crafted of sumptuous materials. The Main Reading Room, easily reached at the rear of the third floor via monumental staircases located just inside the Fifth Avenue entrance, rests atop the stacks, and is, bar none, the best room in New York. Its floor-wide dimensions, high stucco ceiling, large arched windows, and fine furnishings, including long tables set with individual reading lamps, not to mention its steady, hushed sounds of soft voices, books being opened and closed, chairs sliding in and out, and now computer keys being tapped, lend this space an utterly exalting atmosphere of scholarship and learning. It is an absolute privilege for everyone in the world to be able to share this experience.

2 MANUFACTURERS HANOVER TRUST

510 Fifth Avenue, southwest corner of 43rd Street
1954, Skidmore, Owings & Merrill

ISRAEL DISCOUNT BANK

Fifth Avenue, southeast corner of 43rd Street
1917, York & Sawyer
Renovation in 1962, Luss, Kaplan & Associates

A pair of banks right across the street from each other. One is a modern monument, the other a modernization of a Beaux-Arts structure. One is in all the architectural history books, the other is virtually unknown. Yet, though it is hardly the daring design statement that Manufacturers is, the Israel Discount Bank has, I believe, aged better. Nowadays the typical pedestrian scarcely notices Manufacturers a block north of the New York Public Library. When it was built, however, it was the first glass-and-steel building on Fifth Avenue and was extravagantly praised by critics. Lewis Mumford noted the way that, despite its crystalline quality, the architects had nonetheless managed to convey the same sense of solidity and monumentality as the old Beaux-Arts bank architects. Manufacturers, said Mumford, was clearly built for the ages.

I wonder what Mumford thought some years later, for what is clearest of all is that architecture of this sort requires the most painstaking upkeep, lest it look dirty, warped, and bedraggled. This is a mode of modern architecture in which detail is everything. Streaky windows, littered floors, buckling acoustical tiles—little things that in a Beaux-Arts building would hardly detract from the general impression—can murder a building like Manufacturers Hanover Trust. That said, it bears repeating that this is one of the most thorough and intricate high-modern designs in New York, and it marked a revolution in bank planning. Where once banks were built like fortresses, with seemingly impenetrable marble façades and the like, here is one as what Mumford called a "crystal lantern," a glass cube in which interior and exterior seem as one. The old bank architecture obviously did not keep confidence in the banking system from shattering during the Depression, but still one wonders what mental dislocations may have been wrought by such a radical departure in banking practice as, for example, to place the vault, with its thirty-ton door, in the very front, making it the visual focus of the pedestrian outside.

Mumford praised this sign of self-assurance. In 1954 such a gesture seemed thrillingly forward looking. Today it seems a charming *retardataire*. Mumford wrote of Manufacturers, "As a symbol of the modern world, this structure is almost an ideal expression. . . . This architecture is the formal expression of the culture that has explored the innermost recesses of the atom, that knows that visible boundaries and solid objects are only figments of the intellect." The great architectural historian Sir Nikolaus Pevsner wrote of Manufacturers Hanover Trust, "Here is perfection, and, as is the fate of classic achievement, it cannot last long—the Italian High Renaissance less than twenty years, from Leonardo's *Last Supper* to about 1515." A crystal lantern, said Mumford, and this is most apparent at night when this glass cube is lit from within: it is truly a brilliant sight, until the next morning, when the streaky windows, the littered floors, the buckled acoustical tiles reappear.

Across the street, the Israel Discount Bank is a renovation of a 1917 neo-Renaissance bank building by New York's greatest bank architects, York & Sawyer (Bowery Savings Bank, 11.2). Most of the original exterior and much of the interior were restored, and what has been added is tasteful and subdued, though it in no way apes the older forms. The result is that the old is lent a crispness, while the new is given a richness, and somehow it all seems poignantly appropriate as a setting for an Israeli institution. The quality of this renovation is comparable to that of Kajima International for the Bank of Tokyo at 100 Broadway (1.16). Today the Israel Discount Bank looks as fresh as it did in 1962.

3 CENTURY CLUB

7 West 43rd Street, between Fifth and Sixth avenues
1891, McKim, Mead & White

HARVARD CLUB

27 West 44th Street, between Fifth and Sixth avenues
1894, McKim, Mead & White

NEW YORK YACHT CLUB

37 West 44th Street, between Fifth and Sixth avenues
1900, Warren & Wetmore

The blocks in the low forties just west of Fifth Avenue are New York's Pall Mall. Far the most impressive of these clubhouses is the Century Club, and well it should be, being the one club that counts a disproportionate share of architects on its membership roster. Indeed McKim, Mead & White, when chosen to design the Century's new clubhouse, were members, i.e., "Centurions." Stanford White's incredibly rich façade—one of his best—was based on Sanmichele's Palazzo Canossa in Verona. It was Sanmichele's Palazzo Grimani in Venice that White later chose to emulate in his great Tiffany Building (9.6) of 1906 on the southeast corner of Fifth Avenue and 37th Street. Where in the Tiffany Building White simplified Sanmichele's forms in a very modern attempt to reveal structure, fifteen years earlier his wont had been rather to embellish them by adding a Palladian loggia and encrusting the Roman brick façade with richly molded terra-cotta. Note especially the exuberant window frames on the upper level. This block of 43rd Street is very dense, and though when the Century was built it was not nearly so crowded, the clubhouse may look all the better in its now-cramped site. The very gradual way this façade comes into view as one walks eastward from Sixth Avenue gives it a dreamlike quality possessed by few buildings. I do not think it would have this quality if it was more open and thus announced itself sooner to the pedestrian. It is worth pointing out that though this is an extremely ornate building, it was actually constructed on a very modest budget.

McKim, Mead & White's Harvard Club was designed in a Georgian Federal rather than Italian Renaissance style out of deference to the dominant architecture of the Harvard campus in Cambridge, Massachusetts. The inspiration here seems to have been Sir William Chambers's Somerset

House, begun in 1776 in London, though the Harvard Club is made of brick and, of course, qreatly reduced in scale. This is a very sober clubhouse, pleasant and utterly without the dreamlike quality of the Century Club.

The other major clubhouse in these parts is Warren & Wetmore's New York Yacht Club. This is one of the most exuberant façades on earth. It starts with fully modeled Ionic columns set atop a base, with resultantly deep, high-arched windows. Such characteristically Beaux-Arts depth and mass is always impressive by itself. Warren & Wetmore, however, did not stop there. At the bottom of each of the three window bays of the façade is a projecting limestone ship's stern, with limestone cascades of water overhanging the sidewalk. This is clearly the wildest architectural sculpture in New York.

While in the vicinity, note the Algonquin Hotel at 59 West 44th Street, between Fifth and Sixth avenues. It was designed by Goldwin Starrett and built in 1902. The Oak Room restaurant was the site in the 1920s of the famed meetings of the Algonquin Round Table, which included Robert Benchley, George S. Kaufman, Dorothy Parker, Alexander Woollcott, and others. It is also the place where H. L. Mencken lived when he was up from Baltimore. The hotel retains its literary ambience, and a stop for a drink in the very cozy lobby is a must.

On the southwest corner of Fifth Avenue and 44th Street is an old Sidewalk Clock, a remnant of the kind of urban amenity that has largely fallen by the wayside in our advancing times.

4 FRED F. FRENCH BUILDING

551 Fifth Avenue, northeast corner of 45th Street
1927, H. Douglas Ives, and Sloan & Robertson

Viewed from two or three blocks down Fifth Avenue on a sunny day, the crown and tops of the setbacks of the Fred F. French Building explode in Art Deco polychromy, while the orange brick shaft gently twinkles. Up close, the compact entrance arcade and elevator lobby are a concentrated effusion of gilt and bronze. The French Building is a cousin to Goodhue's St. Bartholomew's Church (10.10), an instrument for capturing the brilliant light of the underrated New York sky. There is no wonder that the faience panels on the north and south sides of the top depict a rising sun. The thirty-eight-story slab, with its long side on 45th Street, is massive, but its sculptured bulk still allows for a congenial street presence and a pocket of daylight. This building sparkles even on days when its neighbors sag in shadow.

5 SCRIBNER BOOKSTORE (now Benetton)

597 Fifth Avenue, between 48th and 49th streets
1913, Ernest Flagg

This is exactly what a big downtown general bookshop is supposed to look like. The storefront has a great deal in common with Flagg's Little Singer Building (4.1) on Broadway and Prince Street, while the rest of the façade recalls Lamb & Rich's Bryant Park Studios (9.8). Along with these, Scribner's is one of very few Manhattan buildings that would be completely at home in Paris. The building has large, beautifully framed show windows, but more important to the total effect is the way the upper storefront windows lead into the fine, large vaulted interior, in which the cast-iron motif of the storefront is carried through to the railings of the mezzanine. Thus from the street, there is not only a clear view of a once book-filled interior, but the design does everything to draw the eye ineluctably inward. I would go so far as to say that not only was this the best bookshop façade in the city, but it is the best retail façade of any kind: that the city's best retail façade was that of a bookstore is exactly as things should be in a city renowned as an intellectual center.

6 GOELET BUILDING (aka Swiss Center)

608 Fifth Avenue, southwest corner of 49th Street
1932, E. H. Faile & Company
Lower floors remodeled in 1966, Lester Tichy & Associates

Unique, severely geometrical, not Art Deco, not International Style, but a potential, untapped vein of modernism. The façades are very skillful balances of vertical and horizontal in which there seems strong movement in both directions. The alternating vertical bands of windows and spandrels broken by continuous horizontal piers recalls Howe & Lescaze's Philadelphia Saving Fund Society Building, which was completed the same year as the Goelet Building. It may thus seem odd that the former building should have gone down in history as an early modern classic, while the Goelet Building has been completely ignored. Robert A. M. Stern, Gregory Gilmartin, and Thomas Mellins, in their *New York 1930: Architecture and Urbanism Between the Two World Wars,* give a scant paragraph to this building, calling it "a luxuriously detailed but bastardized interpretation of the International Style." They also refer to its "awkwardly massive penthouse."

Such views are surprising from authors known for championing the stylistically impure. Part of the "bastardization" lies in the flamboyant use of contrasting materials, particularly the white Vermont marble chosen for the spandrels and the dark green marble selected for the piers. As for that "awkwardly massive penthouse," it is very surprising to me that Stern, Gilmartin, and Mellins failed to recognize its source in the architecture of the Viennese Secession, particularly the work of Otto Wagner and Josef Hoffmann. Indeed the Goelet Building and Joseph Urban's Hearst Magazine Building on Eighth Avenue between 56th and 57th streets are the two Manhattan structures that most explicitly recall Viennese Secessionist architecture. On one block of Midtown Fifth Avenue, then, we have vivid glimpses of both fin de siècle Paris (Scribner's) and fin de siècle Vienna.

7 SAKS FIFTH AVENUE

611 Fifth Avenue, between 49th and 50th streets
1924, Starrett & Van Vleck

SWISS BANK TOWER

12 East 50th Street, between Fifth and Madison avenues
1989, Lee Harris Pomeroy Associates

Saks, like Lord and Taylor, also by Starrett & Van Vleck, ten blocks down Fifth Avenue and built ten years earlier, is a conventional, boxy, well-designed, neo-Renaissance, department-store building. The best thing about Saks is its particularly exciting main floor. Like Macy's (9.1), it is a total sensory experience. There is a profusion of polished wood and gleaming glass; a lovely music of muffled voices, hard objects striking glass counters, and display cases sliding open and closed; perfume-scented air; and a soft, kinetic bustle. The best, most elegant, and most easily accessible men's room in midtown is located on the sixth floor of Saks. The stalls are fully enclosed small rooms, a true anomaly.

Utilizing Saks's air rights and rising directly behind the store is the Swiss Bank Tower, a tall office building that strives mightily to be unobtrusive, but does so not by conventional contextualism but by a unique ghostliness. That is, the concrete walls are very plain and very soft, and look unfinished. It is as though Lee Harris Pomeroy's whole intent was to create a tall building that appeared as much as possible simply not to be there. I think many people who gaze upon the Swiss Bank Tower wonder when it is going to be completed. The nicest thing about it is the band of lights along its top, which is a pleasant nighttime skyline element. The worst thing about this largely unexceptionable building is that it cuts Fifth Avenue off from its view—that was there for nearly six decades!—of the clock atop the Newsweek Building.

8 ST. PATRICK'S CATHEDRAL

Fifth Avenue, from 50th Street to 51st Street
1878; towers added in 1888: James Renwick, Jr.

ARCHBISHOP'S RESIDENCE

452 Madison Avenue, northwest corner of 50th Street
1880, James Renwick, Jr.

RECTORY

460 Madison Avenue, southwest corner of 51st Street
1880, James Renwick, Jr.

LADY CHAPEL

1906, Charles T. Mathews

St. Patrick's Cathedral is immensely popular with the public. The critics have not been so kind. I side with the public. Indeed, I think St. Patrick's is a masterpiece. Flamboyant Gothic forms are brilliantly adapted to a tightly constrained site. Typical, though, of "advanced" opinion of St. Patrick's is this from Paul Goldberger of the *New York Times*: "The end result is rather stuffy and dry . . . there is no element of it that works as a lively element in the cityscape . . . the absence of flying buttresses makes for a certain blandness . . . too self-assured, too successful, too proud to prove itself." When St. Patrick's was built, American Catholics, most of them poor Irish, were second-class citizens, victims of virulent prejudice.

8 *St. Patrick's Cathedral*

But their numbers became great enough during the era of mass Irish immigration to warrant a new cathedral for New York. Archbishop John Hughes decided that rather than be a shrinking violet, the new cathedral would be the most magnificent, in-your-face church in the nation. Before St. Patrick's, the only Gothic churches with which Americans were familiar were the ones promoted by the Ecclesiological Movement, best represented in New York by Trinity Church (1846, 1.17) and Grace Church (1846, 6.9, designed, like St. Patrick's, by Renwick). This Anglican Gothic was based on English architecture of the thirteenth and fourteenth centuries, in reaction to Neoclassicism (best represented in New York by St. Paul's Chapel, 1766, 2.6). St. Patrick's would be different. Renwick chose from among various types of Gothic, both French and English, eschewed the Ecclesiological niceties, and organized the disparate parts into a sumptuous, antipuritanical but strongly controlled composition. The plot was not of the right proportions for a "correct" Gothic church of the size and splendor desired. Renwick thus had to adapt to the difficult site, and what he did within these limitations is every bit as impressive as anything by Frank Lloyd Wright. Renwick had to fill a site long in relation to its width. Thus the main body of the church is low in relation to its length; the transepts are stubby; there are single rather than double aisles; and so on. The narrow site left only 32 feet each for the twin 330-foot-high towers. (This ratio of 10 to 1 compares to the 6.5 to 1 of Cologne Cathedral.) I bet the towers of St. Patrick's would rank as the most soaring structures ever built by man. How can Paul Goldberger say that no part of St. Patrick's Cathedral works as a lively element in the cityscape? The interior is based on English precedents: York (early fourteenth century) and Winchester (early fifteenth century). Note the complex system of liernes and tiercerons that forms the lovely series of eight-pointed stars along the crown of the nave vault. Throughout there is a feeling of classical stateliness so different from the dark Gothic of Trinity Church. Trinity is Anglican Gothic; St. Patrick's is cosmopolitan Gothic. What better symbol could there be for a church with universal aspirations adapting itself to the hostile climate of the New World?

9 VILLARD HOUSES

451–457 Madison Avenue, between 50th and 51st streets
1884, McKim, Mead & White

The detailing of the façades of this group of attached houses was the work of Joseph Morrill Wells, at the time Stanford White's chief assistant, and its precision, quality, and dignity set a new standard for the firm of McKim, Mead & White. This detailing, which brought the Italianate to a new height, combined with the novel courtyard, open to Madison Avenue, around which the houses were harmoniously arrayed, to make the Villard Houses perhaps the most admired work of architecture of their time in New York. They were a group of six town houses, designed as though it was a single palazzo or Parisian hôtel, a kind of updating of the Colonnade Row (6.6) concept from the 1830s. Thus were achieved a grandeur and a monumentality usually denied to a row of town houses. Sources included the Palazzo della Cancelleria in Rome, long incorrectly attributed to Bramante, completed in 1498, and the obvious basis for most of Wells's detailing (the rustication, quoining, and lintels); Baldassare Peruzzi's Villa

Farnesina in Rome, completed in 1511 (McKim, Mead & White's Pierpont Morgan Library, 9.11, was also inspired by the work of Peruzzi), a possible source for the courtyard concept; and F. A. Duquesney's Gare de l'Est in Paris, completed in 1852, from which came the Villard Houses' arcaded entrance.

Henry Villard, the railroad magnate who had commissioned the houses, had his own home in the southern wing of the group. The central section comprised two houses, and the northern wing was composed of three, two of which were approached from 51st Street, while all the other houses in the group were entered from the courtyard. The complex later became the headquarters of the Random House publishing firm during the storied tenure of Bennett Cerf, and also served as offices for the Roman Catholic Archdiocese of New York. When the houses were threatened with demolition to make way for what became the Helmsley Palace Hotel, preservationists worked out a plan with developer

10 *Cartier Building*

Harry Helmsley in which the hotel would rise behind the houses, with the central section and southern wing comprising public rooms for it. The northern wing was given to a group of nonprofit organizations concerned with the quality of the urban environment: the Municipal Art Society, the Parks Council, the Architectural League, and the New York Chapter of the American Institute of Architects. The northern wing is now known as the Urban Center, and within it the Municipal Art Society operates the Urban Center Galleries, in which architectural exhibits are mounted, and Urban Center Books, by far New York's best retail source for books and magazines on architecture, urban planning, and interior design.

10 647 FIFTH AVENUE

Between 51st and 52nd streets
1905, Hunt and Hunt

CARTIER (originally Morton F. Plant residence)

651 Fifth Avenue, southeast corner of 52nd Street
1905, Robert W. Gibson
Conversion to a shop in 1917, Welles Bosworth
Extension at 4 East 52nd Street in 1905: C. P. H. Gilbert

This is a heavy-duty Beaux-Arts ensemble of which the centerpiece is the Cartier building, one of the great houses of New York (though it remained one for a mere twelve years before being remodeled into a shop.) It is best viewed from the north along Fifth Avenue. The 52nd Street façade was the front of the house, with the main entrance surmounted by the fluted Ionic pilasters and pediment. When Welles Bosworth, architect of 195 Broadway (2.5), remodeled it into a shop, the entrance was swung around to Fifth Avenue. The rinceaux, or stylized foliate carving, in the frieze shows that the naturalistic ornament of Louis Sullivan, as seen in the Bayard Building (6.2), was very much a product of the École des Beaux-Arts. The house just south, now the Gianni Versace boutique, is notable for its Corinthian pilasters, and had a twin next door that was demolished to make way for Skidmore, Owings & Merrill's Olympic Tower. Around the corner on 52nd Street is a mansarded extension to the Plant house, now also part of Cartier's. These flanking buildings serve only to frame the jewel box that is Cartier's.

11 52ND STREET, FROM FIFTH AVENUE TO SIXTH AVENUE

It is rather hard to believe that megadeveloped West 52nd Street was until the 1960s the center of the international jazz universe, boasting among other clubs Charlie Parker's own Birdland. Now this is a solid strip of tall buildings, punctuated by an occasional holdout such as the **Twenty-One Club** restaurant at number 21, a former speakeasy where a hamburger costs twenty-one dollars and where there is an impressive outdoor display of lawn jockeys. **The Museum of Television and Radio** at number 23 is the new home of what once was called the Museum of Broadcasting, which used to be at 1 East 53rd Street. Johnson's skyscraper museum seems intended to recall the shape of antique radios. With his Elmer Holmes Bobst Library (5.5) at New York University, Johnson has already given us a building that looks like a television set.

11A *CBS Building*

11[B] *Museum of Television and Radio & Tishman Building*

At 666 Fifth Avenue at the northwest corner of Fifth Avenue and 52nd Street is the **Tishman Building**, designed by Carson & Lundin and built in 1957. This is an immense thirty-eight-story, over 1.2 million-square-foot office building, covered in a hideous embossed aluminum skin that looks a lot like the embossed stainless-steel skin of the Mobil Building (11.6) on East 42nd Street. There are some nice things about the Tishman Building, however, foremost among them being the generous arcaded space at its base, complete with a "water wall" designed by the distinguished Japanese-American sculptor Isamu Noguchi. For the indoor lobby, Noguchi designed the back-lit translucent ceiling from which are hung undulating, horizontal, white-enameled aluminum bands. Together the arcade and lobby are an unusually crisp rendering of the midcult 1950s style also exemplified by the lobby of the United Nations General Assembly Building (11.10) and the Mobil Building (11.6). (A block away, on the façade of the Associated Press Building on Rockefeller Plaza between 50th and 51st streets in Rockefeller Center, 13.18, is a relief sculpture that, together with the red cube at 140 Broadway, 2.3E, is Noguchi's best-known public sculpture.) On the top floor of the Tishman Building there used to be a touristy bar called Top of the Sixes, notable for its exciting views. It has been replaced by one of those fancy cigar-smoking establishments. The large B. Dalton Bookseller at the base also recently closed. At this writing, alas, the splendid arcade is endangered.

Thirty-one West 52nd Street, the former E. F. Hutton Building, was designed by Kevin Roche John Dinkeloo & Associates and built in 1987. Like the same firm's 60 Wall Street (1.6) and Three United Nations Plaza (11.11), it is an example of the Postmodern Egyptoid work that seems to be the result of some bizarre, esoteric religious conversion among the designers that gave us the Ford Foundation (11.8), indisputably one of the greatest high-modern buildings in the world. Number 31 is the ungainliest of them all and provides a startling contrast to the **CBS Building** next door at number 51, for Roche Dinkeloo is the successor firm to Eero Saarinen & Associates, architects of CBS, which was built in 1965. "Black Rock," as it is popularly known, is thirty-eight stories sheathed in exquisite, somber, black Canadian granite. Rather than the building being set back on a plaza, it wraps around the building, making it completely freestanding—as freestanding, indeed, as the Flatiron Building (8.3). Unbroken, triangulated piers rise the height of the tower, giving the façade a faceted, rocklike surface. These piers alternate with continuous vertical strips of smoked glass.

Some consider this building to be one of Manhattan's most elegant towers. Others find it funereal. It has been criticized for being aloof from its surroundings, but I feel that there is room in a city for the occasional aloof building, particularly if it is as high quality an object as this. Besides, I do not really feel that CBS is altogether aloof. The way that that wraparound plaza opened 53rd Street to 52nd Street via a narrow passage inside the block tied the two streets together in a way a conventional plaza on dismal Sixth Avenue never could have. Midtown could do with more urbanistic gestures of this kind. Alas, number 31 widened the space behind CBS, creating a more accessible plaza but detracting from the earlier thrill of the through-block sneak peek.

Finally **650 Fifth Avenue,** at the southwest corner of 52nd Street, was designed by John Carl Warnecke & Associates and built in 1978. The base-and-tower form, extending out to the sidewalk with alternating horizontal bands of glass and granite, is a distant and much degenerated descendant of Howe & Lescaze's Philadelphia Saving Fund Society building. The big second-floor window overlooking Fifth Avenue is a Bauhaus touch. Functionally it indicates the floor on which the elevator lobby is located. The bonus trade-off here is the arcade on 52nd Street, in which one of the city's few—the city's only?—outdoor escalators carries workers to the office elevator banks on the second floor.

12 MUSEUM OF MODERN ART

11 West 53rd Street, between Fifth and Sixth avenues
1939, Philip Goodwin and Edward Durell Stone
Additions in 1951 and 1964, Philip Johnson Associates
Addition in 1985, Cesar Pelli & Associates

MUSEUM TOWER

21 West 53rd Street, between Fifth and Sixth avenues
1985, Cesar Pelli & Associates

The Museum of Modern Art was conceived as an American equivalent of the Palais de Luxembourg in Paris, i.e., as a place to exhibit contemporary art before the best of it was passed on to, in the case of the Palais de Luxembourg, the Louvre, or, in the case of MoMA, the Metropolitan Museum of Art (17.20). MoMA's first home was in Warren and Wetmore's Heckscher building (now called the Crown Building, 14.9) on the southwest corner of Fifth Avenue and 57th Street. MoMA's first director, Alfred H. Barr, Jr., however, was fired by an enthusiasm for the Bauhaus, the avant-garde German design academy in which painting, sculpture, architecture, graphic design, film, photography, theater, and industrial design were conceived as a single cultural expression. Barr wanted MoMA to be an American equivalent not of the Palais de Luxembourg, but of the Bauhaus. He wanted it to be a place where people could experience the current cultural totality at its highest level. Thus would MoMA establish the first museum departments of architecture, film, photography, and industrial design, departments now commonplace at even the most conservative art museums.

It was enormously important to Barr that MoMA have a new building of its own. He wanted this building to be itself an embodiment of

12 *Museum Tower on left, Museum of Modern Art at front*

the avant-garde spirit of the museum. He also wanted it to have a prominent midtown location and to be as inviting to the general public as Macy's (9.1). When MoMA was given its 53rd Street site by John D. Rockefeller, Jr., and Mrs. John D. (Abby Aldrich) Rockefeller, Jr., in 1932, Rockefeller Plaza had been built to 51st Street, and there were plans to extend it to 53rd. The front entrance of MoMA was thus deliberately placed on-axis with Rockefeller Plaza. Rockefeller Plaza, of course, was never extended beyond 51st Street, and so there is no formal promenade to the entrance of MoMA. In lieu of extending Rockefeller Plaza, however, a through-block lobby was created in the Time Warner, formerly the Esso, Building, on-axis with Rockefeller Plaza and leading from 51st to 52nd streets, and a through-block arcade was created in the Tishman Building (13.11), slightly off-axis with Rockefeller Plaza, leading from 52nd to 53rd streets. Thus is MoMA tied in, however obliquely, with Rockefeller Center (13.18).

The building Barr got is one of the modern monuments of New York. Barr was very keen that the commission to design the new museum building be given to the Bauhaus's Mies van der Rohe, whose work was introduced to the New York public in MoMA's seminal "Modern Architecture: International Exhibition," organized by Henry-Russell Hitchcock and Philip Johnson in 1932. (Mies went on, of course, to design the Seagram Building, 10.11, thirty-six years later on Park Avenue, which shows just how old the high modern style was by the time of the Seagram Building.) MoMA's trustees, however, gave the job to a pair of little-known architects, Edward Durell Stone and Philip Goodwin. Mies himself could hardly have produced a finer example of the Bauhaus style. At the time Goodwin, an art collector and MoMA trustee, was known as a talented, if very mannered, designer of houses in traditional architectural styles, i.e., as about the last person from whom one would expect a Bauhaus-style monument. Stone had worked on Rockefeller Center as a draftsman for Wallace K. Harrison, and his proclivities were decidedly more modern than Goodwin's.

What these men wrought was a major building that for sheer surprise value may have no parallel in the architectural history of New York. The gleaming white marble and glass façade was an imperious usurper of attention on its street of brownstones. Revolving doors, as in a department store, opened onto a spacious lobby, at the other end of which was a glass wall displaying the museum's outdoor sculpture garden. The art critic Henry McBride said that if Le Corbusier believed houses should be "machines to live in," then Stone's and Goodwin's MoMA was "a machine to show pictures in."

MoMA was substantially renovated and expanded in the early 1980s by Cesar Pelli & Associates. After being more or less closed for four years, the museum reopened with much fanfare in May 1984. Stone's and Goodwin's 53rd Street façade was left unaltered. Within, on the other hand, a great many changes had been wrought, necessitated by the tremendous post-World War II expansion of the museumgoing public, an expansion that had its roots partly in MoMA's early striving to extirpate all traces of traditional museological effeteness from its program. By the 1980s, however, the size and character of the museumgoing public would surely have surprised Alfred Barr. Even if Barr had wanted MoMA to be as inviting to the general public as Macy's, still I doubt he could possibly have foreseen just how literally the renovated and expanded museum would look like a suburban shopping mall. As Hilton Kramer puts it, the new MoMA "is designed . . . for a public nurtured on blockbuster exhibitions—exhibitions that are as much media events as they are art events, and that have the inevitable effect of arousing, by means of high-intensity publicity campaigns, the kind of interest which art in and of itself can probably never fully satisfy."

Today attending major exhibitions at MoMA is about as aesthetically rewarding as attending trade shows at the Javits Center (1.8). Alfred Barr wanted to afford the general public access to a real aesthetic experience—a noble desire in the true American spirit. Alas, nowadays MoMA too often scarcely affords any aesthetic experience at all. One of the central pleasures of urbane existence, museumgoing, has been senselessly destroyed, and it is nothing less than a tragedy that MoMA, one of a handful of the most important institutions of any kind in the history of New York, should so completely have capitulated to ignominious trends. The new MoMA follows Richard Rodgers's and Renzo Piano's Centre Pompidou in Paris and I. M. Pei & Partners's East Wing for the National Gallery of Art in Washington, D.C., in being what Hilton Kramer calls "pioneer examples of blockbuster-inspired museum design." In all fairness, it must be said that MoMA goes nowhere near as far as either of these precursors in creating spaces in which the accommodation of huge crowds takes clear precedence over the exhibition of works of art.

At any rate, Philip Johnson's Abby Aldrich Rockefeller Sculpture Garden remains directly across the lobby from the front entrance, and thus on-axis with Rockefeller Plaza. It is possible to enter the Channel Gardens of Rockefeller Center from Fifth Avenue, pass the Lower Plaza, take a right turn on Rockefeller Plaza, continue through the decently designed Time Warner lobby and Tishman arcade, enter MoMA, and continue straight to the sculpture garden, where one may sit and meditate. (Alas, this progression is greatly impeded if one does not have a MoMA membership card to flash at the guard at the museum's entrance. Would that somehow the sculpture garden could be made accessible to the public without paying!) The architectural historian William H. Jordy says of MoMA's sculpture garden that "no public outdoor space designed in the United States in the quarter of a century following World War II surpasses this one as a lively, yet dignified, urban space, organized for a variety of activities." Jordy wrote this some twelve years before the renovation and expansion, and though the sculpture garden has been intruded upon somewhat by Pelli's glazed space-frame Garden Hall and Museum Tower, still the garden has been left with its integrity largely intact.

Though MoMA is now designed for blockbuster exhibitions, the upstairs galleries housing the museum's permanent collection remain eminently worth visiting, for the quality of many of the works on display is so high that they would be worth seeking out even if housed in a subway rest room. I strongly recommend a visit to MoMA's second floor. To the left at the top of the escalator (which starts in the lobby just in front of the glass wall looking onto the sculpture garden) is the gallery containing Van Gogh's *Starry Night* (1889, the year the arch was erected in Washington Square, 5.2) and Henri Rousseau's *Sleeping Gypsy* (1897, the year Low Library was built at Columbia University, 19.3). Continuing to the left, one encounters Pierre Bonnard's *Breakfast Room* (circa 1931, the year the Empire State Building, 9.4, was completed). New York is a city of awesome artistic diversity, far more so than one might think from perusing the art press. In my opinion, the best young painters in New York today, and they are many even if their names are unknown to the trendmongers, see themselves as working in the tradition of the "painterly realism" of Bonnard (1867-1947).

In the next gallery is Picasso's great *Les Demoiselles d'Avignon* (1907, the year of the U.S. Custom House, 1.1, on Bowling Green, and the Plaza Hotel, 14.7). To the left just beyond the Picasso is the entrance to the gallery containing nothing but paintings from Monet's Water Lilies series, which date from circa 1920 (roughly the period of Bertram Grosvenor Goodhue's St. Bartholomew's Church, 10.10). Exiting the Water Lilies gallery, and continuing directly across to the next entrance, one enters the gallery containing Picasso's *Guitar*, said to be the first assemblage sculpture ever. It was created in 1912 (the year between the completion of the New York Public Library, 13.1, and Grand Central Terminal, 10.1). Continuing straight into the next gallery, one finds Picasso's *Three Musicians* from 1921 (Edith Wharton's *The Age of Innocence* was a best-seller). Taking a right into the next gallery, one comes to Constantin Brancusi's sculptures, *Bird in Space* from 1928 (the year of Joseph Urban's Hearst Magazine Building) and *Fish* from 1930 (the year of William Van Alen's Chrysler Building, 11.4, Howells & Hood's Daily News Building, 11.7, and Joseph Urban's New School for Social Research, 5.10).

Straight through the next two galleries is Umberto Boccioni's futuristic *Unique Forms of Continuity in Space* from 1913, the year of that other great example of unique forms of continuity in space, Grand Central Terminal (10.1). To the right through the next entrance are a number of the rigorously geometrical and surprisingly beautiful paintings of Piet Mondrian, including his most famous work, *Broadway Boogie Woogie*, completed in 1943. In a literal reading, this painting evokes the random animation of the Manhattan grid—it is an attempt, and a strikingly successful one, to capture something like the totality of the Manhattan experience in a single canvas. It is a must on any architectural itinerary in New York.

The next gallery contains what for me is the high point of the MoMA collection, the works of Henri Matisse. *The Red Studio* dates from 1911 (the year of the New York Public Library, 13.1), and *Dance* dates from 1909 (the year of Napoleon LeBrun & Sons' Metropolitan Life Tower, 8.4, and Hoppin & Koen's Police Building, 2.18). In the next gallery are works by Paul Klee, including *Mask of Fear* from 1932 (the year Rockefeller Center, 13.18, was begun), and Wassily Kandinsky, one of the first—if not the very first—to paint a totally abstract painting. This gallery features four Kandinskys—called *Paintings No. 198, 199, 200, and 201*, from 1914 (the year the Frick Collection, 17.11, was built). Klee and Kandinsky were the foremost painters associated with the Bauhaus, and so were colleagues of Mies van der Rohe, architect of the Seagram Building (10.11). There is much more on MoMA's second floor, but these are some of the highlights. I strongly recommend that the reader should take the opportunity to study this staggering collection.

As part of Cesar Pelli's renovation and expansion of MoMA, the museum erected next door a tall, income-producing apartment building, called Museum Tower. This is one of the best tall buildings to go up in Manhattan in the 1980s. Like Mies van der Rohe, Pelli sees the skyscraper curtain wall not as a blank expanse to be composed to decorative effect, but rather in a truly architectural sense, as an expression of architectural, not merely graphic, detail. The architectural critic Ada Louise Huxtable writes: "He divides, frames, and color-codes the thin, light, vitreous wall . . . he treats it as a taut, enveloping membrane . . . the solution never defaults on a meticulous and vigorous reference to an architectonic rationale." I believe that Pelli has here taken the conventional package required by

Manhattan developers to its expressive extreme. To go beyond this would be to enter the realm of Norman Foster or Moshe Safdie, architects who are radically redefining the very premises of "the package," and who have not built in New York (though Safdie came close at Columbus Circle).

13 ST. THOMAS CHURCH

1 West 53rd Street, northwest corner of Fifth Avenue
1913, Cram, Goodhue & Ferguson

St. Thomas, perhaps the most prestigious Episcopal congregation in the city, built this church from 1911 to 1913. The basic plan is by Ralph Adams Cram, and the interior detail by Bertram Grosvenor Goodhue. The first thing to note about St. Thomas is that it is an exceptionally grand church with an almost cathedral-like interior, crammed (no pun intended) into a very tight site, and was built on Fifth Avenue at the very time it was experiencing dense commercial development. There is no greater skill architects can possess than to design something perfectly suited to its site, and St. Thomas is suited to this site in every conceivable way. The interior measures 214 feet long, 43 feet wide, and 95 feet to the crest of the ceiling. St. Patrick's Cathedral (13.8), by contrast, measures 306 feet long, 48 feet wide, and 108 feet to the crest of the ceiling. St. Thomas is not that much smaller than St. Patrick's, given that the former occupies an awkward corner plot, and the latter has an entire city block all to itself.

The demarcation between the nave, which runs seven bays along the south side of the church, and the chancel, which runs two bays, is a thickened rib and a step up (similar to Trinity Church, 1.17). This is one of the devices the architects use to open up the space. The nave is a symmetrical area placed near the southern side of the building. The northern side, along 53rd Street, running west from the corner tower, contains a porch and chantry, surmounted by an east-west gallery, and, just west of the tower, the beginning of a north-running gallery over the narthex. Perhaps if there had been more space, the architects would have duplicated the southern part along the north side, and added a north tower. Given the space limitation, however, they had to forego symmetry. The south tower would look odd if the church was not located on a corner, but it serves to anchor the block and to help turn the corner,

13 *St. Thomas Church*

giving the church a bit of strength among its much higher neighbors.

The long side walls are relatively plain, which increases the sense of spaciousness and also beautifully sets off the two principal decorative features of the church: the magnificent rose window and the reredos behind the altar. Goodhue's reredos was based in part on the one at All Souls College, Oxford, in the perpendicular Gothic mode, although the St. Thomas reredos is larger than any the Middle Ages produced. The reredos contains sixty figures from the history of Christianity, designed by Lee Lawrie (sculptor of the statue of Atlas in front of the International Building at Rockefeller Center, 13.18). Note the carving of the choir furniture, designed by Goodhue: contemporary images, including an airplane, an automobile, World War I generals, and the sinking of the Lusitania are worked in among the Christian iconography. Fifth Avenue street scenes are featured in the carving on the façade, and the door at the base of the tower, intended as the bride's entrance, is ornamented with a dollar sign. Goodhue's humorous gestures did indeed prompt controversy.

The front steps of St. Thomas are, like the steps of St. Patrick's down the street, a popular place for people to sit and rest or eat their lunch. The interior is a softly dark, serene, beautiful, and mysterious space, and the best place I can think of for a few moments' meditative pause from the day's rambling.

14 520 MADISON AVENUE

Between 53rd and 54th streets
1981, Swanke Hayden Connell

535 MADISON AVENUE

Northeast corner of 54th Street
1986, Edward Larrabee Barnes Associates

527 MADISON AVENUE

Southeast corner of 54th Street
1987, Fox & Fowle

A dense forest of new skyscrapers. Leaving aside the question of the quality of any of the individual designs, these blocks of Madison have become an enclave of chill in the midtownscape. The low-rise liveliness, second storiness, diversity of shops, and respite from the adjoining megaoffice precincts are fast vanishing amid the onslaught of yet-more-speculative behemoths born of the 1980s' real-estate fever. Five hundred twenty formerly Continental Illinois Center, is the behemothest of them all: almost a million square feet in forty-three stories. The immense sloping base and conventional rectangular tower are sheathed in ultrasmooth polished red granite. As a way of fulfilling zoning requirements, the slope is an alternative to traditional setbacks, plazas, or atriums. Unfortunately, its effect is to call attention to itself, and this is truly one of the most aggressive buildings in midtown (which is saying a great deal). The best thing about it by far is the way it was forced to build around the venerable Reidys' Bar at 22 East 54th Street, a "holdout" that refused to sell to the developer, and that miraculously continued to operate all through the construction process. (Reidys' was one of my favorite bars. Alas, the space was recently taken over by an upmarket Thai restaurant/brewpub.)

Five thirty-five by Barnes was completed in the same year as his IBM Building (14.10) up the street, and it looks very much as though these two buildings were designed simultaneously. They have similar skins of alternating horizontal bands, but where IBM alternates polished granite and glass, 535, like Citicorp Center (10.14), uses aluminum and glass. While IBM takes a slice out of its lower corner on Madison and 57th, widening the pedestrian walkway, 535 takes out a similar slice, though it is not on the corner, where it would aid pedestrians, but inside the block on 54th Street, where it forms part of the largely useless, bonus plaza. Five thirty-five is smaller than IBM, about 444,000 square feet in thirty-six stories; IBM is about 789,000 square feet in forty-three stories. Yet 535 seems to me to do far more harm to its immediate vicinity than does the better-designed IBM Building.

Five twenty-seven is a somewhat weird building by the usually good Fox & Fowle, located directly across 54th Street from 535. A straight glass and granite façade on Madison gives way to a sloping glass-and-steel façade on 54th Street. This is the land of the sloping façade.

15 UNIVERSITY CLUB

1 West 54th Street, northwest corner of Fifth Avenue
1899, McKim, Mead & White

When I first moved to New York several years ago, I thought the University Club was made, like the Villard Houses (13.9), of brownstone. What a surprise it was when, some years later, the University Club was cleaned, and revealed to be gleaming pink granite. In London there are rather a large number of people who object to the cleaning of building façades. They feel that a building's "character" is enhanced by dirt, which is a sort of record of the passage of time. I am not unsympathetic to this idea in principle. In practice, however, in the New York of our time, the defense of dirt seems somehow inappropriate. It may not be that every building should be cleaned, but nowadays New York is an extremely dirty city, far beyond the call of "character," and a little cleaning shows that there remain a few people who care what the place looks like. I therefore applaud the cleaning of the University Club, particularly at a time when

15 *University Club*

much of the beauty is draining out of Fifth Avenue.

The University Club, like the Pierpont Morgan Library (9.11), is the work of Charles Follen McKim. McKim's design was not adapted from any Italian Renaissance building in particular. The granite used in the façade is the same as that chosen for the terrace of the New York Public Library (13.1). Part of the University Club's imposing presence comes from McKim's use of rustication throughout both the Fifth Avenue and the 54th Street façades. You will notice in your wanderings about the city that such extensive rustication is rare. The balcony railings are bronze in the form of rinceaux, and are interesting to compare with the frieze under the cornice of the Cartier Building (13.10) just a couple of blocks down Fifth Avenue. Note also that McKim reduces the apparent height of the building by using high arched windows to indicate public rooms, and small square windows for bedrooms. The public is not admitted to this or any other clubhouse unaccompanied by a club member, and so I will not say anything about the interiors, except that if you can get in to see them, by all means do so.

16 ST. REGIS HOTEL

2 East 55th Street, southeast corner of Fifth Avenue
1904, Trowbridge & Livingston
Addition to the east in 1925, Trowbridge & Livingston

PENINSULA HOTEL (formerly Gotham Hotel)

2 West 55th Street, southwest corner of Fifth Avenue
1905, Hiss & Weeks

This pair of Belle Epoque hotels, right across the street from each other, make the corner of Fifth and 55th the most Fifth Avenue spot on Fifth Avenue, and one of the most romantic locales in the city. This is what so many people have for so long imagined when they think of Fifth Avenue. For the St. Regis, Trowbridge & Livingston adapted contemporary French design to the tall hotel, with an elongated, relatively plain shaft rising to a rich mansard top. The lobby is surprisingly small, as is appropriate for a hotel conceived as a quiet, dignified, luxurious retreat and built in what in 1904 was an exclusive residential section of Fifth Avenue. Note, nonetheless, the beautiful bronzework in the lobby, in the revolving doors of the front entrance on 55th Street, and in the very romantic doorman's sentry box just outside the front entrance. The King Cole restaurant off the lobby features a famous mural by Maxfield Parrish, originally painted for the Knickerbocker Hotel (12.3) on Times Square. Henry Hope Reed calls it "the best mural in the city." After many years as a Sheraton hotel, during which time it was possible for ordinary people to afford a weekend there, the St. Regis is now once again privately owned, and has been thoroughly refurbished and made into what is reputed to be the most expensive hotel in New York.

The Peninsula was built as the Gotham and completed a year after the St. Regis. It shares the west side of Fifth Avenue between 54th and 55th streets with Charles Follen McKim's University Club (1899, 13.15). Hiss & Weeks designed the Gotham to harmonize with the clubhouse, and though the hotel is twice as tall as its neighbor, it uses a similar Italian Renaissance style and continues the club's string courses, arches, balconies, and rustication, making it appear as though this was conceived as a unified block. The rustication and the large brackets also complement the St. Regis across Fifth Avenue. The Gotham was sadly empty for a number of years in the 1980s until its short-lived tenure as Hotel Maxim's de Paris, which gave way to the Peninsula, part of a prestigious international chain. It appears that in its present guise this hotel is here to stay for a while.

17 712–714 FIFTH AVENUE

Between 55th and 56th streets
1908, Adolf S. Gottlieb
1909, Woodruff Leeming
1989, Kohn Pedersen Fox

The former Coty Building at number 714 was built in 1909, and the windows by Rene Lalique were added in 1912. The former Rizzoli Building at number 712 dates from 1908. When in the mid-1980s it was announced that these buildings were to be demolished to make way for a tall mixed-use building, there was a preservationist uproar. Though these were two perfectly fine small buildings, I do not think the uproar was so much about saving a couple of good buildings as it was about preserving something of the traditional scale of what is the most elegant commercial stretch of Fifth Avenue. Because the preservationists had to sound like they were trying to save good old buildings on their own merits, they emphasized the uniqueness of the Lalique windows—windows that few people had ever paused to look at, but that in the midst of the preservationist uproar became so famous that people began to refer to this as the "Lalique block," as though that was how it had always been known. It was eventually agreed to place the new tower behind the Coty and Rizzoli buildings, which were renovated by Beyer Blinder Belle as the elegant entrance to the Henri Bendel store, relocated from 57th Street.

18 ROCKEFELLER CENTER

48th Street to 51st Street, from Fifth Avenue to Sixth Avenue
1932–40, Reinhard & Hofmeister; Corbett, Harrison & MacMurray; Raymond Hood; Godley & Fouilhoux
Additions in 1947–52, Carson & Lundin

"The Stonehenge of economic man." —Cyril Connolly

18[A] *Associated Press Building*

Rockefeller Center is defined by its T-shaped plaza, which opens off the west side of Fifth Avenue between 49th and 50th streets onto the Promenade, leading to the Lower Plaza, site of the skating rink, and then flares north and south into a three-block-long street called Rockefeller Plaza, which runs parallel to Fifth and Sixth avenues from 48th to 51st streets. The plaza is symmetrical, and the Center's limestone buildings are arranged axially around it. Rockefeller Center is one of New York's rare examples of Beaux-Arts civic planning.

It is also Manhattan's forum. A forum, as the architectural historian William H. Jordy points out, is to a city what a lobby is to a building. A forum gathers and dispenses people and is the setting for civic ceremony. The most important annual civic gathering in New York is the lighting of the Rockefeller Center Christmas tree. The Promenade, with its seasonally changing plantings, walled by human-scaled structures, is one of the warmest spaces in the city. Nothing about the scale and materials of the approach from Fifth Avenue to the RCA (now GE) Building could be improved. The major problem with the plaza is as a dispenser of people. One walks from Fifth Avenue to the Lower Plaza and one wants to turn around and walk back to Fifth Avenue, since there is little of interest beyond. The street called Rockefeller Plaza is a fairly dull stretch of road. The side streets hugging the RCA Building are fairly dull, and lead to the abominable Sixth Avenue. The plaza is a gateway to—what? The Center's underground concourse can be reached via the plaza, but though this concourse is handsomer than its considerable progeny, it is a retailing dud and is used mostly as a conduit for workaday scurrying about, becoming a ghost town on weekends. There was once talk of extending Rockefeller Plaza north to the the Museum of Modern Art, the entrance of which was deliberately placed on an axis with Rockefeller Plaza. The plan was abandoned when the Twenty-one Club restaurant refused to budge from the proposed path of extension.

18[B] *30 Rockefeller Plaza*

Along Fifth Avenue, Rockefeller Center achieves perfection. Closing the eastward vista from the Promenade is the neo-Renaissance box of Starrett & Van Vleck's Saks department store (1924), which in scale, materials, and details could hardly be bettered as the close to the open space. The Promenade opens between two identical, deep, seven-story limestone boxes, their long sides, containing uniformly and elegantly designed shopfronts, walling the Promenade. The northernmost of these buildings is called the **British Empire Building** and was opened in 1933. Above its Fifth Avenue entrance is Carl Paul Jennewein's gilded bronze relief *Industries of the British Commonwealth* (1933), depicting working people throughout the British Empire, e.g., an Indian woman with a bag of salt, a British coal miner, and an Australian shepherd. Such a work could never be done today, for it would be attacked as a glorification of colonialism. (Jennewein's relief work can also be seen at the entrance to the Brooklyn Public Library, 23.4 and his lunette murals are in the lobby of the Woolworth Building, 2.9.) The southernmost of these flanking buildings is called **La Maison Francaise**. Above its Fifth Avenue entrance is Alfred Janniot's gilded bronze relief *The Friendship of France and the United States* (1934). This relief contains a fabulous wealth of naturalistic detail. An allegorical female figure of Paris holds a model of Notre Dame Cathedral, while behind her unfurls a banner with the motto of Paris inscribed in Latin: "fluctuate nec mergitur" (she floats but never sinks). Beside her is New York, seated on the prow of an ocean liner; behind her the Manhattan skyline of the 1920s. The women touch hands over a trio of female figures representing the things these two great cities presumably have in common: Poetry, Beauty, and Elegance. Needless to say, this work, too, could not be done today, for it seems that in the last six decades we have become far too cynical to hold, let alone express, such unembarrassedly lofty ideals—not to mention that the whole notion of allegorical female figures would arouse the ire of feminists.

The **Lower Plaza**, to which the Promenade leads, was originally occupied by benches and ringed with shops. And as with sunken plazas the world over, people simply would not use it. In a desperate attempt to salvage the space in the early years of the Center, a temporary skating rink was installed. It proved a resounding success, for while people will not use a sunken plaza, they will stand at its railings and look down into it, provided there is something worth looking at. The skaters provide colorful, animated theater that people just love to watch. In this context, Paul Manship's rather silly eight-ton gilded bronze *Prometheus* works as a piece of jolly pop sculpture.

Beyond *Prometheus*, fronting Rockefeller Plaza, is **30 Rockefeller Plaza**, popularly known as the RCA Building, even though it is now officially the G(eneral) E(lectric) Building, opened in 1933. Rockefeller Center's focal point, the RCA Building, is an immense slab tower, seventy stories high and, when built, the largest office building in the world (larger even than the Empire State Building). Yet because of its broad plaza, its generous through-block public lobby, its connections to the underground concourse and to the subway, and its suavely sculpted massing, it has no overbearing impact on the streets around it. The vast lobby, leading from Rockefeller Plaza to Sixth Avenue, was conceived not merely as an elevator lobby but as a public corridor lined with shops, newsstands, public telephones, rest rooms, eateries, bank branches, and escalators to the concourse and subway. It is decorated with rather monochromatic murals by the Spaniard Jose Maria Sert and the Englishman Frank Brangwyn. It is the large mural by Sert above the information desk opposite the Rockefeller Plaza entrance that replaced the unfinished mural by Diego Rivera, which was removed under orders of John D. Rockefeller, Jr., who felt, correctly, that it glorified Soviet Communism. The RCA Building is home to NBC Studios. It was here, in NBC's radio days, that Arturo Toscanini led the NBC Symphony Orchestra. Now such popular television shows as *Saturday Night Live,* the *Today* show, and *NBC Nightly News* with Tom Brokaw are produced here.

On Fifth Avenue between 51st and 52nd streets, just north of the British Empire Building, is the forty-one-story **International Building**, opened in 1935. It is entered from a small midblock plaza between two projecting seven-story wings, the design of which echo that of the British Empire Building and La Maison Francaise down the avenue. The northernmost of the wings was originally called Deutsches Haus, but when the United States entered the war against Hitler, the name was changed to the International Building North. Above its Fifth Avenue entrance is Attilio Piccirilli's glass relief *Youth Leading Industry* (1936), made of a special, liquid-seeming Pyrex and best viewed at night when it is illuminated from within. The southernmost of the wings is called Palazzo d'Italia. Between and above the doors of its entrance are bronze reliefs by Giacomo Manzu. In the plaza of the International Building stands Lee Lawrie's bronze, four-story-high *Atlas* (1937), one of the most famous kitsch sculptures in the world. Lawrie designed *Atlas'* globe in an openwork fashion so as not to obscure the views of St. Patrick's Cathedral from the lobby of the International Building. This high-ceilinged lobby is one of the best spaces in Rockefeller Center. Note how the escalators to and from the mezzanine substitute for the grand staircase one might expect to find in such a monumentally scaled space. It is a real treat to ride the escalator down from the mezzanine and look out the front window as St. Patrick's flashes into view through the openwork globe of *Atlas*.

Directly behind the International Building, fronting on Rockefeller Plaza between 50th and 51st streets, is the fifteen-story **Associated Press Building**, which opened in 1938. Above its Rockefeller Plaza entrance is Isamu Noguchi's ten-ton stainless-steel relief, *News* (1940). One of the first stainless-steel bas-reliefs ever executed, it depicts newsmen working with the tools of their trade, e.g., typewriter, telephone, and camera. It is an excellent example of the early work of this modern master, before his almost Art Deco abstracted-realism gave way to total abstraction such as one finds in the arcade "waterwall" and lobby ceiling a block away at the Tishman Building (1957, 13.11) or in the cube in the plaza of 140 Broadway (1967, 2.3E).

Rockefeller Plaza culminates at 51st Street in the thirty-three-story **Time Warner Building**, originally the Esso Building, designed by Carson & Lundin and opened in 1947. Ada Louise Huxtable has written that the Time Warner lobby "is an unusually well-designed interior public space, with a tasteful and meticulous attention to proportion, material and detail that still places it among the best of its type in the city."

The other Rockefeller Center buildings include the thirty-one-story **former RKO Building**, opened in 1932, at 1270 Sixth Avenue, between 50th and 51st streets. Embedded in its southwest corner is the vast and spectacular **Radio City Music Hall**, which, when it opened in 1932, was the largest indoor theater in the world. It seats nearly 6,000, and the proscenium-stage curtain, the largest in the world, weighs three tons. Designed by Edward Durell Stone (co-architect of the Museum of Modern Art, which opened seven years later) and Donald Deskey, it is now used for major pop concerts and for stage spectacles featuring that

New York institution, the long-legged, high-kicking, precision-dancing Rockettes. One cannot explore the interior of this Art Deco monument on one's own, but there are regular guided tours, and readers are urged by all means to avail themselves of the opportunity to gape slack-jawed at the improbable modernistic splendor of this theater. The twenty-story **Simon & Schuster Building**, formerly the U.S. Rubber Company Building, is at 1230 Sixth Avenue, between 48th and 49th streets. The original part of this building, opened in 1940, is directly to the south of the IND subway entrance at the northeast corner of Sixth Avenue and 48th Street, extending eastward on 48th Street about a third of the way to the midblock parking garage. At the southwest corner of 49th and Rockefeller Plaza is the **former Eastern Airlines Building**. The curved windows at the base are one of the most boldly modern touches in Rockefeller Center and were replicated in a 1955 addition to the Simon & Schuster Building. The Eastern Airlines lobby, visible through large plate-glass windows on Rockefeller Plaza, is notable for Dean Cornwell's bold mural depicting the history of transportation; it surrounds a large well in which a curving staircase leads to the concourse, making this the one place in the Center in which the concourse and street levels visually interpenetrate. The thirty-six-story **former Time-Life Building**, opened in 1937, is at One Rockefeller Plaza on the east side between 48th and 49th streets.

Construction of Rockefeller Center began in 1932. The planning of the area, owned by Columbia University and occupied by a red-light district of speakeasies, brothels, and rooming houses, began in the 1920s under the direction of the architect Benjamin Wistar Morris as a scheme to relocate the Metropolitan Opera from its obsolescent facility at Broadway and 39th Street. It was Morris who came up with the idea of a large formal plaza with promenade. But the Met opted out of the development as a result of the 1929 stock market crash. John D. Rockefeller, Jr., who, on the Met's behalf, had leased the land from Columbia, decided to push ahead with a major development. Because of the Depression and the soft market for office space, he felt the development had to be uniquely attractive to lure the office tenants, shoppers, theatergoers, and tourists who would make it pay. He decided to retain Morris's basic scheme but to adapt it to a complex of office buildings. The Center now accommodates 160,000 pedestrians per day.

I want to take the opportunity to comment on what a currently fashionable academic intellectual has recently written about Rockefeller Center. Richard Sennett, Professor of Sociology and of the Humanities at New York University, writes in *The Conscience of the Eye: The Design and Social Life of Cities* (1990): "Tourists are to be found at all hours in the esplanade. . . . The scene here is lively enough, but its picture-postcard pleasures have not proved very attractive to natives. . . . All around these structures in the heart of the city there is pressure, too many people walking too fast on the streets, yet the internal grounds of Rockefeller Center are seldom used as a shortcut." For Sennett, Rockefeller Center is an authoritarian place that imposes an arbitrary regimentation on the streets around it. It is worth mentioning what Sennett says because, though his is far from the majority view of Rockefeller Center, he is representative of what passes for the most advanced thought in current academia. I doubt very strongly that Sennett has ever worked in or near Rockefeller Center. His basic unfamiliarity with the area is evident when he mistakenly notes that St. Patrick's Cathedral is directly across Fifth Avenue from the Promenade, when in fact it is across from the International Building, and when he uses "esplanade" to refer to what no one refers to by that word but rather as Promenade or Channel Gardens. Perhaps Sennett read somewhere that natives seldom use Rockefeller Center's internal grounds as a shortcut. I have spent most of my working life in and around Rockefeller Center, and I have not spent a single working day in the area without using the Center's internal grounds as a shortcut. Sennett adduces native resistance to the Center as a major element of his case that the Center represents authoritarian design. But in fact there is no such native resistance—it is a figment of Sennett's perfervid imagination.

In 1974, a Marxist architectural historian of an earlier generation, James Marston Fitch, writing with Diana S. Waite, got it right: Rockefeller Center "has not only demonstrably raised the whole tone of this area: it has also held it there for thirty years." Make that fifty years.

19 ROCKEFELLER CENTER EXTENSION

West side of Sixth Avenue, from 47th Street to 52nd Street
1959–73, Harrison, Abramovitz & Harris, and Emery Roth & Sons

Through the 1960s, Rockefeller Center was added to along the west side of Sixth Avenue, which had already been pompously renamed the Avenue of the Americas, though New Yorkers have continued, justly, to call it Sixth Avenue. This is perhaps the most overpowering and banal street in Manhattan, a frightening phalanx of monstrous towers rising sheer behind plazas. Once Sixth Avenue was a honky-tonk strip in the shadow of the elevated. Used book and record stores, workingmen's dives, coffee shops, smoke shops, cut-rate clothing stores, and the like were swept away in favor of this antiseptic march of towers.

The buildings that belong to Rockefeller Center include the forty-five-story, 1.9 million-square-foot **Celanese Building** at 1211 Sixth Avenue, between 47th and 48th streets, designed by Harrison, Abramovitz & Harris, and opened in 1973. How fitting that this row should include the headquarters of a major world supplier of polyester fabrics!

The fifty-one-story, 2.5 million-square-foot **McGraw-Hill Building** at number 1221, between 48th and 49th streets, was designed by Harrison, Abramovitz & Harris and opened in 1972. Its sunken plaza includes the entrance to the McGraw-Hill Bookstore, one of the city's best sources for technical and business books.

The fifty-four-story, nearly 2.3 million-square-foot former Exxon Building at **1251 Sixth Avenue**, between 49th and 50th streets, was designed by Harrison, Abramovitz & Harris and opened in 1971.

The only one of these buildings that is of any interest at all is the forty-eight-story, nearly two million-square-foot **Time-Life Building** at number 1271, between 50th and 51st streets, designed by Harrison & Abramovitz and opened in 1959. Like the Tishman Building on 52nd Street (13.11), the Mobil Building (11.6), and the United Nations General Assembly Building (11.10), it is a sterling example of 1950s midcult. The pavement out front has an undulating pattern based on contemporary Brazilian design. This was at the height of the vogue for Rio, the time when schoolchildren were being taught about the marvels of Brasilia, and the era of "The Girl from Ipanema." The Time-Life pavement brings all this back to life. The elevator lobby walls are covered in stamped steel panels, which circa 1959 stood for bold, and that remind the viewer of the skins of the Mobil and Tishman buildings.

Between 51st and 52nd streets, outside the Rockefeller Center boundaries, at 1285 Sixth Avenue, is Skidmore, Owings & Merrill's crisply detailed forty-two-story, 1.7 million-square-foot **Paine Webber Building,** built in 1960, formerly the Equitable Building until the opening of the Equitable

Center (12.10) directly behind it in 1985.

Thirteen hundred and one Sixth Avenue, between 52nd and 53rd streets, is Shreve, Lamb & Harmon's twenty-one-story, nearly 1.5 million-square-foot former J.C. Penney headquarters, dating from 1963.

At 1335 Sixth Avenue, between 53rd and 54th streets, is William B. Tabler's 1963 **New York Hilton Hotel.** The forty-six-story Hilton was hilariously lampooned by Tom Wolfe in a *New York* piece entitled "The Automated Hotel," reprinted in Wolfe's 1968 collection, *The Pump House Gang:* "My cab pulls up to the entrance amid a magnificent outlay of glass, architectural cedar bushes or something, some kind of Neo-Prehistoric stone sculpture and a lot of dramatic ceiling spotlights. There seemed to be about a thousand men in alumicron suits with name tags standing out there. Alumicron is a new wonder fabric made of aluminum and silicon. Its advantage is that it shimmers and bends rather than folds, so that it never wrinkles." Sounds like something the Celanese company might make.

Number 1345, between 54th and 55th streets, is Emery Roth & Sons' fifty-story, 1.8 million-square-foot **Burlington Building,** built in 1970.

CHAPTER 14

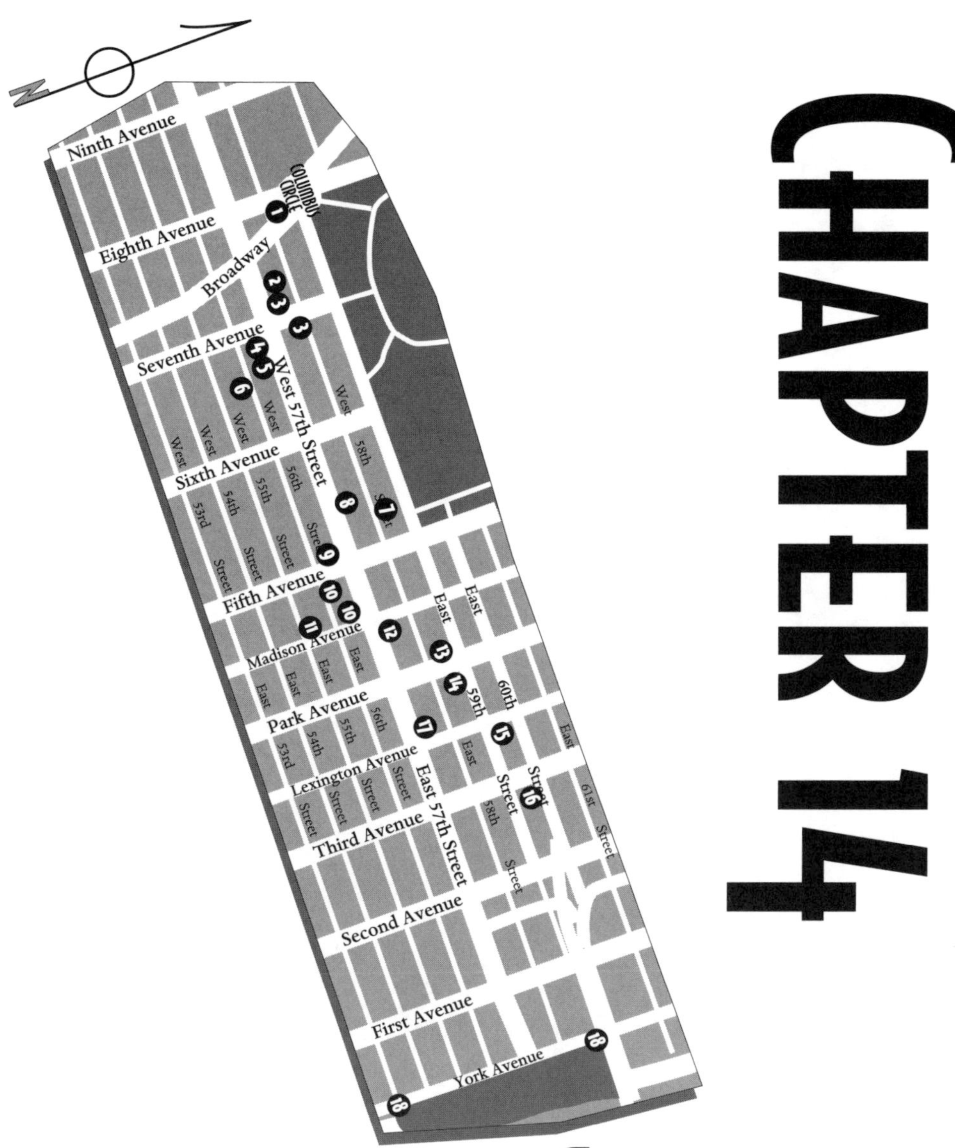

From Columbus Circle to Sutton Place

5 *Carnegie Hall Tower and Metropolitan Tower (left)*

Chapter 14 From Columbus Circle to Sutton Place

1 2 COLUMBUS CIRCLE

Between Broadway and Eighth Avenue
1965, Edward Durell Stone

Built as Huntington Hartford's Gallery of Modern Art, and now headquarters of the New York City Department of Cultural Affairs, this is one of the most ridiculed buildings in Manhattan. Hartford, the eccentric heir to the A&P supermarket fortune, hated the Museum of Modern Art's idea of what was best in the art of our time. Formalist abstraction was Hartford's *bête noir.* His taste ran more to what others would call kitsch and camp. When he decided to build his own anti-MoMA, he chose an architect of similar persuasion. That architect, of course, had also codesigned, nearly thirty years before, the MoMA itself.

2 ART STUDENTS LEAGUE

215 West 57th Street, between Seventh Avenue and Broadway
1892, Henry J. Hardenbergh with Walter C. Hunting and John C. Jacobson

Fifty-seventh Street is world famous for its concentration of art galleries. But virtually all those galleries are housed in the upper stories of buildings. The storefronts of 57th Street are occupied mostly by shops and restaurants; among the latter are some of the city's most touristy, such as the **Russian Tea Room,** the **Hard Rock Café,** and **Planet Hollywood.**

Few things at street level indicate that this is a street renowned for high culture. One such thing, obviously, is Carnegie Hall (14.4). Another, a true landmark in the artistic history of New York, is the French Renaissance *palais* that houses the Art Students League. Among the league's teachers in the late nineteenth and early twentieth centuries were William Merritt Chase, Thomas Eakins, Augustus Saint-Gaudens, Joseph Pennell, and Robert Henri. The league was instrumental in breaking the straitjacket of academic technique and introducing Impressionistic effects into American painting.

3 THE OSBORNE

205 West 57th Street, northwest corner of Seventh Avenue
1885, James E. Ware

ALWYN COURT

180 West 58th Street, southeast corner of Seventh Avenue
1909, Harde & Short

Two of the city's most distinguished apartment houses, and a marvelous study in contrasts. The Osborne could be a Chicagoan with its robust, Richardsonian Romanesque stonework. Alwyn Court, on the other hand, is an essay in filigreed delicacy: French Renaissance encrusted nearly to overkill with terra-cotta ornament.

4 CARNEGIE HALL

156 West 57th Street, southeast corner of Seventh Avenue
1891, William B. Tuthill
Renovated in 1986, James Stewart Polshek & Partners

For over a century, New Yorkers' musical mecca. The twenty-eight-hundred-seat (about one hundred more than Avery Fisher Hall at Lincoln Center) hall is a six-story neo-Renaissance structure with a fifteen-story tower that houses studios. Carnegie Hall has never been much admired as architecture, although since its recent renovation, it is a shimmering presence in this part of town. Dvorak's *New World Symphony* had its premiere here in 1893. Tchaikovsky, Toscanini, Mahler, Stravinsky, Caruso—and The Beatles—are just some of the names that have graced the stage of America's most famous concert hall.

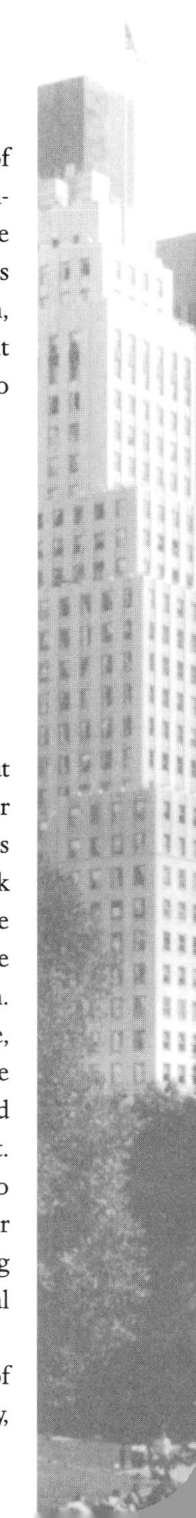

5 CARNEGIE HALL TOWER

152 West 57th Street, between Sixth and Seventh avenues
1990, Cesar Pelli

Hats off to Cesar Pelli! This fifty-nine-story mixed-use building is one of the best skyscrapers built in Manhattan since the 1930s. It defers so completely to Carnegie Hall that it seems an organic growth from that venerable building. Were there more such deferential buildings in Manhattan, this would be a more civilized city. Just compare it to Schuman, Lichtenstein, Claman & Efron's horrid Metropolitan Tower (1987), a few doors east at 140 West 57th Street, a slick, aggressive, black glass wedge that tries to upstage everything around it.

6 CITYSPIRE

150 West 56th Street, between Sixth and Seventh avenues
1987, Murphy/Jahn

CITY CENTER

135 West 55th Street, between Sixth and Seventh avenues
1924, Harry P. Knowles and Clinton & Russell

CitySpire fails exactly where Carnegie Hall Tower succeeds. While Helmut Jahn pays lip service to contextualism by topping his sixty-nine-story tower with a dome in tribute to the Moorish dome atop City Center, he is utterly unable to submerge his ego. CitySpire is a monstrous midblock intrusion, all the sadder because these blocks of the West Fifties continue to harbor various attractions, fast disappearing from our city, that once made midtown side streets some of the most enticing places on earth. These attractions include City Center itself, originally the Masonic Temple, later purchased for the city by Mayor LaGuardia. Fanciful polychrome Spanish tile on the façade and the dome make this a pleasing, quirky, and unostentatious structure, perfectly appropriate for a midtown side street. Converted by the city to a three thousand-seat theater, it was home to the New York City Ballet and New York City Opera before Lincoln Center was built. Today it continues as a dance mecca (no pun intended), hosting visiting companies as well as being the permanent home of such local ensembles as that of the late Martha Graham.

Also worth noting as examples of the once-and-present uses of streets like these are a pair of shops, modest in the space they occupy, that are so preeminent in their specialties that they serve an international clientele: **Joseph Patelson Music House,** 160 East 56th Street, on the same block as CitySpire, seller of sheet music and music books; and the **Mysterious Bookshop,** 129 West 56th Street, again on the same block, the city's premier source of mystery and crime novels, with thousands of them packed onto shelves in a charming two-level shop.

7 PLAZA HOTEL

Grand Army Plaza, from 58th Street to 59th Street
1907, Henry J. Hardenbergh

GRAND ARMY PLAZA

Fifth Avenue, from 58th Street to 60th Street
1912, Thomas Hastings

In this rock 'em, sock 'em city of the splendiferous skyline and more world-weight megastructures than any other place, it makes one glad to know that no image more immediately conveys *New York* than that of the Plaza Hotel fronting Grand Army Plaza. This is Gotham *luxe.* The extravagant French Renaissance pile, the fountain, General Sherman, the crowds relaxing, the hansom cabs with their horses, the entrance to Central Park—this is as much New York as any scene in the city. It tells as much about this city's values and aspirations as the World Trade Center (3.5) or graffiti-spattered subway cars.

In the northern half of Grand Army Plaza is the statue of General William Tecumseh Sherman, designed by Augustus Saint-Gaudens and completed in 1903. It is one of the greatest equestrian monuments in the history of art. Note the beautiful contrast between the powerfully realistic Sherman and the fancifully allegorical Winged Victory. The equine musculature is beautifully rendered. The monument was recently, controversially, jarringly regilded to its original appearance. In the southern half of Grand Army Plaza is the beautiful, marble, Italian Renaissance–style Pulitzer Memorial Fountain, designed by Thomas Hastings and built in 1916. The bronze statue of Pomona, goddess of abundance, is by Karl Bitter.

Directly across the street from Grand Army Plaza, on Fifth Avenue between 58th and 59th streets, is Edward Durell Stone's fifty-story **General Motors Building** (1968), which when built was harshly criticized for two reasons: by being set back from the street line with a large, astroturf-covered,

7 *Plaza Hotel*

sunken plaza of its own, it destroyed Grand Army Plaza's fine sense of enclosure; and, horror of horrors, it had the sheer unmitigated gall—in 1968!—to be clad in shining white marble.

8 9 WEST 57TH STREET

Between Fifth and Sixth avenues
1974, Skidmore, Owings & Merrill

A fifty-story, nearly 1.4 million-square-foot behemoth and one of the most derided buildings in Manhattan. It *is* a bit imperious, but is it really more so than most other modern buildings? It is clearly no more imperious than CitySpire (14.6) or Metropolitan Tower (14.5). Imperious buildings exist as pure objects, and 9 West 57th has a quality as pure object that most other modern buildings in the city lack. The meticulously detailed, sloping, black-glass 57th Street façade is elegantly framed in white travertine. The side facing out toward Fifth Avenue has the travertine-framed glass recessed behind steel cross-braces. The 57th Street façade is one of the most stunning examples ever of the pure curtain wall. If one allows that big American cities are going to have their imperious buildings—whether to exploit land values or to stroke developers', architects', or corporations' egos—then at least they should be as well detailed as the vast majority of buildings that come from the offices of Skidmore, Owings & Merrill.

9 CROWN BUILDING (formerly Heckscher Building)

730 Fifth Avenue, southwest corner of 57th Street
1921, Warren & Wetmore

Architectural critics have never thought much about this building. It was the first tall building in the city after the 1916 zoning resolution, but unlike the later Shelton Towers Hotel (now the New York Marriott East Side, 10.8), it made no effort to pioneer a new skyscraper massing. It has in recent years, however, been quite a popular building, i.e., since its restoration, gilding and flood lighting. It is a very visible and pleasant building, and to many people symbolizes Fifth Avenue elegance. It is interesting to note that it was in this unapologetically classical skyscraper that the Museum of Modern Art had its first home.

10 TRUMP TOWER

725 Fifth Avenue, northeast corner of 56th Street
1983, Der Scutt and Swanke Hayden Connell

IBM BUILDING

590 Madison Avenue, between 56th and 57th streets
1983, Edward Larrabee Barnes & Associates

Talk about Fifth Avenue elegance! It is of course very tempting to dump on Trump Tower, and to do so would not in my opinion be wrong, but—and I am almost afraid to admit this—the atrium, I think, has shown itself to work. Tourists move through this place as though on a conveyor belt. The movement never subsides, there is no "gridlock," and credit for that has to go to what at first sight seems an awkward, too-vertical design. The slick, faceted black form of the exterior is obviously all wrong for Fifth Avenue, but as for that atrium, which could easily be in Hong Kong, I refuse for the sake of snobbery to quibble with something that so

10 *Trump Tower*

magnetically draws passersby in from the street. The materials are lush; the "water wall" works both visually and, more important in this context, aurally; and the lower-level café space is an entirely civilized place in which to pause over an espresso.

Barnes's pentagonal, forty-three-story IBM Building covers only 40 percent of its lot, so it, too, makes a generous gift of public space. The northeast corner of the gray-green, polished-granite and green-glass tower is cantilevered over the sidewalk to create more pedestrian space at the busy intersection of Madison and 58th. The southwest corner of the building is given over to a large, exceptionally pleasant, bamboo-bedecked garden plaza/atrium, at its best when decorated for Christmas and there are carolers. This plaza/atrium connects with the god-awful Nike Town store, and a few steps across the main floor leads to an entrance to the Trump atrium. IBM Plaza had, alas, become a haven for homeless people and fell into disuse among the general public. It has recently been refurbished, with the addition of some inappropriate modern sculptures. IBM's granite skin somehow manages not to have that brittle veneer look that most 1980s granite skins do. I think Barnes has done about as well as possible with this mode of building.

11 SONY BUILDING (Former AT&T Building)

550 Madison Avenue, between 55th and 56th streets
1984, Philip Johnson/John Burgee

Postmodernism was not new in 1978, when plans were unveiled for the new headquarters for American Telephone & Telegraph, but no major urban high-rise had yet been built in that mode. Here was Philip Johnson, acolyte of Mies van der Rohe, designing a forty-two-story building with a broken-pediment, "Chippendale" top, a high-arched entranceway, and the promise of a decisive break from the standard of glass-and-steel boxes. The AT&T was the most controversial, talked about, and hyped American building in a generation. It was completed in 1984.

Thirty-two years earlier, Lever House (10.13), two blocks east and a block south, had initiated the glass-and-steel revolution that would at first astonish and exhilarate critics and public alike before getting down to the business of destroying much of the city's architectural character. The mode was still fresh in 1958 when Johnson collaborated with Mies van der Rohe on the elegant, neoclassical Seagram Building (10.11). By 1978, the mode was all too clearly played out. Skidmore, Owings & Merrill had so skillfully exploited advanced technology in the service of the Miesian aesthetic in such works as 140 Broadway (2.3E) that the high-modern mode had been dissolved by its own harsh logic into pure Platonic prisms. There were two alternatives. One was the complete reinvention of the skyscraper, such as the British architect Norman Foster was doing in Hong Kong. The other was to try to go back to earlier modes. New York got, and continues to get, the latter.

Unfortunately, in most cases, postmodernism has given us not a reprise or serious reinterpretation of earlier styles, but cartoon or Pop Art versions of them. Sony, in the last analysis, is a superscaled, facile hulk of a building. Its squat, unsculptured, rectangular mass bears down hard on Madison Avenue. When first built, the vaunted vaulted entranceway led to a dank recess of an arcade, compared with which the most pedestrian Emery Roth shoebox was all sweetness and light. Today, in recognition of

11 *Sony Building from Central Park*

the awfulness of the original space, the arcaded plaza has been replaced with some sort of huge Sony exhibit, replete with what can only be called interactive advertisements. Is this an improvement? I'm not sure. It would be better, perhaps, if the whole building were replaced. Classical architecture, like classical music and formal poetry, is about measure and modulation, with meanings enriched through judicious counterpoint. The AT&T is all counterpoint, all sophomoric "deconstruction" of the classical. Johnson is capable of much better, as the elegant lobby of 190 South LaSalle Street in Chicago attests.

12 FULLER BUILDING

41 East 57th Street, northeast corner of Madison Avenue
1929, Walker & Gillette

Forty stories that have all the impact on the street of a four-story row house. This is as good as urban high-rise architecture gets. Not the least of this building's virtues is that it greets the street with an entrance sculpture by Elie Nadelman.

13 500 PARK AVENUE

Southwest corner of 59th Street
1960, Skidmore, Owings & Merrill

500 PARK TOWER

59th Street, south side, between Madison and Park avenues
1986, James Stewart Polshek & Partners

Five hundred Park Avenue was originally the headquarters of Pepsi-Cola, then of Olivetti, both companies one associates with the 1960s. This twelve-story ice cube is, with Lever House (10.13) and the Seagram Building (10.11), one of three high-modern classics on Park Avenue. Five hundred Park Tower, the Polshek addition to the west, is a forty-story office and apartment building designed to harmonize with the Skidmore, Owings & Merrill building. The office floors are sheathed in aluminum and glass to recall the earlier building, and the apartment floors are sheathed in gray granite with discreet, punched windows, an obviously more appropriate look for a residential building.

14 499 PARK AVENUE

Southeast corner of 59th Street
1984, I. M. Pei & Partners

A black chamfered prism, rather like a dark version of Roche Dinkeloo's One United Nations Plaza (11.11).

15 BLOOMINGDALE'S (department store)

59th Street to 60th Street, from Lexington Avenue to Third Avenue
1930, Starrett & Van Vleck

This department store was the work of the same architects who did Lord & Taylor at Fifth Avenue and 38th Street, and Saks Fifth Avenue (13.7), at Fifth Avenue and 49th Street. Much of what I said about Macy's (9.1) applies here as well. This is a big, bustling department store, with all that implies about sensory stimulation. The main difference is that this store is the most aggressive of all purveyors of chic. On the main floor, the air is positively viscous with the perfume sprayed by attractive young people standing in the aisles. The bustle can be overwhelming. The aisles are narrower than at other stores, the salespeople and customers more desperately chic, the din less hushed, and the layout deliberately mazelike. If you're in the wrong mood, this can be a terrible experience. In the right mood, it can be very exciting.

16 CINEMA I and CINEMA II

1001 Third Avenue, between 59th and 60th streets
1962, Abraham W. Geller & Associates

Does anything in Manhattan say *1962* the way these duplex theaters do? The only real competition is Butterfield House (5.11) on West 12th Street in the Village. This was the Jackie Kennedy era in the history of American taste. Geller's Cinemas were the last word in midcult Manhattanite taste.

17 135 EAST 57TH STREET

Northwest corner of Lexington Avenue
1987, Kohn Pedersen Fox

A superscaled concave shaft fluted with continuous vertical strip windows à la the suburban Paris housing projects of the Spaniard, Ricardo Bofill. The unfinished-seeming, tempietto-adorned corner plaza is less an urban amenity than a windswept receptacle for street debris. The lower-level Place des Antiquaires, a high-toned antiques mall entered off 57th Street, is so cold and lacking in animation it makes one long for Manhattan Mall (9.3).

18 SUTTON PLACE

53rd Street to 59th Street, west of the F. D. R. Drive

Sutton Place, one of the most elegant enclaves in Manhattan, is actually the northern extension of Avenue A, which continues beyond it as York Avenue. The original Sutton Place development is the portion from 57th to 59th streets. This is an enclave of town houses that became instantly fashionable in 1921 when one family named Vanderbilt and another named Morgan erected houses here. The portion from 53rd to 57th streets was developed later as Sutton Place South, and was conceived as an enclave of luxury apartment houses. **Number 1 Sutton Place South** is one of the city's most prestigious apartment addresses. It was designed by Cross

& Cross and Rosario Candela and dates from 1927. At the eastern end of 57th Street, at the East River, is the small **East River Park.** Standing guard is a bronze boar, one of three identical boars copied from an ancient Greek original by the sculptor Pietro Tacca. The others are in the Straw Market in Florence and Country Club Plaza in Kansas City. The original is in the Uffizi in Florence. This park will be remembered as the place where Woody Allen and Diane Keaton sat overnight on a bench gazing out at the Queensboro Bridge in *Manhattan.*

Number 1 Sutton Place, on the north side of 57th Street on the park, is the house built in 1921 for Mrs. William K. Vanderbilt. It was designed by the fashionable high-society architect Mott B. Schmidt. **Number 3 Sutton Place,** also designed by Schmidt and also built in 1921, was originally the home of Anne Morgan, daughter of J. Pierpont Morgan, and is now the official residence of the secretary general of the United Nations. At the eastern end of 58th Street on the East River is another small park, this one called **Sutton Square.** Running for a block north of Sutton Square along the river is an elegant private street, Riverview Terrace, paved with Belgian blocks and comprising just six town houses.

CHAPTER 15

Broadway in the Upper West Side

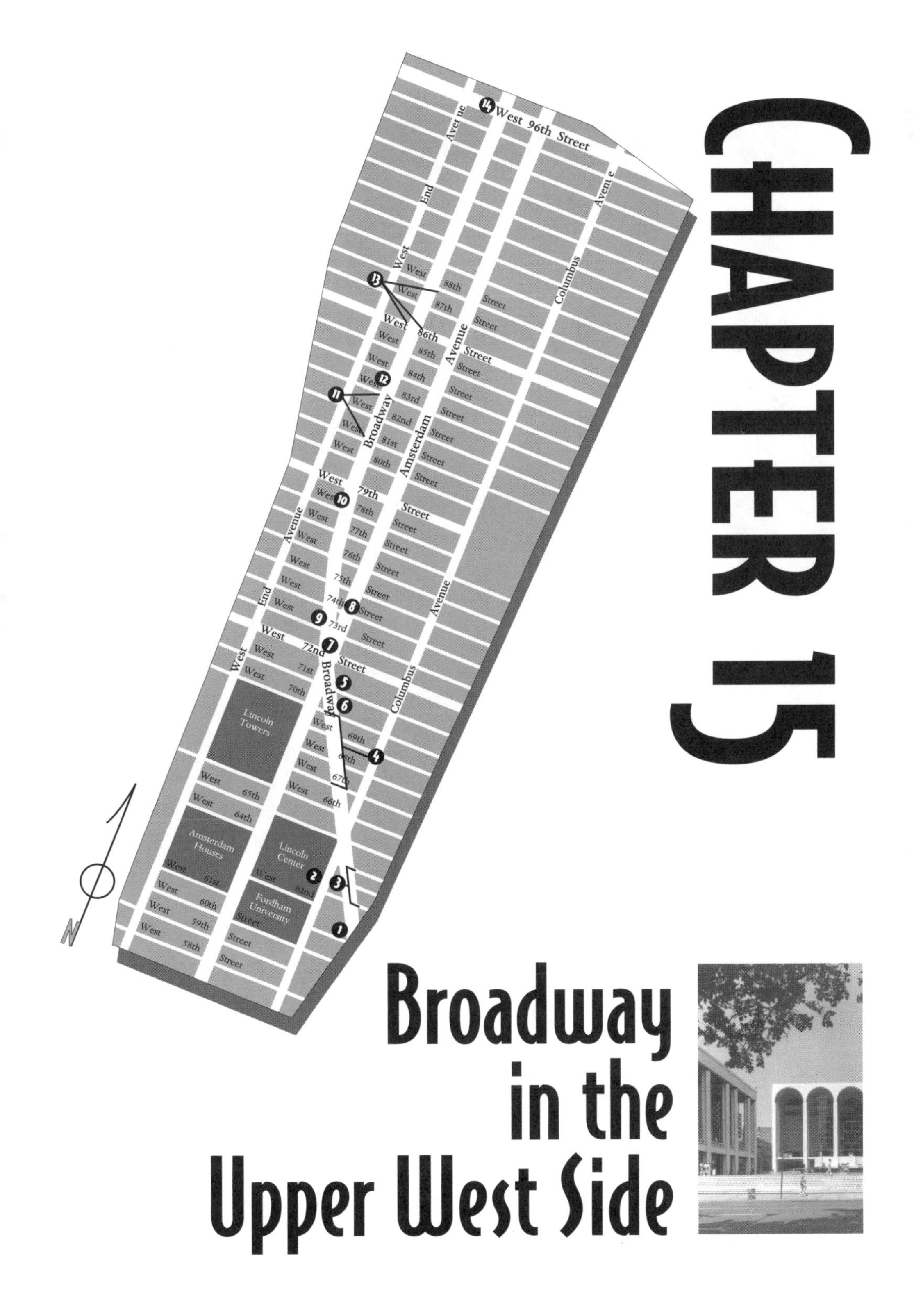

2A *Lincoln Center*

Chapter 15
Broadway in the Upper West Side

1 AMERICAN BIBLE SOCIETY BUILDING (Bible House)

1865 Broadway, northwest corner of 61st Street
1966, Skidmore, Owings & Merrill

Vintage midsixties Skidmore, Owings & Merrill: a bravura cast-in-place concrete grid asserting itself on behalf of Fundamentalist Christianity.

2 LINCOLN CENTER FOR THE PERFORMING ARTS

62nd Street to 66th Street, from Columbus Avenue to Amsterdam Avenue

It made no sense in the early sixties. It makes no sense now. Alas, it is a fact, and one that can hardly be altered. For all the nay-saying, I doubt there is anyone who has visited this complex who has not enjoyed something about it. The long views out the glazed foyers of the Avery Fisher Hall during intermission at an evening concert are thrilling, as is the downstairs mass procession, amid resplendent midcult surroundings, following a concert. One feels one is in a movie with David Niven and Capucine. The library can be one of the most pleasant places in town on a hot summer day. Air conditioned, uncongested, and one can sit comfortably with headphones, listening to rare recordings. No, Lincoln Center is not a total bust.

One enters off Columbus Avenue onto the broad plaza, which even

2[B] *Avery Fisher Hall*

Ada Louise Huxtable, who has been mercilessly critical of Lincoln Center, praises for its scale and its relationship to the other plazas in the center. Surrounding the plaza are the three main buildings of Lincoln Center. All are designed in a style that architectural historian William H. Jordy, in an article in 1960, labeled New Formalism. New Formalism takes up the neoclassical element in the work of Mies van der Rohe and sheathes it in luxurious materials like travertine, often adding historical allusions or exotic ornament. If it sounds like postmodernism, that's because it is like postmodernism without the irony and cynicism. It is the total absence of irony and cynicism that makes this style the architectural equivalent of what Dwight Macdonald in the 1950s so disparagingly called midcult. (Macdonald's favorite examples of midcult were the novels of James Gould Cozzens and the musicals of Rodgers and Hammerstein.) New York's premier New Formalist architect was Edward Durell Stone, a devotee of the International style when he codesigned the Museum of Modern Art, who later decided that modernism had become a rather joyless affair, and that he would spruce his buildings up by covering them in white marble and adding Moorish screens and Orrefors chandeliers. The style was quite popular in the early 1960s. Stone's most notable work in New York, and one of the city's most critically reviled buildings, is the former Gallery of Modern Art at Two Columbus Circle (14.1), about which Ada Louise Huxtable charmingly said, "Stone's little seraglio for Huntington Hartford's Gallery of Modern Art is more suggestive of houris behind its pierced marble screen than art."

Well, Lincoln Center is like a whole City Beautiful civic center made out of New Formalist buildings. Dead ahead is the almost thirty-eight hundred-seat Metropolitan Opera House, designed by Wallace K. Harrison and built in 1966. Travertine, plush red carpeting, crystal chandeliers, a Chagall mural—the whole shebang. Today it is almost quaint. The Metropolitan Opera House is home to the Metropolitan Opera and the American Ballet Theatre. Facing the south side of the plaza is the New York State Theater, designed by Philip Johnson and Richard Foster and dating from 1964, home to the New York City Ballet and New York City Opera. It seats over twenty-seven hundred. This is my favorite Philip Johnson building in the city. To the extent that Mies van der Rohe can be integrated with Claude Perrault's east façade (completed in 1674) of the Louvre, Johnson has done it. Facing the north side of the plaza is the Avery Fisher Hall, home of the New York Philharmonic. It was designed by Max Abramovitz and built in 1962, and renovated in 1976 by Johnson/Burgee.

The rest of Lincoln Center moves away from the New Formalism of the three main buildings. To the west of the New York State Theater and south of the Metropolitan Opera House, along 62nd Street with its back to Amsterdam Avenue, is Damrosch Park, setting of the Guggenheim Bandshell, where outdoor concerts are performed. The park and bandshell date from 1969 and were designed by Eggers & Higgins. To the west of the Avery Fisher Hall and the north of the Met is the Vivian Beaumont Theater, 1965, by Eero Saarinen & Associates, generally considered the best work of architecture at Lincoln Center. The Beaumont is an elegant, austere pavilion, vaguely Greek, though very clearly a product of twentieth-century technology, with Skidmore, Owings & Merrill's New York Public Library for the Performing Arts cantilevered over the

Beaumont's rear seating area. The Beaumont is now home to the Lincoln Center Theater, which produces Broadway-style plays by major playwrights with all-star ensembles. The Library is entered between the Beaumont and the Met, and houses the New York Public Library's collection of books on the performing arts (including film), as well as recordings, sheet music, and much more. It is truly a remarkable metropolitan resource. It can also be entered from the rear on grim Amsterdam Avenue.

The Beaumont rests serenely before a large reflecting pool, set in the middle of which is a reclining figure by Henry Moore. From this plaza, a bridge crosses 65th Street, connecting the main Lincoln Center island with the Juilliard School complex. The Juilliard School and the connected eleven hundred-seat Alice Tully Hall were opened in 1969, and were designed in a sort of Brutalist style by Pietro Belluschi with Eduardo Catalano and Westermann & Miller. Juilliard, of course, is the most prestigious educational institution in the world dedicated to music, dance, and theater. The latest addition to the Center is the mixed-use Lincoln Center North building by Davis, Brody & Associates, opened in 1989. It is at the northeast corner of 65th Street and Amsterdam Avenue. This crisply detailed and demurely handsome building—perhaps the best building in the Lincoln Center Complex—includes dormitory and rehearsal space for Juilliard, luxury apartments, and the Walter Reade Theater, the new home of the Film Society of Lincoln Center, sponsors of the annual New York Film Festival.

3 30 LINCOLN PLAZA (apartments)

1884–96 Broadway, between 62nd and 63rd streets
1978, Philip Birnbaum

ONE LINCOLN PLAZA

1900–16 Broadway, between 63rd and 64th streets
1971, Philip Birnbaum

Thirty Lincoln Plaza is a huge, thirty-three-story, beige brick apartment building with a few tricks. First, it has an arcaded sidewalk along Broadway: 1970s midcult Rue de Rivoli. Second, it has a very pleasant courtyard plaza that can be entered from the Broadway arcade and is open to 63rd Street. The plaza is exceptionally well designed, with a waterfall, plenty of seating, plenty of green, and facing shops. Best of all, the plaza is superbly enclosed, particularly by the rear of the Century apartments on Central Park West. One Lincoln Plaza is much reviled for its forty-two-story bulk, but 30 Lincoln Plaza continued One Lincoln Plaza's Broadway arcade. One Lincoln Plaza's arcade is filled with sidewalk restaurants, which at night in fair weather lend excitement and chic to these otherwise drab parts. One Lincoln Plaza is a mixed-use structure that, among other things, is headquarters of the American Society of Composers, Authors and Publishers (ASCAP).

COPLEY (apartments)

2000 Broadway, northeast corner of 68th Street
1987, Davis, Brody & Associates

BEL CANTO (apartments)

1991 Broadway, between 67th and 68th streets
1986, John Harding

CORONADO (apartments)

2040–52 Broadway, northeast corner of 70th Street
1990, Schuman, Lichtenstein, Claman & Efron

Thirty Lincoln Plaza and One Lincoln Plaza were part of the first wave of mega-apartment development along Broadway near Lincoln Center. These three are part of the second wave. The twenty-nine-story Copley, with its rounded corners, alternating horizontally banded windows and buff brick spandrels, and wraparound concrete belt courses, is obviously derivative of the 1931 Starrett-Lehigh Building (7.5) in Chelsea. The twenty-six-story Bel Canto has a red-brick apartment tower set back over a seven-story base, enclosing a handsome public atrium opening onto Broadway. Within the atrium is Ollie's Noodle Shop, an exceptionally comfortable, well-designed café/restaurant in which, because of the provisions of the zoning bonus awarded the building, one can sit as long as one likes without ordering. If one chooses to order, what one gets is fairly decent and modestly priced. This is a very New York space. The twenty-one-story Coronado, with its turreted corner and fanciful 70th Street entrance, desperately tries to be contextual, though its ends up being scarcely preferable to a Philip Birnbaum buff box.

5 DORILTON (apartments)

171 West 71st Street, northeast corner of Broadway
1902, Janes & Leo

It is well to compare the twelve-story Dorilton to the Coronado (15.4): luxury apartment houses from two eras. In 1902, high-class apartment houses were among the most substantial buildings in the city. By 1990, they were cheaply constructed and trendily appliqued. I doubt the Coronado will still be a prestigious building in the year 2078, when it will be as old as the Dorilton is now. I have no doubt the Dorilton will still be admired in 2078. Janes and Leo pulled every stop with the Dorilton: rustication, statuary, huge brackets holding up a fourth-floor cornice, projecting bay windows, high chimneys, a monumental side-street entrance with globe-topped gateposts, and a bridge connecting the two wings and forming a high archway, all surmounted by an in-your-face mansard.

6 BLESSED SACRAMENT CHURCH (Roman Catholic)

150 West 71st Street, between Columbus Avenue and Broadway
1921, Gustave Steinback

This is one of the best church buildings in New York—a dream of an urban church. Without breaking the street line of West 71st Street, without remotely lording it over the neighbors, still Steinback managed a façade of true ecclesiastical splendor. The fitting of this building into its site is as masterful a piece of urban architecture as you will ever see. The Gothic façade is given just the right amount of articulation for optimum effect on the passerby. The entrance is carved with beautiful shallow reliefs. The pointed arches are ever so slightly elongated to correct for the tight siting. There is a magnificent blue and red rose window. Like the old IRT subway stations, which are shallow and only a few steps from the sidewalk, the sanctuary of Blessed Sacrament Church can seemingly be entered in a single bound from the sidewalk. From 71st Street, one enters a superbly dark and mysterious long Gothic space of, surprisingly, nearly cathedral scale—as fine a church interior as those by Goodhue at St. Thomas (13.13) and St. Vincent Ferrer (17.8). No Art Deco skyscraper or twisty Greenwich Village lane more enthrallingly evokes urbanity. To have a church like this tucked away on a side street by definition makes a city great.

6 *Blessed Sacrament Church*

7 72ND STREET IRT CONTROL HOUSE

Broadway and Amsterdam Avenue, south of 72nd Street
1904, Heins & LaFarge

Philip Copp, the indefatigable cataloguer of the New York City subway system and author of the monumental, still-unfinished *Silver Connections: A Fresh Perspective on the New York Area Subway Systems,* writes, "Heins and LaFarge designed this house in the Flemish Renaissance style; so now we know what the Flemish Renaissance looked like." This is one of the handful of neighborhood landmarks (see the Jefferson Market Library, 5.9) that tell you where you are. It is the sign that says you are entering the Upper West Side, the point at which Amsterdam Avenue begins to run east of Broadway. Here you will find what may be the most throbbingly diverse neighborhood in America: yuppies and burnouts, bourgeois Jewish grandfathers and sullen juvenile decadents, a free melange of the genteel and the polymorphous perverse. All announced by a little

Flemish Renaissance subway control house in which, says Copp, "it seems as if Time stood still, but had sagged a bit while hanging around." At the northwest corner of Broadway and 72nd Street is the twenty-five-story Alexandria apartments, designed by Frank Williams & Associates and Skidmore, Owings & Merrill, and opened in 1990. This is another gimmicky postmodern apartment house, this time a polychromed brick-and-sheet-metal Egyptoid ziggurat.

8 CENTRAL SAVINGS BANK (now Apple Bank)

2100 Broadway, northeast corner of 73rd Street
1928, York & Sawyer

When I first moved to New York, I made a point of meeting a number of distinguished architects and architectural historians to supplement my reading on New York architecture. One question I asked each of them

8 *Central Savings Bank*

was what their favorite buildings in New York were. The only building mentioned as often as the Central Savings Bank was City Hall (2.10). Designed by America's greatest bank architects, York & Sawyer, the Central Savings Bank combines two of those architects' other great buildings: the Bowery Savings Bank (11.2) on 42nd Street and the Federal Reserve Bank (2.3B) on Liberty Street. Like the Bowery, the Central has a vast, almost cathedral-like banking room. Like the Federal Reserve, the Central is a freestanding palazzo, using much the same late-Gothic Tuscan vocabulary. Also like the Federal Reserve, the Central features magnificent ironwork by Samuel Yellin.

Unlike either of those structures, the Central occupies an island unto itself at the intersection of Broadway and Amsterdam Avenue. As a sentinel of the Upper West Side, it unostentatiously, but unmistakably, bespeaks the solid bourgeois values of the middle-class Jewish community that once was housed in the grand apartment blocks running north up the great Broadway Boulevard. It is this bourgeois heritage that remains the backbone of the Upper West Side, so solid it still has not withered amid the merciless onslaught of misguided modernity. An excellent view of the east façade of the Central Savings Bank can be had while savoring an incredibly cheesy slice of pizza at Vinnie's across Amsterdam Avenue.

9 ANSONIA HOTEL

2109 Broadway, between 73rd and 74th streets
1904, Graves & Duboy

As wondrous an architectural experience as this largely foursquare city permits is the sighting of this grand edifice as one walks north on Broadway toward the 72nd Street convergence of Broadway and Amsterdam Avenue. At 72nd Street, the improbably ornate mass of the Ansonia seems to float into view. It is utterly dreamlike. This is high-style fin de siècle Parisian architecture by an actual Parisian firm, pitched a stunning seventeen stories in the air: real French design at all-American scale, and as such unique in world architecture. From its rusticated base to its turreted and dormered wedding-cake mansard, the entire façade is slathered with ornament: rounded corner towers, and filigreed iron balustrades, and what may be the biggest brackets in town.

9 *Ansonia Hotel*

10 APTHORP (apartments)

2211 Broadway, between 78th and 79th streets
1908, Clinton & Russell

The ultimate bourgeois apartment block, as evocative of the graces and stolidities of that bygone way of life as anything on the boulevards of Paris or Bucharest. Here the principal early tenants were German Jews, whose quest for refinement and respectability led to the patronage of much of what continues to give vibrancy to the culture of this city. The building is absolutely enormous, occupying the full block bounded by Broadway and West End Avenue and 78th and 79th streets. Midblock on Broadway is a huge arched entrance, through which one enters the vast interior courtyard, which affords privacy, air, and light to those who desire such amenities, though they may equally desire the bustling life of the boulevard. The cavernous, well-appointed apartments of this palatial block may represent the highest level to which the modern urban ideal has been pushed.

Just south of the Apthorp, at 2127 Broadway between 74th and 75th streets, is the vast Fairway Market, a warehouse/cornucopia spilling its fruits, vegetables, and sundry other delicacies onto the sidewalk out front. It is the very picture of metropolitan abundance.

11 BROADWAY (apartments)

2250 Broadway, southeast corner of 81st Street
1987, Beyer Blinder Belle

Former KEITH'S 81st STREET THEATER

1913, Thomas W. Lamb

BROMLEY (apartments)

225 West 83rd Street, northeast corner of Broadway
1987, Costas Kondylis

The Broadway is a fairly plain, twenty-story, red-brick apartment tower, built behind and using the air rights to Thomas Lamb's very lovely, three-story, glazed-white, terra-cotta mock-Palladian theater, beautifully renovated into a large retailing space. The Bromley replaced Loew's 83rd Street Theater, built in 1921 and also designed by Thomas W. Lamb. We now have an enormous twenty-three-story apartment building that looks as if it is oozing out of its site like a blob of silly putty. Set into its base on Broadway is the impressively scaled, very suburban Loew's 84th Street Sixplex, six movie theaters seating almost three thousand people.

12 BROADWAY FASHION BUILDING

2315 Broadway, southwest corner of 84th Street
1931, Sugarman & Berger

If the diner façade—sheet metal and exploding semiotica—of Big Nick's Pizza and Burger Joint down the street defines upper Broadway, circa 1962, then the Broadway Fashion Building defines upper Broadway, circa 1931. Note that all along this pulsing commercial boulevard, interspersed with the big bourgeois apartment blocks, are a number of well-designed,

14 *The Columbia*

low commercial buildings, known in real-estate parlance as taxpayers. Most are in a classical idiom. This four-story one is exuberant Art Deco.

13 BOULEVARD (apartments)

2373 Broadway, between 86th and 87th streets
1989, Schuman, Lichtenstein, Claman & Efron and Alexander Cooper & Partners

BELNORD (apartments)

2360 Broadway, between 86th and 87th streets
1909, H. Hobart Weekes

MONTANA (apartments)

247 West 87th Street, northeast corner of Broadway
1984, Gruzen Partnership

The Boulevard is a twenty-one-story polychromed apartment building with rounded corner windows and a subterranean Gristede's supermarket. It occupies the entire west side of Broadway from 86th to 87th streets. Directly across the street, occupying the entire east side of Broadway from 86th to 87th streets, is the massive, twelve-story, neo-Renaissance Belnord, similar in its courtyard design to, if not as well detailed as, the Apthorp (15.10). Here until his death resided Isaac Bashevis Singer, the quintessential Upper West Side boulevardier. The Montana, directly north of the Belnord, and occupying the entire east side of Broadway from 87th to 88th streets, is a twenty-six-story apartment building that attempts, albeit in a brittle buff brick façade, to emulate the twin-towered classics of Central Park West.

14 COLUMBIA (apartments)

275 West 96th Street, northwest corner of Broadway
1983, Liebman Williams Ellis

Occupying the entire west side of Broadway from 96th to 97th streets is this enormous thirty-six-story apartment building. What is refreshing here is that the terms of apartment development—pack the site, create units with balconies and views, do it at low cost—are met head-on, unflinchingly, in a neo-Bauhaus design that eschews fashionable contextualism and does not try pretentiously to conceal its inherent tawdriness. What a breath of fresh air!

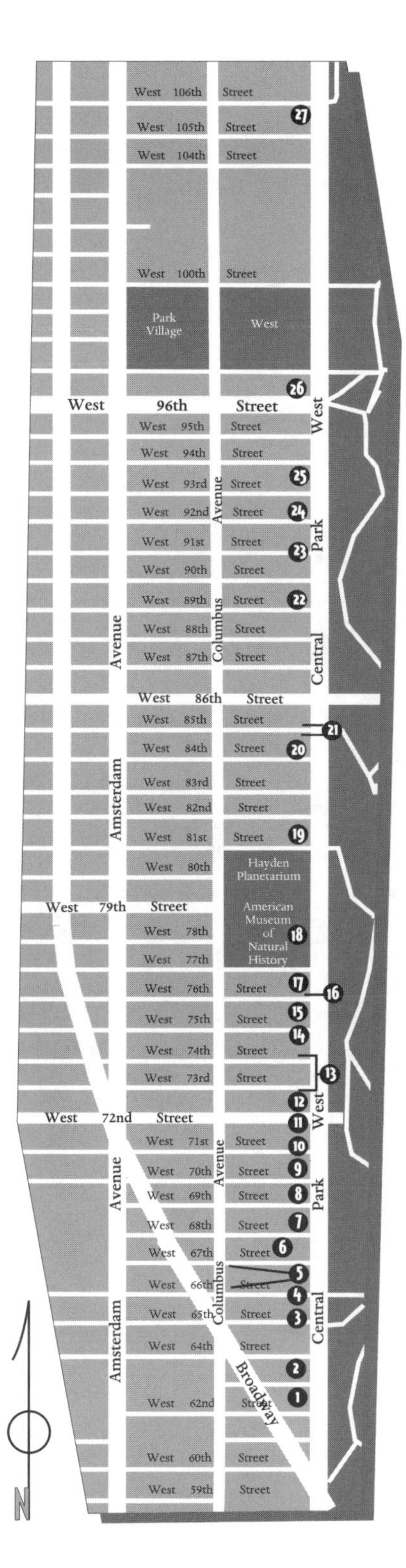

CHAPTER 16

Central Park West

5 *ABC Studios*

Chapter 16
Central Park West

1 THE CENTURY (apartments)

25 Central Park West, between 62nd and 63rd streets
1931, Jacques Delamarre for Irwin S. Chanin

Twin towers, each of which is topped with intersecting vertical and horizontal fins, perhaps inspired by Frank Lloyd Wright. The west side of the building is crowned with curved forms reminiscent of old radios or jukeboxes. Vincent Scully characterized the style of the old McGraw-Hill Building (12.1) as "jukebox modern." That is also an apt characterization of this building. This romantic Art Deco apartment building is, at thirty-two stories, the tallest of the Central Park West towers. It replaced Carrère & Hastings's spectacular Century Theater, built in 1909 in the hope that it would become a national repertory theater. Alas! Its location proved too far uptown, and it never really caught on.

2 NEW YORK SOCIETY FOR ETHICAL CULTURE

2 West 64th Street, southwest corner of Central Park West
1910, Robert D. Kohn

Kohn was New York's principal purveyor of the Art Nouveau style in architecture, as evidenced here and in his Evening Post Building (2.7) on Vesey Street.

3 PRASADA (apartments)

50 Central Park West, southwest corner of 65th Street
1907, Charles W. Romeyn and Henry R. Wynne

Ornate French Second Empire, with arched windows all around the base. It possesses those banded limestone "marshmallow" columns that I have always regarded as one of the truly tasteless architectural elements of all time.

4 55 CENTRAL PARK WEST (apartments)

Southwest corner of 66th Street
1930, Schwartz & Gross

High Deco. Note how the brick shades from purple at the base to yellow at the top. This increases the appearance of height and also makes the building perpetually seem to be in sunlight.

5 ABC STUDIOS

47 West 66th Street, between Columbus Avenue and Central Park West
1985, Kohn Pederson Fox

CAPITAL CITIES/ABC HEADQUARTERS

77 West 66th Street, between Central Park West and Columbus Avenue
1988, Kohn Pedersen Fox

WABC BUILDING

149–155 Columbus Avenue, southeast corner of 67th Street
1981, Kohn Pedersen Fox

A riot of Kohn Pedersen Fox. Three huge buildings, three kinds of brick, three kinds of fenestration, all hyperactive with this firm's trademark doohickeys. The twenty-three-story number 77 is the best, with lovely red brickwork. This street is the "campus" of ABC-TV. Number 47 is the building from which "World News Tonight" with Peter Jennings is broadcast.

6 HOTEL DES ARTISTES (apartments)

1 West 67th Street, between Central Park West and Columbus Avenue
1918, George Mort Pollard

This was built by a syndicate of artists as a studio and apartment building, hence the double-height windows that are the most conspicuous feature

6 *Hotel des Artistes*

of the neo-Gothic façade. The artists rented half the building to nonartists, and realized enough of a profit that there was a rush to erect similar buildings. The Hotel des Artistes is in fact the fourth such studio building put up on this street, all designed by Pollard: the others are the **Central Park Studios** at number 15 (1906), the 67th Street **Atelier Building** at number 33 (1906), and **numbers 39–41** (1907). Together they make a marvelous street wall. At the base of the Hotel des Artistes is one of Manhattan's most venerable restaurants, the Café des Artistes.

7 SECOND CHURCH OF CHRIST, SCIENTIST

77 Central Park West, southwest corner of 68th Street
1900, Frederick R. Comstock

Outside, part modern French, part neo-Grec. Inside, Neoclassical after Wren. Or what to do when you are designing a church for a religion without a tradition.

8 BRENTMORE (apartments)

88 Central Park West, southwest corner of 69th Street
1909, Schwartz & Gross

Early Schwartz & Gross, who went on to become masters of Art Deco.

9 CONGREGATION SHEARITH ISRAEL

99 Central Park West, southwest corner of 70th Street
1897, Brunner & Tryon

It is somewhat unusual, and very pleasing, to see a Beaux-Arts synagogue. This building houses the oldest Jewish congregation in New York, founded by Spanish and Portuguese immigrants to New Amsterdam in 1655. The building is Greek in its severity, the composition dominated by four large Corinthian columns and a pediment inset with rinceaux. Part of the interior is dedicated to a reproduction of the first house of worship built by the congregation, a Georgian building from 1730. Included are many of the original furnishings.

10 WEST 71ST STREET

From Central Park West to Columbus Avenue
1890s

A marvelous collection of turn-of-the-century row houses.

11 MAJESTIC (apartments)

115 Central Park West, between 71st and 72nd streets
1930, Jacques Delamarre for Irwin S. Chanin

Dinner jackets. Martinis, very dry. Witty badinage. Skyline views out the window. Cole Porter. Fred Astaire. You thought it was just the movies? The movies got it from Irwin Chanin.

12 DAKOTA (apartments)

1 West 72nd Street, northwest corner of Central Park West
1884, Henry J. Hardenbergh

After visiting New York and being entertained by the music publisher Gustav Schirmer, Tchaikovsky wrote in his diary: "The American publisher, Mr. Schirmer, is rich beyond dreams. He lives in a palace bigger than the czar's! In front of it is his own private park!" Schirmer's "palace" was the Dakota. The composer was obviously a bit confused about the building, but it is also true that the upstart nouveaux riches who colonized the territory west of Central Park concocted the superluxury apartment house as a form of urban palace to dwarf the mansions of the Four Hundred.

Today, however, the startling impact of this building type has long since diminished. What is now thought special about the Dakota is that it represents not something new and progressive, but something old and reactionary. Just a few years ago there was a great vogue of the Dakota, coinciding with the high tide of the movement to renovate nineteenth-century row houses, so fragrant with the bourgeois grace of bygone times. The Dakota stood for that moment in architectural taste, and seemed to be the antithesis to the sterility of suburban living and the East Side's glazed-white-brick high-rises. What makes the Dakota so successful is Hardenbergh's skill in modulating diverse elements.

This is picturesque Beaux-Arts. There is the undeniable flavor of high Victorian Gothic in the tawny brick and contrasting brownstone quoins, in the octagonally domed oriels, and especially in the finialed gables. This is not, however, your conventional picturesque composition. Rather, the whole is organized on strictly symmetrical lines, and details—arches, lintels, railings—are pure Renaissance. What Hardenbergh created, then, is neither a goofily picturesque monster nor a statelier-than-thou temple of good taste, but a tasteful monster, a rich, looming presence on Central Park.

13 WEST 73RD STREET and WEST 74TH STREET

From Central Park West to Columbus Avenue

Delicate row houses: numbers **15A** to **19** and **41** to **65 West 73rd Street** were designed by Henry J. Hardenbergh, architect of the Dakota (16.12), and were built in 1885. **One hundred one** and **103 West 73rd Street** were also designed by Hardenbergh and were built in 1879. At 135 Central Park West, occupying the entire block from 73rd to 74th streets, is the **Langham** apartments, designed by Clinton & Russell, architects of the Apthorp (15.10), and built in 1905. This neo-Renaissance prism is a riot of rustication. From **18** to **52 West 74th Street** is a group of neo-Georgian row houses designed by Percy Griffin and built in 1904.

13 & 14 *The Langham and San Remo*

14 SAN REMO (apartments)

145–46 Central Park West, between 74th and 75th streets
1930, Emery Roth

One of the finest sights in New York is the view from Broadway around 70th Street of the twin towers of the San Remo floating above the city. This is exactly the kind of sight the world never saw before New York started pitching temples thirty stories into the air. The tops of the towers, which actually conceal water tanks, are modeled on the Choragic Monument of Lysicrates, like the Municipal Building (2.12) downtown. It was in this building that Rita Hayworth died from Alzheimer's disease.

15 KENILWORTH (apartments)

151 Central Park West, northwest corner of 75th Street
1908, Townsend, Steinle & Haskell

A French Second Empire, limestone-frosted, red-brick cake in which those banded columns I dislike so much are rendered relatively inoffensive by the context of a kinetic base.

16 UNIVERSALIST CHURCH OF NEW YORK and PARISH HOUSE

4 West 76th Street, southwest corner of Central Park West
1898, William A. Potter

A fairly bland neo-Gothic church. The tower is modeled on the one at Magdalen College, Oxford, as is that of the First Presbyterian Church (5.12) on Fifth Avenue and 12th Street, erected fifty-two years earlier.

17 NEW YORK HISTORICAL SOCIETY

170 Central Park West, between 76th and 77th streets
1908, York & Sawyer
North and south wings in 1938: Walker & Gillette

One of the city's great research libraries, specializing in New York and American history and genealogy, and the repository of treasures which include the files of McKim, Mead & White, the original watercolors of the *Birds of America* series by John James Audubon, and the world's largest collection of Louis Comfort Tiffany lamps and stained glass.

18 AMERICAN MUSEUM OF NATURAL HISTORY

Central Park West to Columbus Avenue, from 77th Street to 81st Street
1874–77, Calvert Vaux and Jacob Wrey Mould
1888–1908, Cady, Berg & See
1912–34, Trowbridge & Livingston
Theodore Roosevelt Memorial in 1936: John Russell Pope
Hayden Planetarium in 1935: Trowbridge & Livingston

The largest museum in the world is one of the most imposing groups of buildings in New York, and also one of the most deliciously varied. The museum was founded in 1869 during the golden age of natural history. It grew, in the wake of Darwin's writings, from the same wide interest in natural history that led middle-class families to amass seashell collections. The cornerstone of the present complex was laid in 1874 by President Ulysses S. Grant, and the museum opened in 1877. The original Vaux and Mould, high Victorian, Ruskinian, Gothic structure—very similar

18 *American Museum of Natural History*

to the same architects' Metropolitan Museum of Art (1874–80, 17.20) directly across Central Park—is barely visible in a court on Columbus Avenue. The Columbus Avenue and 77th Street fronts date from the Cady, Berg & See years, and are in a very impressive, Richardsonian Romanesque style, towered and turreted, and executed in rockfaced pink granite. I feel that with Heins & LaFarge's crossing in the Cathedral of St. John the Divine (1892–1911, 19.1), this portion of the American Museum of Natural History is Manhattan's most striking example of that robust style. These parts of the museum also have a good deal in common with Charles Haight's Chateauesque former New York Cancer Hospital (1885–90, 16.27) twenty-four blocks up Central Park West. The Central Park and 81st Street fronts belong to Trowbridge & Livingston, whose Beaux-Arts classical design used a smooth version of the same New Brunswick granite found in the Cady, Berg & See portions.

The museum was finished off in 1936 by the completion of John Russell Pope's magnificent Beaux-Arts Theodore Roosevelt Memorial in the center of the Central Park front. Not only is this the formal entrance to the museum, but it is the state's official monument to one of its greatest—perhaps even its greatest—native son. It is a fairly relaxed design, with four widely spaced Ionic columns framing a deep, barrel-vaulted archway and surmounted by a broad attic. Atop the columns are statues by James Earle Fraser of Daniel Boone, John James Audubon, William Clark, and Meriwether Lewis. In front of the arch, seeming to have just emerged from it, is James Earle Fraser's bronze equestrian Roosevelt (dedicated in 1940). This is another of the city's many wonderful examples of politically incorrect civic sculpture: on either side of Roosevelt are guides, one African, one American Indian. The interior of the Theodore Roosevelt Memorial, the main hall of the museum, is a beautiful, stirring, barrel-vaulted, Corinthian-columned monumental space. There is something marvelously apposite about a monument to this great president acting as the entrance to a museum dedicated to science and nature, rather than seeming aloof and uninvolved in the manner of the Grant memorial.

The museum is a wonderland of fascinating exhibits, whether you're an expert or an ignoramus on natural history. One-and-a-half-million square feet encompass an unparalleled collection of dinosaurs, meteorites, gems, minerals, fossils, insects, and almost campy, utterly delightful nature dioramas. The collection of bird specimens, representing 96 percent of known species, is an astonishing resource for birders, appropriately located in a building bordering the birders' paradise of Central Park.

19 BERESFORD (apartments)

211 Central Park West, northwest corner of 81st Street
1929, Emery Roth

Forming a fine wall along wide 81st Street across from the American Museum of Natural History, and occupying the entire block of Central Park West from 81st to 82nd streets, is this twenty-two-story, triplet-towered apartment building. Two towers are visible from the south, surmounting the 81st Street elevation, and two towers are visible from the east, surmounting the Central Park West elevation. Otherwise this is pretty much of a Park Avenue neo-Renaissance box.

20 CENTRAL PARK WEST (apartments)

Northwest corner of 84th Street
1930, Schwartz & Gross

High Deco. Sproutlike organic forms are appliquéd to the red brick façade at the base and at the top, providing upward thrust.

21 ROSSLEIGH COURT (apartments)

1 West 85th Street, northwest corner of Central Park West
1906, Mulliken & Moeller

ORWELL HOUSE (apartments)

257 Central Park West, southwest corner of 86th Street
1905, Mulliken & Moeller

Purple brick with limestone trim.

22 ST. URBAN (apartments)

285 Central Park West, southwest corner of 89th Street
1905, Robert S. Lyons

A lovely building with a rounded and domed corner tower and a total of sixteen dormers along the tops of the east and north façades.

23 ELDORADO (apartments)

300 Central Park West, from 90th Street to 91st Street
1931, Margon & Holder and Emery Roth

By 1931 Emery Roth had moved from the Beaux-Arts of the Beresford (16.19) and the San Remo (16.14) to the Art Deco of this building. The thirty-story Eldorado is the most insistently vertical of the Central Park West towers. This is the northernmost of the twin-towered Central Park West buildings. The towers are stepped in pointy finials. The base features bronze relief work, a la the Chanin Building (11.3).

24 ARDSLEY (apartments)

320 Central Park West, southwest corner of 92nd Street
1931, Margon & Holder and Emery Roth

More Art Deco Roth. Stacked, receding cubes (hence "cubist," though it has nothing to do with Picasso and Braque), with the cubic forms underscored by Art Deco ornament, as in the Town House apartments on East 38th Street (9.13) and the Goelet Building (13.6) on Fifth Avenue and 49th Street. Later the same form would be stripped of ornament and become prevalent as the glass-and-steel ziggurats of the 1950s. The base is enriched with polychromed sandstone and concrete decoration.

25 336 CENTRAL PARK WEST (apartments)

Southwest corner of 94th Street
1929, Schwartz & Gross

Sixteen stories, Art Deco. The terra-cotta cornices at the top of the main structure and the water tower are Egyptoid Art Deco, considerably more graceful than Egyptoid Postmodern, e.g., Roche Dinkeloo's 60 Wall Street (1.6) or the Alexandria (15.7) apartments at Broadway and 72nd Street.

26 FIRST CHURCH OF CHRIST, SCIENTIST

1 West 96th Street, northwest corner of Central Park West
1903, Carrère & Hastings

The only church in Manhattan done full throttle in Hawksmoor Baroque. High Ionic columns flank the pedimented entrance beneath the tower

26 *First Church of Christ, Scientist*

with its obelisklike spire. Everything is slightly exaggerated, distended or elongated, or rendered stark, and a powerful sense of mystery pervades.

27 Former NEW YORK CANCER HOSPITAL

2 West 106th Street, southwest corner of Central Park West
1887, Charles C. Haight

Now apartments. Red brick and brownstone. Fat corner towers with conical slate roofs. The style is late French Gothic, in which the Romanesque round arch reappeared, thence refined by the Renaissance. Though a hospital, it is like an overblown chateau, the only chateauesque building on Central Park West, though that style is superbly suited to such a street, where the forms seem to rise and loom from the park the way they might from across the Loire Valley.

CHAPTER 17

The Upper East Side

1 *Sherry-Netherland Hotel and General Motors Building*

Chapter 17
The Upper East Side

1 SHERRY-NETHERLAND HOTEL

781 Fifth Avenue, northeast corner of 59th Street
1927, Schultze & Weaver

PIERRE HOTEL

795 Fifth Avenue, southeast corner of 61st Street
1929, Schultze & Weaver

A pair of large hotels by the same firm that designed the Waldorf-Astoria (10.9) on Park Avenue. Together, these towers define the southeast corner of Central Park, and announce the beginning of residential Fifth Avenue. The Sherry-Netherland sports a peaked roof with a pointy finial. At its base, at the northeast corner of Fifth Avenue and 59th Street, is a shop called à la Vieille Russie, whose tiny wood-framed windows feature beautiful changing displays of objets d'art; Russian art and antiquities, including icons and Fabergé eggs, are the stock in trade. The Pierre has a high slender mansarded tower atop a palazzo base, in the mode of Cass Gilbert's United States Courthouse (2.15) on Foley Square. The base is like another clubhouse presence on the avenue, while the tower works as a skyline element to be viewed from Central Park.

2 METROPOLITAN CLUB

1 East 60th Street, between Fifth and Madison avenues
1893, McKim, Mead & White
East wing: 1912, Ogden Codman, Jr.

On the walk up Fifth Avenue, it is when one comes to 60th Street and sees the corner of this chillingly stately marble Renaissance palazzo, rusticated and quoined with sharp-angled cornices, that one knows one has entered the rarefied precinct of the upper classes.

3 667 MADISON AVENUE

Southeast corner of 61st Street
1987, David Paul Helpern

An attempt to fit a huge office building into the delicate low-rise fabric of retail Madison Avenue. Helpern's massing and use of stone are skillful, but I'm not sure about the dainty iron railings on the setbacks.

4 695 MADISON AVENUE

Northeast corner of 62nd Street
1928, McKim, Mead & White
Renovated in 1986, Beyer Blinder Belle

Originally Louis Sherry's restaurant. Take tea there, according to a guidebook from the 1930s, "and you are sure to see a certain number of Our Best People." Today it is a particularly opulent outpost of the Indianapolis-based The Limited women's clothing-store chain, specialists in outfitting modestly pecunious young careerists. When it was transformed into The Limited, Beyer Blinder Belle added the skylight and the gilding, turning this from a building no one looked at twice to a conspicuously stylish one.

5 MODERN TOWN HOUSES

Between Lexington and Park avenues

The East 60s and 70s between Lexington and Park avenues are, with the East 50s between Second and Third avenues, one of the two best places in the city to study the modern town house. **One Hundred One East 63rd Street** was designed by Paul Rudolph and renovated in 1968 from a stable built in 1881. The dark glass-and-steel grid fronts what was once the home of the fashion designer, Halston. **One Hundred Ten East 64th**

3 *667 Madison Avenue*

Street dates from 1988 and is the only New York work of the firm of Agrest & Gandelsonas, who are particularly admired among architecture students. The fortresslike, six-story, limestone, bow-fronted house, in a style recalling the stripped classicism of Paul Philippe Cret, occupies a tight site between the rhythmic piers and double lancets of the north side of the robust, rough-textured-stone, neo-Gothic **Central Presbyterian Church** (1922, Henry C. Pelton and Allen & Collens, the same architects who designed Riverside Church, 19.8), on the southeast corner of Park Avenue and 64th Street, and Philip Johnson's high-modern former Asia House (17.12). **One Twenty-Four East 70th Street** was designed by William Lescaze, probably Manhattan's most prolific designer of modern town houses, and dates from 1941. It was included in the Museum of Modern Art's seminal exhibition, *Built in USA, 1932–1944*. **One Twenty-Five East 70th Street,** also known as the Paul Mellon house, dating from 1965, is one of very few Manhattan buildings since World War II that have been designed in traditional styles. H. Page Cross, a distinguished architect of classical country houses, including Paul Mellon's on Cape Cod, designed a "French Provincial" house cut off from the street by a high wall. The four-story cream-colored stucco house, its façade dominated by shuttered French windows with curved iron balcony railings, rises to what is surely the only true dormered-mansard roof built in Manhattan in half a century. The two-story east wing is similarly "anachronistic" and is topped by a balustrade. Thirty-two East 74th Street dates from 1935 and is another product of William Lescaze: it is in the classic glass-block and white-stucco mode that was a trademark of Lescaze's work.

6 WILDENSTEIN GALLERY

19 East 64th Street, between Fifth and Madison avenues
1932, Horace Trumbauer

I do not know if there is another building in New York built expressly to house a single art gallery. This is one of those exceptionally tony old-line establishments, and it is suitably housed in an almost-too-elegant-to-believe French eighteenth-century limestone palais. It is a very beautiful building, and in its large windows great paintings are often displayed. The 1930s may be unique in the history of architecture for having so many clients committed to so diverse a range of architectural styles, from the most full-blown Beaux-Arts to International-style modern, and everything in between. One need only compare the Wildenstein Gallery with the William Lescaze town house, described above at 32 East 74th Street: the two buildings were built three years and eleven blocks apart in the 1930s.

7 TEMPLE EMANU-EL

840 Fifth Avenue, northeast corner of 65th Street
1929, Robert D. Kohn, Charles Butler, Clarence Stein, and Mayers Murray & Philip

This is the home of the largest Reform Jewish congregation in the world. Just as St. Patrick's Cathedral (13.8) was built at colossal scale on fashionable Fifth Avenue as a declaration of self-confidence by the city's burgeoning Roman Catholic population, so Temple Emanu-El, in moving from its landmark building (now demolished) on Fifth Avenue and 43rd Street, was determined to assert itself in the most upper-class residential district in the city, and to be comparable in scale to the Catholics' St. Patrick's or the Episcopalians' Cathedral of St. John the Divine (19.1). Unlike the Catholics and Episcopalians, the Jews had no strong traditions of ecclesiastical architecture. Among the architects were Robert D. Kohn, who in his Society for Ethical Culture (16.2) and Evening Post buildings (2.7), had pioneered Art Nouveau architecture in New York, and Clarence Stein, who had worked with Bertram Grosvenor Goodhue and would go on to design, with Henry Wright, the seminal planned community of Sunnyside Gardens in Long Island City, Queens. These were not architects who felt bound to any particular style. What they chose was a variety of the southern Italian Romanesque that was liberally laced with Moorish influences. They felt this style represented the intermixture of western European and Near Eastern forms, which they felt to be particularly expressive of the Jewish Diaspora. The auditorium is 150 feet long (St. Patrick's nave is 144 feet), 77 feet wide (St. Patrick's is 48 feet), and 103 feet high (St. Patrick's is 108 feet). The auditorium of Temple Emanu-El is the one place in New York that looks most like a set for a Cecil B. DeMille Biblical spectacle. The fine mosaics are the work of Hildreth Meiere, whose work also adorns St. Bartholomew's Church (10.10).

8 CHURCH OF ST. VINCENT FERRER (Roman Catholic)

Lexington Avenue, southeast corner of 66th Street
1918, Bertram Grosvenor Goodhue

Goodhue, four years after St. Thomas's (13.13), a year before St. Bartholomew's (10.10). The first Catholic church by a man who had an anti-Catholic prejudice. Unlike St. Thomas's, the bulky tower rises right over the entrance. It is a remarkably straightforward and powerful Gothic design, with its towered narrow front on Lexington, and its long, dynamic north side along 66th Street. The exterior of rough-hewn granite makes this a manly church indeed. The interior, of sandstone and Guastavino tile, is simple and cold. The nave, which seats 1,670 (about the size of the largest Broadway theaters), is 130 feet long, 40 feet wide, and 77 feet high. (St. Thomas's is 214 feet long, 43 feet wide, and 95 feet high.)

Of particular note is the stained glass. The blue rose window is by Charles Connick, the Boston-based former newspaper cartoonist who became the leading theorist of the neomedieval stained-glass movement in America, and the man who, inspired by Viollet-le-Duc, was as responsible as anyone for the dominance of blue in neo-Gothic glasswork. Connick also did the chancel, clerestory, and chapel windows. The two small narthex windows are by J. Gordon Guthrie and Henry Wynd Young, who were also leading figures in the neomedievalist movement. These windows depict St. Augustine and St. Louis.

9 COUNCIL ON FOREIGN RELATIONS

60 East 68th Street, southwest corner of Park Avenue
1919, Delano & Aldrich
Addition to west: 1954, Frederick Rhinelander King

Originally the home of Harold I. Pratt, son of Charles Pratt, kerosene magnate and founder of Brooklyn's Pratt Institute. It now houses the organization that publishes *Foreign Affairs* magazine. This is a very simple, very elegant neo-Georgian box. Particularly notable is the ground floor. Nine arched windows are deeply incised in the rusticated base on the north and east faces of the building. Note also the ten octagonal attic windows below the balustrade-topped cornice. The addition to the west, by King, is in the same neo-Georgian style, continuing the base treatment of the original. It is fascinating to think that this addition was built in the same year as Skidmore, Owings & Merrill's Manufacturers Hanover Trust Company (13.2) branch at Fifth Avenue and 43rd Street.

10 HUNTER COLLEGE, SOUTH AND EAST BUILDINGS

Lexington Avenue, southwest and southeast corners of 68th Street
1986, Ulrich Franzen & Associates

The Hunter "campus" had long been in several buildings scattered about the blocks around here. Franzen's buildings have tied the campus together into a unified, readily definable whole. The twin towers connect to the 68th Street IRT station, which has been dramatically augmented with a glass-enclosed bridge across the tracks, allowing overhead views of trains entering the station. But there are terrible drainage problems that make this station a nightmare to use on rainy days. And circulation within the towers is prone to bottlenecks. Modern architecture was once hailed as a functional style, better suited than classicism to the everyday needs of people. It has turned out that modern architecture is in fact far more purely aesthetic than classicism. Classicism offered the architect a much larger vocabulary and much more flexible grammar, meaning that functional requirements seldom had to be sacrificed to aesthetic aims because the aesthetic could adapt. In most modernism, purity of form is the goal, and when that is the case, functional requirements can hardly be easily accommodated.

Note the older **Hunter Building**, occupying the entirety of the east side of Park Avenue from 68th to 69th streets. Built in 1940 and designed by Shreve, Lamb & Harmon and Harrison & Fouilhoux, it is, with its early modern strip fenestration, very much of the same family as the Museum of Modern Art (13.12).

11 FRICK COLLECTION

1 East 70th Street, northeast corner of Fifth Avenue
1914, Carrère & Hastings
Renovated in 1935, John Russell Pope
Addition to east: 1977, John Barrington Bayley

The Indiana-limestone former home of Henry Clay Frick is designed in an elegant, shallowly modeled, delicately detailed, French eighteenth-century style by Thomas Hastings. In 1935, following the death of Frick's widow, the house was transformed into the great museum it is today. John Barrington Bayley's addition on 70th Street is without question the best classical building in New York since the 1930s, and is in my opinion the finest work of post–World War II architecture in New York. The addition is based on Jules Hardouin-Mansart's Grand Trianon at Versailles, built in the late seventeenth century. The one-story addition, like the original building, is of Indiana limestone, with Ionic pilasters and entablature, beautifully executed by a new generation of craftsmen at the Indiana Limestone Company. The elaborate bronzework throughout the addition was the work of Arthur Ward of P. E. Guerin and Company of Greenwich Village.

To the east of the addition, and an integral part of its design, is a formal garden, visible from inside, through floor-to-ceiling arched windows, and from 70th Street through Louis Quinze gates that were originally at the house's entrance drive. The lush garden, designed by the English landscape architect Russell Page, features a large pool with water lilies, and is fronted on its north and east sides by walls removed from the original building at the time of the construction of the addition. Below the addition and the garden are two stories of exhibition and storage space and educational facilities.

It is often said that there may be no museum in the world in which as high a percentage of the pictures permanently on display are true masterpieces. The Frick has never been devoted to anything but quality, and in this age in which most museums have dedicated themselves to overhyped blockbuster shows and to identifying and cashing in on whatever the latest trends happen to be, the Frick reigns serene as one of the few remaining oases of civilization in the city. Don't miss: Giovanni Bellini's *St. Francis in Ecstasy*, Ingres's *Comtesse d'Haussonville*, Georges de La Tour's *Education of the Virgin*, Rembrandt's *Polish Rider*, Titian's *Portrait of Pietro Aretino*, and Vermeer's *Mistress and Maid*. If you want to see what an honorable man looks like, you can go to the Federal Hall National Memorial (1.12) to see John Quincy Adams Ward's statue of George Washington, or to Madison Square (8.4) to see Augustus Saint-Gaudens's statue of Admiral Farragut. Even better, come to the Frick to see Holbein's incomparable portrait of the incomparable Saint Thomas More. This painting is the very image of honor, in this the most honorable of New York's arts institutions.

12 ASIA SOCIETY

725 Park Avenue, northeast corner of 70th Street
1981, Edward Larrabee Barnes Associates

Former ASIA HOUSE

112 East 64th Street, between Lexington and Park avenues
1959, Philip Johnson & Associates

This is a rare opportunity to compare modern structures built by the same organization twenty-two years apart. What I find most striking is how much less aesthetic difference there is than there would have been in the twenty-two years between 1937 and 1959, or between 1915 and 1937, and on back in twenty-two-year increments to the beginning of American architecture. The earlier building sports a glass-and-steel-grid curtain wall at double-plot width tucked between two town houses, with a kind of small plaza in front, corresponding to the front gardens of the neighboring town houses. The Barnes building substitutes masonry for

12 *Asia Society*

steel and glass, but it is a brittle, polished, brown-granite veneer, as flat and lacking in modeling as Johnson's curtain. In twenty-two years, we have gone from the curtain to the veneer, with no more substantive changes.

13 LYCEE FRANCAIS

7 East 72nd Street, between Fifth and Madison avenues
1899, Flagg & Chambers
9 East 72nd Street, between Fifth and Madison avenues
1896, Carrère & Hastings

Number 7 was originally the Oliver Gould Jennings house, number 9 the Henry T. Sloane house. How fitting that today both houses should be occupied by a school for the city's French community! For these are two extravagantly French works of architecture. Number 7 is a double-bay-width town house with a very active tension between the verticality of its high, arched windows and its creamy mansard, and the horizontality of its rusticated and vermiculated stonework and its lacy iron balcony railings. Number 9, four bays wide, continues the French windows of the second story of number 7, also above a rusticated base, but here the windows are sandwiched by double-story engaged Ionic columns. Both façades pack a wallop, number 7 with its vertical-horizontal tension, number 9 with its tight intercolumniation. There is no classical serenity here. Henry Hope Reed, the foremost connoisseur of New York's classical architecture, calls these two houses "the epitome of the Beaux-Arts."

14 45 EAST 66TH STREET (apartments)

Northeast corner of Madison Avenue
1908, Harde and Short

The Gothic ornament, the glassiness, the profusion of double-hung windows, and the rounded corner combine to make this one of the most distinctive—and beautiful—apartment houses in the city. It comes as no surprise that its architects were also responsible for the Alwyn Court (14.3) a year later. The block of 67th just west of Madison is quite interesting. Ernest Flagg's Regency Whist Club at number 15, built in 1904, discernibly resembles the same architect's Scribner Building (13.5) of nine years later. Next door, at 13 East 67th Street, is a premodern postmodern house, built in 1921; architect Henry Allen Jacobs took a Palladian window and blew it up into a house. A block south, at 5 East 66th Street, is the superb French Second Empire-style Lotus Club, originally the William J. Schiefflin residence, built in 1900 and designed by Richard Howland Hunt, the son of Richard Morris Hunt, who designed the Metropolitan Museum.

15 867 MADISON AVENUE

Southeast corner of 72nd Street
1898, Kimball & Thompson

This was originally the Gertrude Rhinelander Waldo house, and is now the Ralph Lauren clothing and home-furnishings boutique. It is the principal remaining monument of the chateau style that was once de rigueur for plutocrats' mansions. The chateau style consists largely in a combination of Gothic form and Renaissance detail. The romantic appeal of the varied, irregular silhouette is made respectable by the stateliness of the individual elements. This is having your cake and eating it, too. Eight sixty-seven Madison is some piece of cake. Of particular note are the two stories of ten very deeply incised arched windows on the west façade with their fortresslike quality, and the profusion of magnificent stone carving.

16 Former JOSEPH PULITZER HOUSE

11 East 73rd Street, between Fifth and Madison avenues
1903, McKim, Mead & White

This is about as wide a side-street residence as there is in Manhattan. Stanford White was the designer here, and for inspiration he turned to two Venetian works by Baldassare Longhena—the Palazzo Pesaro (begun in 1663) and the Palazzo Rezzonico (begun in 1667)—both of which are in the tradition of Sanmichele's Palazzo Grimani of more than a century

16 *Pulitzer House*

earlier, the Venetian palazzo on which White based his design for the Tiffany Building (9.6) on Fifth Avenue and 37th Street, begun the year the Pulitzer house was completed. Because of Pulitzer's near blindness, White had to make a model of the façade that could be "read" by touching. This seems the ideal method of judging the sensuous, modeled qualities of classical architecture.

17 WHITNEY MUSEUM OF AMERICAN ART

945 Madison Avenue, southeast corner of 75th Street
1966, Marcel Breuer & Associates and Hamilton Smith

No current work of so-called deconstructivist architecture goes further than Breuer's Whitney in upsetting our every notion of what makes a building. The gray granite-clad reinforced-concrete structure is cantilevered in tiers over a sunken sculpture garden, and is entered from Madison Avenue via a bridge over this sunken garden. The windows are randomly disposed about the west and north façades. A city composed of buildings like these would lead to mass insanity. The interiors are among the most carefully detailed modern rooms in the city.

18 INSTITUTE OF FINE ARTS (former James B. Duke house)

1 East 78th Street, northeast corner of Fifth Avenue
1912, Horace Trumbauer

FRENCH EMBASSY CULTURAL SERVICES (former Payne Whitney house)

972 Fifth Avenue, between 78th and 79th streets
1906, McKim, Mead & White

UKRAINIAN INSTITUTE IN AMERICA (former Isaac D. Fletcher house)

2 East 79th Street, southeast corner of Fifth Avenue
1899, C. P. H. Gilbert

The former Duke house is now home to New York University's graduate program in art history, the most highly regarded in the country. The house is very large, very simple, very elegant, very self-assured. A certain strand of postmodernism, centered around the figure of Leon Krier, has elevated Trumbauer, along with a few others such as Henry Bacon and John Russell Pope, into the pantheon of American architects, a place formerly reserved for Frank Lloyd Wright, Louis Sullivan, and H. H. Richardson. Trumbauer was based in Philadelphia, and there are only a few of his works in New York. Of them, the most notable are the Duke house and the Wildenstein Gallery (17.6). The severe and sparsely ornamented façade is similar to such works as Charles Follen McKim's Pierpont Morgan Library (9.11) in that it achieves its greatest effect through sheer perfection of proportion. In this, it is also similar to the later, modernist work of Mies van der Rohe, e.g., the Seagram Building (10.11). Indeed, I find Mies van der Rohe to have more in common with Trumbauer and McKim than with any of his supposed modernist forebears, such as Wright and Sullivan.

The former Whitney house was designed by Stanford White, and appears to have been inspired by Longhena's Palazzo Pesaro in Venice, also a source for White's Joseph Pulitzer house (17.16), on which he was working simultaneously. White gave Fifth Avenue at around the same time another Venetian palazzo in his Tiffany Building (9.6), forty-one blocks south of here. The former Fletcher house is the most picturesque of the extant chateauesque buildings in the city, a much more flamboyant production than either the former Gertrude Rhinelander Waldo house at 867 Madison Avenue (17.15) or the former New York Cancer Hospital (16.27). This one looks positively like the setting for an H. P. Lovecraft story.

19 25 EAST 83RD STREET

Northwest corner of Madison Avenue
1938, Frederick Lee Ackerman, and Ramsey & Sleeper

Another of the staggeringly diverse products of the decade of the 1930s, when we are accustomed to think that nothing was built because nothing big could be built during the depression. This is an example of what many progressive thinkers of the time considered excellent modern architecture. It was the first apartment house built with central air-conditioning, though it also had openable casement windows. Large expanses of glass block admitted light while maintaining tenants' privacy. Alas, the glass block was removed in the 1980s and replaced by regular glass. The façades exhibit nothing but the functional aspects of the building. Ackerman was a disciple of Thorstein Veblen, and it is indeed hard to conceive of housing for the well-to-do that is less an essay in "conspicuous consumption" than this. Ackerman was also a founding member—with Lewis Mumford, Clarence Stein, Henry Wright, Benton MacKaye, and others—of the progressive Regional Planning Association of America.

20 METROPOLITAN MUSEUM OF ART

Fifth Avenue, from 80th Street to 84th Street
Central façade: 1902, Richard Morris Hunt
Flanking façades: 1906, McKim, Mead & White
Front stairs and pools: 1975, Kevin Roche John Dinkeloo & Associates
Lehman Wing: 1975, Kevin Roche John Dinkeloo & Associates
Sackler Wing: 1979, Kevin Roche John Dinkeloo & Associates
American Wing: 1980, Kevin Roche John Dinkeloo & Associates
Michael C. Rockefeller Wing, Dillon Galleries, Andre Meyer Galleries: 1981, Kevin Roche John Dinkeloo & Associates
Wallace Galleries: 1986, Kevin Roche John Dinkeloo & Associates
Cantor Roof Garden: 1987, Kevin Roche John Dinkeloo & Associates
Tisch Galleries: 1988, Kevin Roche John Dinkeloo & Associates
European Sculpture and Decorative Art Wing: 1989, Kevin Roche John Dinkeloo & Associates

About four million people a year visit the Metropolitan Museum, which is the most popular tourist attraction in New York. The Metropolitan is the largest art museum in the United States, and perhaps the foremost encyclopedic art museum in the world. With the New York Public Library, it is one of the two great institutions that have made New York the cultural capital that it is. The reason so many artists feel it is imperative to live in New York is proximity to this museum. The Metropolitan is to American artists what the Louvre has always been to French ones. The Metropolitan is the reason that the Harvard and Yale, so to speak, of graduate art-history programs, those of Columbia and N.Y.U., are located here. For New York not only has more artists than any other city, it also has more art historians. A lifetime can profitably be spent aimlessly wandering the floors of the Metropolitan. Forget about the special "blockbuster" exhibition of the moment, and lose yourself in the permanent collection,

20 *Metropolitan Museum of Art*

which is the glory of this, as of any serious, art museum. The best approach is, I believe, simply to wander, to scan the contents of the galleries, and to pause when something strikes your fancy. It may be Sassetta's *Saint Anthony in the Wilderness* (circa 1444), or the Egyptian fragment of a queen's head (Eighteenth Dynasty, circa 1417–1379 B.C.), or the T'ang Dynasty seated Buddha, or the glazed earthenware bowl from tenth-century Iran, or Seurat's *La Parade* (1888), or the New Hebrides slit gong.

The Metropolitan building itself, in light of the collections it houses, tends, I think, to be underrated as a work of architecture. I speak here of the main body of the museum—the central section by Hunt and the wings by McKim, Mead & White—before the modern additions by Roche Dinkeloo. The Great Hall, entered up Roche Dinkeloo's front stairs off Fifth Avenue, is as magnificent a room as there is in New York. Across the hall from the front entrance is the grand staircase by Richard Morris Hunt, which culminates in Tiepolo's *Triumph of Marius*. On these stairs, the heightening of sensibility is palpable. The Main Reading Room of the New York Public Library, the concourse of Grand Central Terminal—only a very few spaces in this or any other city have this kind of effect.

The Metropolitan was founded in 1870, and moved to Central

Park ten years later. The original front of Calvert Vaux and Jacob Wrey Mould's high Victorian Gothic building faced the park, and still stands as the east wall of Roche Dinkeloo's Lehman Wing. Hunt's Beaux-Arts Fifth Avenue façade was added in 1902, and McKim, Mead & White's wings came four years later. The Fifth Avenue façade is a masterpiece, more so, in my opinion, than that of the Guggenheim up the street. To do something so huge, so monumental, and make it seem so easy, so fluid, is consummate architecture. Look at the stately, but relaxed, rhythm of Hunt's central section, with the three broad arches framed by paired fluted Corinthian columns. It is a façade that welcomes the passerby even as it gives away nothing of its dignity: a true palace of the people, in that moving ideal of the American Renaissance. The huge, broken entablatures atop the columns, crowned by uncut masses of stone, originally intended to be carved into sculpture, further increase the sense of openness. The sweeping staircase was added in 1970 by Roche Dinkeloo, and has been criticized for obscuring the rusticated base and damaging Hunt's careful composition.

The museum's greatest strengths are Egyptian, Greek, and Roman art; European painting; arms and armor; and American decorative and fine arts. There are many things in the museum's collections that are of great architectural interest. In the Medieval Sculpture Hall, there is the immense wrought-iron Spanish choir screen from the Cathedral of Valladolid, which dates from 1668 and is the equivalent of three stories high. In the courtyard of the American Wing, there is the fine Greek Revival façade of Martin Thompson's Assay Office of 1824, which stood on Wall Street. There is the dining room from the Lansdowne House, London, of 1768, decorated by the great Robert Adam. There is a beautiful Paris shopfront from the Ile Saint-Louis, dating from the late eighteenth century, the age of Louis XVI. Its windows display rare Parisian silver of the day.

The Lehman Wing is a cool concrete atrium with a pyramidal skylight and some of New York's best paintings, including Giovanni Bellini's *Madonna and Child*, Holbein's *Portrait of Erasmus* (Holbein's portrait of Erasmus's mentor, Saint Thomas More, hangs in the Frick Collection, 17.11), Ingres's *Princesse de Broglie*, and Balthus's *Girl in Front of a Mirror*. In the European painting galleries on the second floor, don't miss: Jan Van Eyck's *Crucifixion and Last Judgment*, Hans Memling's *Tommaso Portinari and His Wife*, Rembrandt's *Aristotle Contemplating a Bust of Homer*,

Vermeer's *Young Woman with a Water Jug*, Georges de La Tour's *Penitent Magdalen*, Watteau's *Mezzetin*, and Jacques Louis David's *Antoine Lavoisier and His Wife*.

21 CHURCH OF ST. IGNATIUS LOYOLA (Roman Catholic)

980 Park Avenue, southwest corner of 84th Street
1900, Schickel & Ditmars

At the time St. Ignatius was built, Park Avenue just below 96th Street was considered part of Yorkville—a district of immigrants living in tenements. It was not until after World War I that Park Avenue began to take on its present character as a street lined with neo-Renaissance apartment skyscrapers for the rich. The Roman Catholic Church of St. Ignatius Loyola is one of the oldest extant buildings on Park Avenue above Grand Central. The architects were William Schickel and Isaac Ditmars, who were known as Catholic architects. (Paul W. Reilly, architect of the Church of

21A *St. Ignatius Church*

21[B] *Interior of Church of St. Ignatius Loyola*

Our Saviour (9.13), at Park Avenue and 38th Street, was the head of the successor firm to William Schickel and Company.) The limestone façade of St. Ignatius is severe and logical. The basic scheme derives from Giacomo da Vignola's Baroque Church of the Gesù in Rome (begun in 1568, twelve years after the death of Ignatius), though Schickel and Ditmars incorporated other elements as well. One is the upper central opening, which features the Palladian motif of a tripartite window, the central section of which is round arched and higher than the flanking, linteled windows. Here the central section is glazed, and the flanking sections are "blind." Among New York churches, the earliest extant use of the Palladian motif is in St. Paul's Chapel (2.6) of 1768, where the Palladian elements appear via the influence of the English Neoclassicist, James Gibbs. The façade of St. Ignatius is flattened out, with pilasters but no fully modeled columns. In its flatness, the façade acts as a wall for the broad avenue it faces, in much the same way as the flat façades of the neo-Renaissance apartment houses that line the avenue.

If the façade is a little on the somber side, in character with the rest of Park Avenue, the interior, which shares with the exterior the quality of being strongly controlled, nonetheless is as rich a church interior as there is in New York. The barrel-vaulted nave, with its rich applied ornament, is one of the most splendid interiors in Manhattan. The decoration, though lavish, is carefully modulated and set off by unadorned expanses of wall and ceiling. The nave is flanked by aisles that are marked off by rows of polished granite Corinthian columns. The space, as well as the ornament, is well handled. Few classical churches in my experience are as focused toward the chancel as are many Gothic churches. Here, however, the quality of the space is almost Gothic. The nave is long and narrow and high. There is no grandiose crossing space to provide manifold distractions for the eye to travel en route to the altar. The chancel is well scaled and well decorated and draws the eye. Un-Gothic, however, is the way natural light floods in through the clerestory windows, making the bejeweled interior fairly shimmer.

The Jesuit priest and paleontologist Pierre Teilhard de Chardin was nineteen when St. Ignatius was completed. Like many Jesuits, he worked in China. As an archaeologist, he achieved renown as one of the discoverers of Peking Man. In 1946, at the age of sixty-five, he came to St. Ignatius to serve out his days. On Easter Sunday morning, 1955, he said mass at St. Ignatius, then attended mass at St. Patrick's Cathedral. Later that day he died. Only in a city as great as New York can there be a building as architecturally rich and with such historic associations as this, yet one that virtually nobody has heard of.

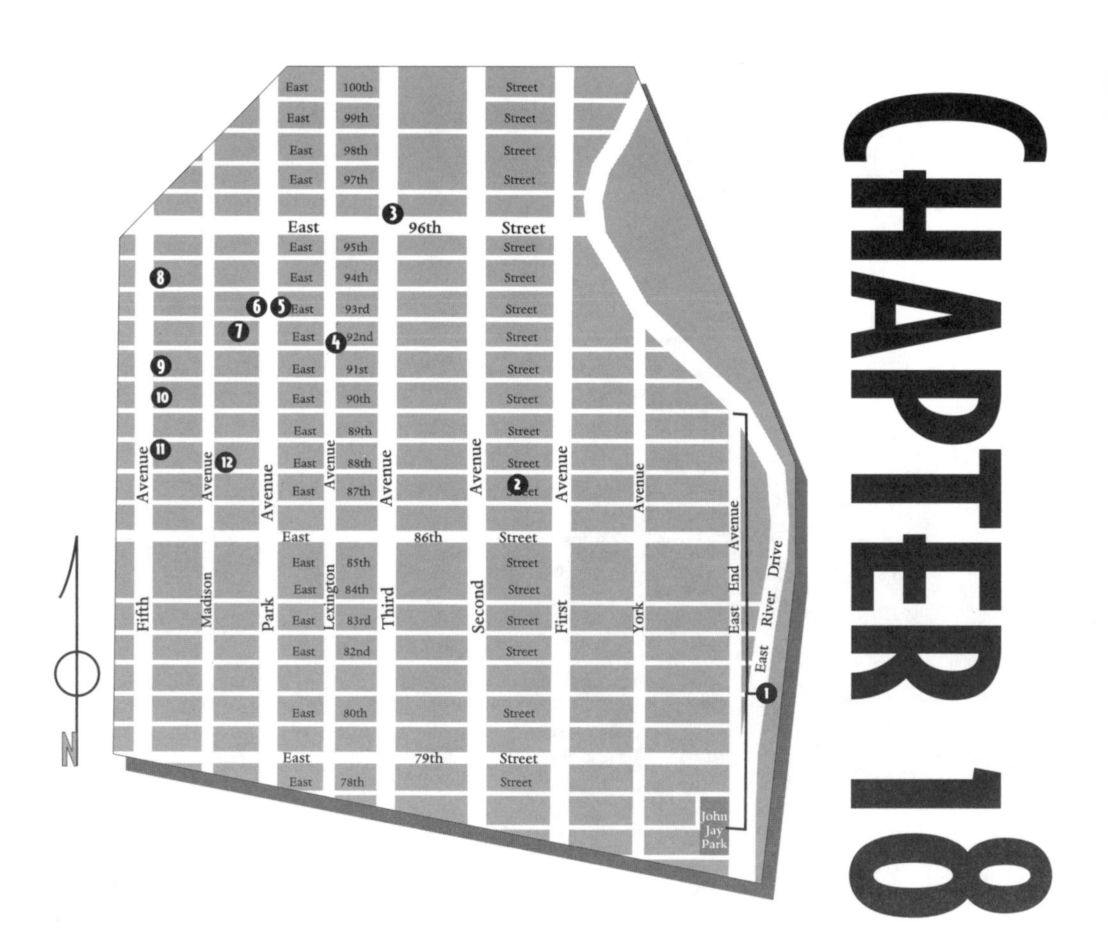

CHAPTER 18

Yorkville and Carnegie Hill

2 *Church of the Holy Trinity (Episcopal)*

Chapter 18 Yorkville and Carnegie Hill

1 CHEROKEE PLACE AND EAST END AVENUE

From 77th Street to 90th Street

Cherokee Place is a one-block-long north-south street that runs from 77th to 78th streets, one block east of York Avenue. The entire south side of 77th Street between York Avenue and Cherokee Place is occupied by the supercolossal **Pavillion** apartments, a strong contender for the title of largest glazed-white-brick pile in Manhattan. There are pleasant fountains in front of its circular driveway. Directly across 77th Street is a group of four large apartment houses originally called the Shively Sanitary Apartments, a name that gives a fair indication that these were not intended as dwellings for the rich. Indeed, they were built by Mrs. William Kissam Vanderbilt in 1911 as model tenements embodying the ideas of Dr. Henry Shively, a proponent of environmental reform to help stem the mass contagion of tuberculosis. Now that these buildings are yuppie-occupied co-ops, they are called the **Cherokee Apartments**. The architect was Henry Atterbury Smith. These buildings impart to 77th Street and Cherokee Place a powerful, brooding, romantic sense of enclosure. Atop rusticated limestone bases rise yellow brick façades rhythmically festooned with iron balconies. Each building has an interior courtyard entered through Guastavino tile-vaulted entrances. Guastavino tile also fills the soffits of the Spanish-tile cornices.

To the east of the Cherokee Apartments and the Pavillion, between Cherokee Place and the F.D.R. Drive, is the wonderful, intensively used, compact **John Jay Park**. This tree- and bench-filled utilitarian recreational space, which includes a public swimming pool, provides a burst of river light at the end of the heavily shaded block of 77th Street just to the west. Contrasts like this are one of the things that make walking in cities such a pleasure. Note also that between the Pavillion and John Jay Park is a fine brick-paved plaza, which extends Cherokee Place to 76th Street for the pedestrian.

Across 78th Street from the Cherokee Apartments and the north end of Cherokee Place are the **City and Suburban Homes**, which occupy the full block bounded by York Avenue, the F.D.R. Drive, and 78th and 79th streets. Like the Cherokee Apartments, these six-story walk-up apartment houses were built as model tenements. Five hundred three to 509 East 78th Street were designed by Percy Griffin and built in 1904. Five nineteen to 541 East 78th Street were designed by Philip Ohm and built in 1913. Five hundred ten to 528 East 79th Street, by Ohm, date from 1912, and 536, also by Ohm, dates from 1913. There was a preservationist uproar in the 1980s when these buildings were threatened with demolition by a developer who wanted to erect a mega-high-rise apartment complex on the site. At this writing, however, the Manhattan real-estate market is experiencing a major recession, a far more potent force for architectural preservation than any amount of civic agitation, and the City and Suburban Homes seem safe for the time being.

Cherokee Place finds its northward extension at 79th Street in the form of the eleven-block-long East End Avenue, which runs from 79th to 90th streets between York Avenue and the F.D.R. Drive. Like Sutton Place South (14.8) and Beekman Place (11.12), this is a tranquil enclave of monied, but unostentatious, gentility. There is not much here of architectural note, but it is worth experiencing for the pleasing anomaly of its clean streets and its pedestrian access to the East River. The latter takes the form of the John Finley Walk (named for a former editor-in-chief of *The New York Times*), which begins on 81st Street and the F.D.R. Drive, and runs to 90th Street. For its first three blocks, this is an ugly concrete promenade, bordered on its west by the rear ends of plain apartment houses, and on its east by the river and a rather uninspiring prospect of Roosevelt Island and Astoria, Queens. There is not even any seating. It gets better at 84th Street, where its west side opens to the fine, formal **Carl Schurz Park**, and where, finally, there is some seating. Note the excellent views of, to the south, the **Queensboro Bridge** (1909, Gustav Lindenthal and Palmer & Hornbostel), a lovely, classical, cantilever bridge spanning the East River from 59th Street in Manhattan to Long Island City, Queens; to the north, the **Triborough Bridge** (1936, O. H. Ammann and Aymar Embury II), a single structure with three separate spans, connecting Manhattan with Randalls Island across the Harlem River, the Bronx with Randalls Island across Bronx Kills, and Queens with Wards Island across the East River; and, also to the north, the **Hell Gate Bridge** (1917, Gustav Lindenthal and Henry Hornbostel), an arch bridge connecting Queens with Wards Island across the East River. Also visible are **Randalls Island**, home of a stadium where major international track-and-field meets are held, and **Wards Island**, home of a city park, a mental hospital, and a sewage-disposal plant.

Carl Schurz Park, located at a splendid bend in the East River, took its present form in 1938, when the F.D.R. Drive was constructed under it. In the park is **Gracie Mansion** at 88th Street. The merchant Archibald Gracie built his elegant Federal-style country house in 1799 well north of what was then the city limits. At this house, the socially prominent Gracie entertained such luminaries as Alexander Hamilton, the Marquis de Lafayette, President John Quincy Adams, and France's King Louis-Philippe. The city bought the house in 1887, and from 1924 to 1930 it housed the Museum of the City of New York. In 1942, during the administration of Mayor Fiorello LaGuardia, the house became the official mayoral residence. By 1964, during the administration of Robert F. Wagner, the need for new reception and office space was pressing. Mott B. Schmidt, aged seventy-five, a renowned designer of classical houses who had been in practice since 1913, and John Barrington Bayley, architect for the New York City Landmarks Preservation Commission, were given the daunting task of adding to one of the city's oldest and best-loved landmarks. The two-story Susan B. Wagner Wing replicates the clapboard siding, attic balustrade, and shuttered windows of the original.

But the new wing's glory is its canopied porch, a delicate composition framed by pairs of slender fluted columns with Composite capitals. Of the five orders of classical architecture—Doric, Ionic, Corinthian,

Composite, and Tuscan—it is the Composite, a combination of the Ionic and Corinthian that had its widest use in Baroque Rome, that is the rarest in New York. Indeed, I can think of only one other place where the Composite order is found in Manhattan: the building that is now the Smithers Alcoholism Center (18.7), built in 1931 on East 93rd Street. In addition, the porch has an arched entrance with a spidery fanlight, and is entered from either side by graceful curved stairways with wrought-iron railings. The porch was modeled on that of the Lyman house in Waltham, Massachusetts, designed by Samuel McIntyre and built in 1793. The beautiful fireplace in the ballroom of the Wagner Wing was originally in the landmark house at 7 State Street, once the home of Elizabeth Bayley Seton, America's first Roman Catholic saint and an ancestor of the very John Barrington Bayley who codesigned the Wagner Wing.

Back on East End Avenue, there is, from 86th to 87th streets, a fine row of Queen Anne town houses, known as **Henderson Place**, designed by Lamb & Rich and built in 1882.

2 CHURCH OF THE HOLY TRINITY (Episcopal)

312–16 East 88th Street, between First and Second avenues
1897, Barney & Chapman

This Episcopal complex of church, bell tower, parsonage, and parish house is the finest high Victorian ensemble in the city. The style is French Renaissance, and has a great deal in common with such chateauesque buildings as 867 Madison Avenue (17.15), the Ukrainian Institute in America (17.18), and the former New York Cancer Hospital (16.27). There is superb Roman brickwork, and the tower, with its bold, high, faceted, receding Gothic arches, is topped with intricate filigreed ornament. The main entrance to the church is on its long side, midblock, at the base of the tower. A fine pointy iron fence separates 88th Street from the shallow tree-studded garden around which the buildings are disposed. It is one of the most beautiful sights in Manhattan.

3 MOSQUE OF NEW YORK

201 East 96th Street, northeast corner of Third Avenue
1991, Skidmore, Owings & Merrill and Swanke Hayden Connell

This is the first deliberately constructed mosque in New York. The copper dome and 130-foot minaret are the work of Swanke Hayden Connell, and the severely rectilinear, almost industrial-feeling interior is by Skidmore, Owings & Merrill. The tower and the mosque are both clad in granite. The mosque is turned twenty-nine degrees off the Manhattan street grid so it faces Mecca.

4 KAUFMAN AUDITORIUM, 92ND STREET YM/YWHA

1395 Lexington Avenue, southeast corner of 92nd Street
1930, Necarsulmer & Lehlbach and Gehron, Ross & Alley

This is hardly noteworthy purely in architectural terms. The 92nd Street Y is nearly as important a cultural institution as New York possesses. It is a major venue for chamber concerts, recitals, lectures, readings, and symposia. The auditorium is a nicely enough designed and comfortable room in a 1930, modern sort of way. What makes it speak volumes, though, is the series of names inscribed atop the proscenium: Moses, Maimonides, George Washington, Thomas Jefferson. The New York Jews who created this great cultural center were at once faithful to their own religious and philosophical traditions and highly respectful of their new nation and its democratic principles. This is the way New York was always meant to be, and that simple series of four names lays to rest any and every argument about multiculturalism or political correctness.

5 1185 PARK AVENUE (apartments)

Between 93rd and 94th streets
1929, Schwartz and Gross

This gargantuan building makes an outstanding limestone-accented, red-brick, massive street wall on the north side of 93rd Street. It also has the most imposing façade on Park Avenue, filling the entire blockfront and featuring a Gothic-arched entrance which leads to an interior courtyard that is visible from the street.

6 67 EAST 93RD STREET

Between Madison and Park avenues
1931, Delano and Aldrich

69 EAST 93RD STREET

Between Madison and Park avenues
1929, Delano and Aldrich

75 EAST 93RD STREET

Northwest corner of Park Avenue
1918; north addition in 1928, Delano and Aldrich

A magnificent neo-Georgian group. Number 67 was originally the George F. Baker house. Number 69 was originally the addition to and courtyard of the George F. Baker, Jr., house. Number 75 was originally the Francis F. Palmer house, and later the George F. Baker, Jr., house. Numbers 69 to 75 are now the Synod of Bishops of the Russian Orthodox Church outside Russia. Baker, Jr., had the garden courtyard added, making this ensemble, with the Villard Houses (13.9), Manhattan's only groups of town houses with a common courtyard open to the street. Number 75, a small red-brick neo-Georgian house, shows its simple, balconied side to Park Avenue, reserving for 93rd Street its marble-arched front entrance, flanked by beautiful marble Doric columns. To the west of number 75 is the garden, at the rear of which runs a wing connecting numbers 75 to 69. Number 69 faces the courtyard with massive upper-level double Ionic columns, while this time 93rd Street gets the sideview. The neo-Georgian style unifies the group, while the superb details and the varying orientations to the courtyard provide variety and keep the ensemble from being a static composition. Residential urban design gets no better than this.

7 SMITHERS ALCOHOLISM CENTER

56 East 93rd Street, between Madison and Park avenues
1932, Walker and Gillette

With the three houses just described, this house makes 93rd Street between Madison and Park avenues my candidate for most beautiful block in Manhattan. The same firm that designed the Fuller Building (14.12) on 57th Street, completed three years earlier, did something quite different in this house for William G. Loew. What a rich period in American architecture when the same firm could, so close together in time, design an Art Deco skyscraper and a grand Beaux-Arts mansion! This was the last of Manhattan's great freestanding mansions. It is the one New York exterior most in the vein of the great eighteenth-century

English Neoclassical architect, Robert Adam. This is evident in its simplicity and fluidity, in its concave front, Palladian windows, and scrollwork. (An authentic Adam-designed interior can be seen in the room from the Lansdowne House in the Metropolitan Museum of Art, 17.20.) Henry Hope Reed says the columns of the entrance aedicule may be the only ones in New York designed in the Composite order, a combination of Corinthian and Ionic that was popular in the Italian Baroque, but actually Mott B. Schmidt's and John Barrington Bayley's Susan B. Wagner Wing (1966) for Gracie Mansion (18.1) also uses the Composite order.

8 INTERNATIONAL CENTER OF PHOTOGRAPHY

1130 Fifth Avenue, northeast corner of 94th Street
1914, Delano and Aldrich

This is Delano and Aldrich country. Simple neo-Federal and neo-Georgian designs on leafy streets, making for one of the most urbane residential areas in the city. This was originally the home of Willard Straight, founder of *The New Republic*. As in other Delano and Aldrich works, the design is severely logical, but with a delicacy, even a demureness, that lends a great warmth to the street. While in this area, take a look at Madison Avenue, which up here is no longer the world-famous street of high-fashion boutiques, but rather a genteel neighborhood shopping strip for the Carnegie Hill community. It has something of the feeling of a shopping street in the handsome center of an exclusive old railroad suburb.

9 CONVENT OF THE SACRED HEART

1 East 91st Street, northeast corner of Fifth Avenue
1918, J. Armstrong Stenhouse with C. P. H. Gilbert

DUCHESNE RESIDENCE SCHOOL

7 East 91st Street, between Fifth and Madison avenues
1905, Warren and Wetmore

CONSULATE OF THE RUSSIAN FEDERATION

9 E. 91st Street, between Fifth and Madison avenues
1903, Carrère and Hastings

One of Manhattan's several magnificent Beaux-Arts ensembles—Henry Hope Reed has called it the finest block of mansions in the city. The

French-limestone Convent of the Sacred Heart is the former Otto Kahn house, a huge, unostentatious, supremely well-proportioned, and self-assured Renaissance palazzo running the length of four large town house lots on 91st Street. I always find it heartwarmingly appropriate when an Italian Renaissance–style building is taken over by a Roman Catholic institution. The Duchesne Residence School, the former James A. Burden, Jr., house, is notable for its heavy bracketed balcony above the first story, and for the bold chamfering of the upper arches. The Consulate of the Russian Federation—and I am proud to say that mine is the first guide to New York that has not had to identify this building as the Consulate of the U.S.S.R.—with its fine Ionic colonnettes was originally the John H. Hammond house.

10 COOPER-HEWITT MUSEUM

2 East 91st Street, southeast corner of Fifth Avenue
1901, Babb, Cook and Willard

The former Andrew Carnegie mansion is now the Smithsonian Institution's National Museum of Design, one of New York's principal venues for architectural exhibitions. Its hyperactive red-brick and Indiana-limestone façades are the perfect complement to the serene Convent of the Sacred Heart across 91st Street. This and the Frick Collection (17.11) are the

10 *Cooper-Hewitt Museum*

only remaining Manhattan mansions with front lawns. Once Fifth Avenue had a number of such houses, common in the outer boroughs of New York City and other American cities, though quite uncommon in land-crazy Manhattan. The lush lawn fronts both Fifth Avenue and 90th Street, and is enclosed by a fine spiky black iron fence. Across 90th Street from the lawn is the stripped-Gothic/Art Deco Church of the Heavenly Rest (Episcopal), built in 1929 and designed by Mayers, Murray and Philip, the successor firm to Bertram Grosvenor Goodhue.

11 GUGGENHEIM MUSEUM

Fifth Avenue, between 88th and 89th streets
1959, Frank Lloyd Wright
Addition to east: 1992, Gwathmey Siegel and Associates

In the countryside, Wright adapted his designs to nature. Nature was Wright's god. It was the works of his fellow human beings that Wright

11 *Guggenheim Museum*

could not abide, and so when he designed in the city—which was not very often—he refused to adapt his designs to what surrounded them, i.e., to buildings designed by other human beings. The central point of the Guggenheim is that it totally ignores its setting. Wright did everything in his power to make his building stand completely apart. Like 9 West 57th Street (14.8), it is an imperious object, flagrantly violating the street wall. Like the Marriott Marquis Hotel (12.5), it is self-contained, turned in on itself and not acknowledging its surroundings. Unlike the Church House of the First Presbyterian Church (5.12) by Wright's former apprentice Edgar Tafel, it does not extend to the dense urban setting the Wrightian principles of design in context.

Gwathmey Siegel's new nine-story annex is exceedingly deferential to Wright's building, which has just been renovated and is being allowed to exist more as the pure object its architect intended it to be. Inside Wright's building, the spiral rotunda is now open all the way to the top, and the glass panes of the dome have been replaced, letting in a flood of natural light. The smaller rotunda at the north end, long used as office space, is now open, and is connected to the galleries in the annex. And a roof garden has been created between the small rotunda and the annex. The effect has been to put Wright's building on display as the most treasured of the museum's holdings.

12 60 EAST 88TH STREET (apartments)

Between Madison and Park avenues
1987, Beyer Blinder Belle

A sincere and successful attempt to revive an older style of luxury-apartment construction in which the building looks like a luxury building, and not like a housing project or an airport hotel. A nicely detailed red-brick shaft surmounts a rusticated limestone base, with a resulting quality of design that is at about upper-middle 1920s' level, which is very far ahead of most apartment architecture of the post–World War II period.

CHAPTER 19

Morningside Heights

1 *Cathedral of St. John the Divine*

Chapter 19

Morningside Heights

1 CATHEDRAL CHURCH OF SAINT JOHN THE DIVINE (Episcopal)

Amsterdam Avenue at 112th Street
1892–1911, Heins & LaFarge
1911–42, Cram & Ferguson

The original architects, Heins & LaFarge, were responsible for the apse, choir, and crossing that remain today. They are in a robust Romanesque style that the architects intended to use for the entire church. After these architects' deaths, Cram & Ferguson took over. Ralph Adams Cram was his era's foremost champion of the Gothic in church design. It was then that St. John's was transformed from a Romanesque church to a Gothic one. Construction halted in 1942, the year of Cram's death. By then the nave and west front had been completed. Construction did not resume until 1979. James Bambridge, a master stonemason from England, was brought in to teach traditional stone carving to the ghetto kids who are now at work on the continuing construction of the church. This stone-carving program is one of the happiest things in New York today. Not only are disadvantaged kids eagerly learning a time-honored craft, but a new generation of Americans is being trained in a once-obsolescent architectural craft, whose revival may bode well for future design. The first goal of the young stone-workers is the completion of the south tower on the Amsterdam Avenue front. The north tower and the crossing lantern are scheduled to follow. If and when St. John's is completed, it will be the largest cathedral in the world. The total length of the interior is

601 feet (compared to St. Patrick's Cathedral, which is 306 feet). It is 146 feet wide (St. Patrick's is 48 feet), and 124 feet high (St. Patrick's is 108 feet).

The nave is very dark, even on the sunniest days. The long aisle walls feature a series of meretricious, horrendously maintained exhibits that look like something from an abandoned provincial museum. Why the cathedral feels these exhibits should be here is beyond me. At best, they are good for a laugh, and perhaps I am old-fashioned, but laughs do not seem to me an appropriate reason to visit a cathedral. These aisle exhibits are in stark contrast to the great gray granite piers, unfinished arches, and temporary Guastavino tile vaulting of Heins & LaFarge's crossing: a majestic, brooding space fragrant with a whiff of the ramparts. The pulpit (1916) of Tennessee marble was designed by Henry Vaughan. In the crossing are the early seventeenth-century Barberini Tapestries, depicting scenes from the life of Christ and a map of the Holy Land. This is the best place from which to turn and look at the rose window, designed by Charles Connick and containing ten thousand pieces of glass. Just beyond the crossing is the breathtaking sequence of ambulatory chapels; from north to south they are:

1) St. Ansgar's Chapel (1918), designed by Henry Vaughan in a fourteenth-century English Gothic style;
2) Chapel of St. Boniface (1916) by Vaughan;
3) St. Columba's Chapel (1911) by Heins & LaFarge, with a fifteenth-century polyptych altarpiece by the Sienese master, Giovanni di Paolo;
4) St. Saviour's Chapel (1904), designed by Heins & LaFarge in a Gothic style;
5) Chapel of St. Martin of Tours (1918), designed by Ralph Adams Cram in a thirteenth-century French Gothic style, with windows by Charles Connick;
6) St. Ambrose's Chapel (1914), designed by Carrère & Hastings in a Renaissance style, with a statue of St. Anthony by Luca della Robbia (1400?–82); and
7) Chapel of St. James (1916), designed by Henry Vaughan in a fourteenth-century English Gothic style.

Several other buildings make up the cathedral complex. At the northeast corner of Amsterdam Avenue and Cathedral Parkway is Cram & Ferguson's neo-Gothic Synod House (1913). Moving east, the next buildings are: Heins & LaFarge's Diocesan House (1912), containing the cathedral library and archives; Cram & Ferguson's chateauesque Cathedral House (1914); Cram & Ferguson's Deanery (1914); and Walter Cook's and Winthrop A. Welch's Cathedral School (1913). The best place to view the cathedral's west front is anywhere on 112th Street west of Amsterdam Avenue, from which point the cathedral closes the eastern vista. Cathedral Parkway (aka 110th Street), running west from Amsterdam Avenue, is a lovely street, wide and bordered on both sides by massive, stately apartment houses. It is the kind of dense, embracing street that is one of the glories of Manhattan.

2 CHURCH OF NOTRE DAME (Roman Catholic)

Morningside Drive, northwest corner of 114th Street
Apse: 1910, Daus & Otto
Rectory: 1915, 1928, Cross & Cross

The Corinthian portico on Morningside Park. Like St. John's, this church is unfinished. Anywhere else in the city, the Church of Notre Dame would probably be famous. In the shadow of the Cathedral Church of St. John the Divine, however, it is virtually unknown. It is one of the truly fine Beaux-Arts churches in New York. The skylight dome was never completed, and the interior has to be artificially illuminated. The original congregation was French speaking, and the design was inspired by that of Barthelemy Vignon's and Jean-Jacques Huvé's Church of Sainte-Marie-Madeleine (1845) in Paris.

3 COLUMBIA UNIVERSITY

114th Street to 120th Street, from Broadway to Amsterdam Avenue
Begun in 1892

Columbia is a distinguished private university, one of eight composing the Ivy League, the elite of American institutions of higher education. John Dewey, Lionel Trilling, and Jacques Barzun are among the illustrious scholars who have graced the Columbia faculty. It is a tight urban campus contained by the Manhattan grid. The older buildings were uniformly

3 *Low Memorial Library, Columbia University*

designed in the Beaux-Arts mode, making the appearance of this campus very different from schools dominated by collegiate Gothic. The unity and beauty have been somewhat compromised in recent years by modern intrusions, but it is still possible to say that for enthusiasts of the classical, Columbia ranks with Thomas Jefferson's University of Virginia as one of the two most beautiful campuses in the country. The plan of the campus was the work of Charles Follen McKim. (Columbia students probably get a kick out of hearing that the campus was built on the site of the Bloomingdale Asylum for the Insane.)

The best way to see the campus is to enter at College Walk (116th Street) at Broadway. To the north, on your left, is **Dodge Hall**, a seven-story structure, designed by McKim, Mead & White and completed in 1924, that houses Columbia's business school. Opposite Dodge Hall, across College Walk, is the six-story **School of Journalism**, designed by McKim, Mead & White and completed in 1913. The bronze Thomas Jefferson in front of the School of Journalism dates from 1914 and was designed by William Ordway Partridge. Continuing east on College Walk, you next come to the main quadrangle, containing, to the north on your left, the focal point of the campus: Charles Follen McKim's fine Pantheon-like **Low Library**, completed in 1898. The broad sweep of steps, Daniel Chester French's bronze Alma Mater (1903), the ten Ionic columns, the octagonal drum, the huge dome—here is a monumentality nearly on a par with the Metropolitan Museum of Art (17.20) or the New York Public Library (13.1).

Just to the northeast of Low Library is the superb **St. Paul's Chapel** (Episcopal), completed in 1907 and designed by Howells & Stokes. This brick-and-limestone Roman church is notable for its vaulted portico, domed crossing, and three apse windows by John LaFarge. The codesigner was Isaac Newton Phelps Stokes, author of the monumental six-volume *Iconography of Manhattan Island,* published in 1909, and to date the single most important reference book on the physical history of Manhattan. North of St. Paul's Chapel is **Avery Hall,** designed by McKim, Mead & White and dating from 1912. This building houses the greatest architectural reference library in the Western Hemisphere, open only to certified scholars. Opposite Low Library, across College Walk, is the **Butler Library,** the main general library of Columbia University. It was designed by James Gamble Rogers and built in 1934.

4 RIVERSIDE DRIVE and 116TH STREET

It is this immediate vicinity that I personally consider the most beautiful part of Manhattan, the equivalent in every way of Paris. Riverside Drive is well worth strolling from its beginning at 72nd Street. It is the most beautiful street in Manhattan. Like Park Avenue, it is a solid row of neo-Renaissance apartment houses and town houses. Like Fifth Avenue, these lush residences face a park across a broad avenue. Unlike Park or Fifth, however, Riverside Drive is curvy, with constantly changing vistas. The park it faces likewise has a curvy border and is narrow, with the mighty Hudson just on the other side. The quality of the façades is much finer than on Park or Fifth. The thrilling thing about Riverside Drive is the combination of strong classical façades with the romantic, leafy setting. Riverside Drive reaches a climax at 116th Street, a broad thoroughfare that leads into the Columbia campus. One is swept from Riverside Drive onto 116th Street by a pair of majestically convex apartment façades: the **Colosseum** at the southeast corner, and **440 Riverside Drive** at the northeast corner. Both date from 1910 and were designed by Schwartz & Gross, the architects who twenty years later would design

4 *Colosseum Apartments*

the classic Art Deco apartment house at 55 Central Park West (16.4). The Riverside buildings are elaborately detailed, red-brick-and-limestone, classical façades: massive, stately, but dynamic. They suck Riverside Drive into 116th Street going east, and into Claremont Avenue going north. A block east at Broadway is the main gate of College Walk, leading to the main quadrangle of the Columbia campus, dominated by Low Library. This is one of the finest classical sequences in America, and an absolutely bravura, hugely underrated piece of urban design.

5 CLAREMONT AVENUE

From 116th Street to Tiemann Place

Claremont Avenue is a four-block-long street that runs north from 116th Street between Broadway and Riverside Drive. Its first block runs along the west side of the Barnard College campus. The west side of Claremont from 116th to 119th streets is dominated by three large apartment buildings:

Peter Minuit Hall at number 25, **Eton Hall** at number 29, and **Rugby Hall** at number 35. All three were designed by Gaetan Ajello and built in 1910. Together they make up an imposing cliff of white terra-cotta ornament. At number 120, at the northeast corner of 122nd Street, is the **Manhattan School of Music**, located in the original home of the Juilliard School until its removal to Lincoln Center. The building dates from 1910, the same year as Ajello's apartments down the street and Schwartz & Gross's apartments at Riverside and 116th (19.5), and was designed by Donn Barber. Additions were made in 1931 by Shreve, Lamb & Harmon (the same year those architects finished the Empire State Building, 9.4), and in 1970 by MacFadyen & Knowles. The Manhattan School is second only to Juilliard in prestige among New York music schools. Claremont is one of those well-enclosed and very comfortable streets that were the models for the residential sections of Battery Park City (3.2).

5 *116th Street and Claremont Avenue*

6 BARNARD COLLEGE

116th Street to 120th Street, from Broadway to Claremont Avenue

Barnard, one of the group of prestigious women's colleges known as the Seven Sisters, was long the female counterpart to Columbia College across Broadway. In this day of women's liberation, the two schools are fully integrated. At 606 West 120th Street (here renamed Reinhold Niebuhr Place after the distinguished theologian who served on Columbia's faculty) is **Milbank Hall**, designed by Lamb & Rich who also planned the Barnard campus, and completed in 1898. Charles A. Rich, successor to Lamb & Rich, contributed **Brooks Hall** (1907) and **Hewitt Hall** (1924), and Arnold W. Brunner designed **Barnard Hall** (1917), the focal element of Lamb & Rich's quadrangle. The most recent building on campus is James Stewart Polshek & Partners' dormitory building of 1988.

7 121ST STREET, FROM AMSTERDAM AVENUE TO BROADWAY

A thrilling street. On the south side is the north side of the Teachers College block. Teachers College is the renowned graduate school of education that, inspired by the theories of John Dewey, pioneered progressive education in America. The mostly red-brick Victorian Gothic blockfront includes, from east to west: **Whittier Hall** (1901, Bruce Price); **Macy Hall** (1894, William A. Potter); the sleek, modern, high-rise **Thorndike Hall** (1973, Hugh Stubbins & Associates, four years before the same architects completed Citicorp Center, 10.14); and the neo-Romanesque **former Horace Mann School**, fronting on Broadway (1901, Howells & Stokes and Edgar H. Josselyn). On the north side of the street, of particular note is **Bancroft Hall** at number 509, built in 1911 and designed by Emery Roth, architect of such Central Park West classics as the San Remo (16.14) and the Beresford (16.19). Here, as in his other buildings, Roth uses an Italian Renaissance vocabulary, but perhaps nowhere in Manhattan is that vocabulary employed so wildly as in Bancroft Hall, which sports copper oriels and a timber, pitched, almost-Wrightian roof.

The vista west on 121st is closed by the solid, stolid neo-Gothic Broadway front of the **Union Theological Seminary** (1910, Allen & Collens). The prestigious seminary, which has close ties both to Columbia

University (19.3) and Riverside Church (19.8), occupies the full block bounded by Broadway and Claremont Avenue and 120th and 122nd streets. With its quiet interior courtyard, the seminary is very much in the Oxford Gothic mode, in striking contrast to the Beaux-Arts campus of Columbia. Rising behind the seminary is the skyscraper tower of Riverside Church. The Belgian architect Leon Krier has remarked how sad he thinks it is that New York, with all its great skyscrapers, could find so few opportunities to include them in axial Beaux-Arts plans. Here is one of those rare instances where a skyscraper does close a Manhattan vista, other examples being Park Avenue (closed by the former New York Central, now Helmsley, Building, 10.5) and Chambers Street (closed by the Municipal Building, 2.12).

8 RIVERSIDE CHURCH

490 Riverside Drive, from 120th Street to 122nd Street
1930, Allen & Collens, and Henry C. Pelton
South wing: 1960, Collens, Willis & Beckonert

Riverside Church is one of the most imposing and sumptuous architectural piles in Manhattan. It was built from 1928 to 1930, with Burnham Hoyt as the principal designer. The congregation is jointly associated with the Baptist Church and the United Church of Christ. It has long been known as an activist congregation in the service of liberal social goals, and is involved in an array of community services that it is safe to say is the most extensive of any church congregation in New York. This is in part the legacy of John D. Rockefeller, Jr. (1874–1960), billionaire philanthropist, with whose money Riverside Church was built, and Harry Emerson Fosdick (1878–1969), the liberal theologian who was the congregation's pastor from 1926 to 1946, and whose sermons, books, and radio broadcasts made him one of the most prominent clergymen of his day. Riverside's roots can be traced back to 1841 and the Lower East Side. After several successive uptown moves, in 1922 the congregation located on Park Avenue at the southeast corner of 64th Street. Called the Park Avenue Baptist Church, it was designed, like the present Riverside Church, by Pelton, and Allen & Collens. (It is now the Central Presbyterian Church, 17.5.) As its Park Avenue location suggests, this had become an affluent congregation. It is easy to see how, equipped with the vision of Fosdick and the money of Rockefeller, this grew to be an extremely

8 *Riverside Church*

ambitious congregation, destined not to remain for long in its modest edifice in the middle of Manhattan's "silk stocking district."

The exact opposite was what Fosdick and Rockefeller wanted: a magnificent structure that would serve as a locus for community services and a beacon of hope in an economically and racially diverse neighborhood. No location could better fulfill such a goal than Riverside Drive and 120th Street, near to both the ivory towers of Columbia University (19.3) (as well as the ivory towers of Union Theological Seminary, 19.7, where Fosdick was professor of practical theology from 1915 to 1946) and the festering slums of black Harlem. The location was also an ideal setting for a magnificent building. Riverside Church sits on the crest of a steeply descending bluff, with a view of the Hudson River to the west, Harlem to the north and east, and the west side of Manhattan to the south. The vista from the top of the tower of Riverside Church, where there is a public observatory, is arguably the most splendid in Manhattan.

To take advantage of the site, the congregation used the best stone, glass, and wood craftsmanship that Rockefeller's money could buy. To serve as a symbol of hope and aspiration, the church was designed in the French Gothic style of Chartres Cathedral. Beneath its Gothic veneer, however, Riverside is a thoroughly 1920s building, steel-framed and with a 392-foot tower (approximately as high as a thirty-story office building) that is one of New York's most remarkable eclectic skyscrapers. Riverside's 265-foot-long west and east sides run along Riverside Drive and Claremont Avenue, respectively. The main entrance is on the west side. The doors are elaborately carved and are modeled on the portal of Chartres. The "cloister entrance" on the east side is graced by a bronze Madonna and Child by Sir Jacob Epstein (1880-1959), who in 1912 created the tomb of Oscar Wilde in Paris's Père Lachaise Cemetery, and who was the most important sculptor in the Vorticist movement, centered around the novelist and painter Wyndham Lewis in England. Epstein pioneered the use of primitive and non-Western forms in modern art, and his work was consistently controversial. The Riverside Madonna and Child is modeled on a Native American mother and her child, using forms influenced by Native American design that also fit the spirit of 1920s Art Moderne.

From Riverside Drive, one enters a spacious, tile-vaulted narthex, with the nave entrance on the left and the chapel entrance on the right. Directly ahead on the east wall are four outstanding early sixteenth-century Flemish glass lancet windows, the only ones at Riverside not made expressly for the building. These windows are believed originally to hail from Antwerp or Bruges. Three of the sixteen scenes that are depicted were copied from Dürer. The scenes, four per lancet, are beautifully complex compositions, making full use of the refined techniques of perspective, foreshortening, and shading, and the figures are anatomically correct. Unfortunately, these windows, which are rather dark to begin with, are so situated that they do not catch much sun; hence, despite their great beauty, they are easy to miss unless deliberately sought out. The windows somehow ended up in England during the Napoleonic Wars, and at some point after that the English captions were painted onto the glass. The windows arrived in New York in 1924 and were installed in the original Park Avenue Baptist Church before being incorporated into the congregation's new home.

To see Riverside's most notable modern glass, turn left into the nave and walk straight up to the chancel. The central ambulatory windows, whose title and subject is *Mercy*, were created by Wright Goodhue (1905-31), the nephew of Bertram Grosvenor Goodhue, architect of St. Thomas Church (13.13). The younger Goodhue committed suicide at the age of twenty-six, cutting short a brilliant, if iconoclastic, career as a stained-glass artist. Like his uncle, he did highly imaginative and original work within an eclectic, medieval mode. His two ambulatory windows at Riverside demonstrate his great illustrative ability (which his uncle's partner, Ralph Adams Cram, claimed was second only to that of Aubrey Beardsley), and his great talent as a colorist. Unfortunately, again, the windows are not shown to the best advantage, as a gigantic cross with a spotlight trained on it is suspended between them, dissipating their lighting effects. Still, these are among the most original windows in New York, and well worth seeking out.

The clerestory windows are copies of those at Chartres. The American neomedievalist stained-glass artists prominent at the time were opposed to the exact copying of medieval precedents, and refused to accept the commission from Riverside to reproduce the Chartres windows. So these windows ended up being made by French firms. James L. Sturm, the historian of stained-glass art, says that the interior of Riverside is brightly lit, unlike the dark interior of Chartres. Hence, windows that are ideally suited to Chartres, and to the soft light of northern France, are inappropriately dull in Riverside, and in fact look best on dark, rainy days.

The nave is 215 feet long and 89 feet wide and crests at 100 feet. (St. Patrick's Cathedral is 306 feet long and 144 feet wide and crests at 108 feet). Riverside Church seats about twenty-five hundred people. The nave, like the exterior, is sheathed in Indiana limestone. The pulpit, on the west side of the chancel, is carved out of limestone and weighs nine tons. (I do not know it for a fact, but I would bet that Riverside has the heaviest pulpit in New York.) In the base of the pulpit are carvings of famous French cathedrals. On the chancel floor is a medieval-style maze, modeled on the larger one at Chartres, which worshippers would traverse on their knees while praying. On the south wall of the nave is Christ in Majesty, plaster cast and covered in gold leaf, by Sir Jacob Epstein. There are no transepts and no side chapels, which is unusual for a Gothic church of this size. Because of this, the exterior massing—the main body plus the tower—is very reminiscent of certain skyscrapers of the day, e.g., Hood and Fouilhoux's American Standard Building (1924) on Bryant Park (9.8).

Reentering the narthex, you will notice, to your left and the left of the Flemish windows, a tiny chapel containing the painting *Christ in*

Gethsemane by Heinrich Hofmann (1824–1902), said to be the single most reproduced religious painting in history. Christ Chapel, entered through a door in the south wall of the narthex, is modeled after the eleventh-century Romanesque nave of the Chapel of Saint-Nazaire in Carcassonne, France. The chapel at Riverside is a stolid, but finely wrought, piece of neo-Romanesque design. Its south windows were blocked, however, when Riverside added its southern wing in 1960. Since then, the stained-glass windows have had to be artificially backlit. (Throughout Riverside Church, the natural lighting has been botched one way or another.)

The narthex, in its scale, dimensions, and construction, is very similar to the lobbies of tall office buildings of the time. From it, one can ascend via elevator and stairway to the top of the carillon tower. From the stairway, there is a clear view of the bell chamber of the carillon. The Laura Spelman Rockefeller Memorial Carillon, a gift from John D. Rockefeller, Jr., in honor of his mother, is the world's largest carillon, the most superlative of all Riverside's superlatives. It contains seventy-four bells. The largest, at twenty tons, is the largest tuned bell ever cast; the smallest is ten pounds. The bells date from 1925, 1930, and 1956, and were cast in England and Holland. This was the first carillon ever to exceed five octaves, and the heaviest bells can be played only with the aid of electric motors. The tower also houses offices, classrooms, meeting rooms, and a gymnasium.

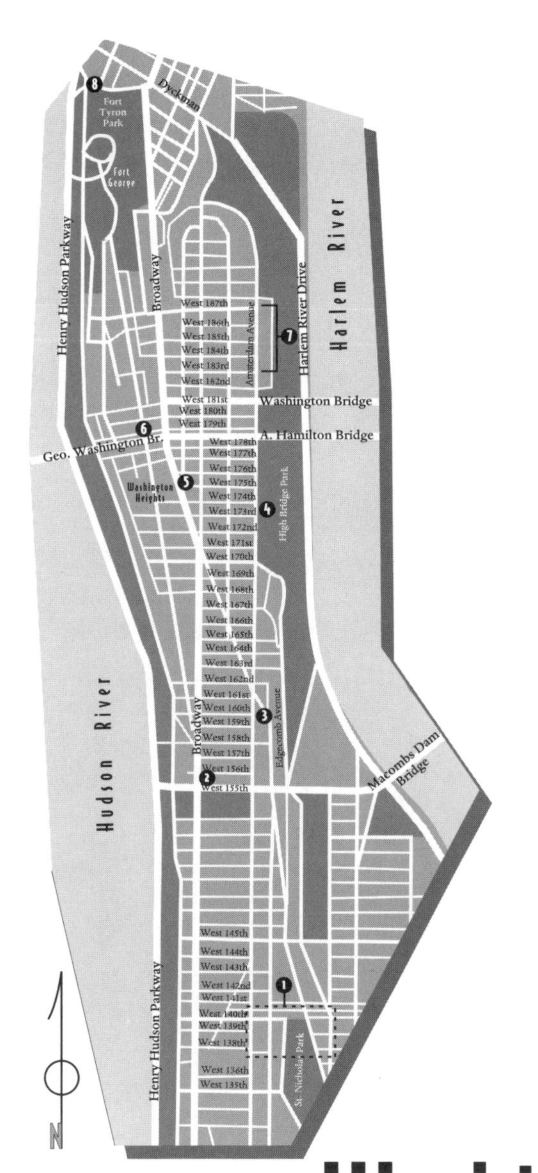

CHAPTER 20

Washington Heights and Harlem

1 *City College*

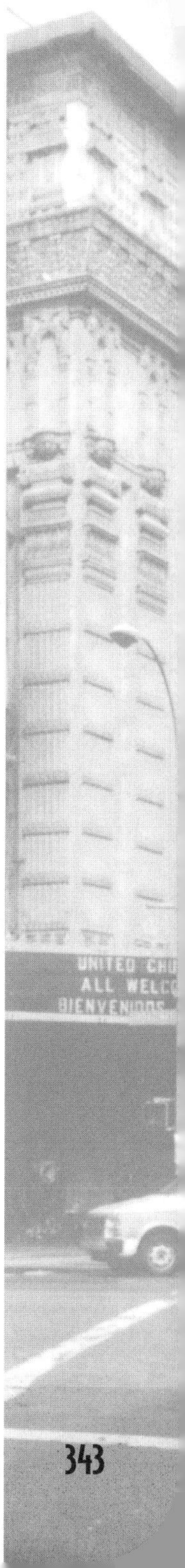

Chapter 20
Washington Heights and Harlem

1 CITY COLLEGE

138th Street to 140th Street, from St. Nicholas Terrace to Amsterdam Avenue
1897–1930, George B. Post

A remarkably attractive and tranquil enclave amid a teeming, tumble-down corner of Harlem: it seems almost to be a movie set. **Townsend Harris Hall** was completed in 1906; **Shepard Hall**, **Baskerville Hall**, **Compton Hall**, and **Wingate Hall** were completed in 1908; and **Goethals Hall** was completed in 1930. These six buildings, along with the three gates (on 138th, 139th, and 140th streets), are faced in dark Manhattan schist, quarried on the site, trimmed in white terra-cotta. It is a compact, but powerfully concentrated, romantic version of collegiate Gothic. In the 1910s, Lewis Mumford attended night classes at City College. He describes the physical setting this way:

> . . . the college buildings, in their dark stone masses and white terra-cotta quoins and moldings, rising like a collection of crystals above the formless rocks of the hill. Below, the plains of Harlem spread a vapor of light beneath the twinkle and flood of a large beer sign. The Gothic architecture of the main building, which followed the curve of the escarpment and dominated it with the tower of the Great Hall, did magnificent justice to its setting. In the afterglow, or on a dark night, these buildings could awaken nostalgic tremors as easily as might those of Trinity or Magdalen.

In those years, about 90 percent of the student body was Jewish, the sons of poor immigrants determined to see their children succeed in America. City College has an almost mythical status as the incubator of the city's Jewish professional elite. Today the student body, like the population of the surrounding community, is predominately black and Hispanic. At the eastern edge of the campus is a precipitous overlook across St. Nicholas Park toward the Harlem River, with a spectacular view of the Bronx, in particular historic Yankee Stadium. Below 138th Street stretches the large modern addition to the campus.

North of the old campus, along Convent Avenue from 141st to 145th streets, is an extension of the City College enclave, a well-preserved group of houses built from 1886 to 1906. At 287 Convent Avenue is the Federal-style house called **Hamilton Grange**, built in 1802. Once the home of Alexander Hamilton, whose estate comprised the land where this group of houses stands, it was originally located nearby at Amsterdam Avenue and 143rd Street, and was moved to its present site in 1889. It was designed by John McComb, Jr., coarchitect of City Hall (2.10). The large Romanesque Revival church looming over Hamilton Grange is R. H. Robertson's **St. Luke's Episcopal Church** of 1895.

Just on the other side of St. Nicholas Park from City College is an even finer group of houses than the one on Convent Avenue. **Strivers' Row**, 138th and 139th streets between Seventh and Eighth avenues, built in 1891, is one of the handsomest residential enclaves in the city, and a bastion of the black elite. Originally known as the King Model Houses after their developer, David H. King, Jr., these houses earned the sobriquet "Strivers' Row" in the 1920s and '30s when they became the desired homes of upwardly mobile blacks. Residents at that time included the musicians W. C. Handy and Eubie Blake. More recently, this is where Wesley Snipes and Lonette McKee lived in Spike Lee's *Jungle Fever*. The red-brick neo-Georgian houses along the south side of 138th Street were designed by James Brown Lord, architect of the Appellate courthouse on Madison Square (8.4). The yellow-brick neo-Georgian houses along the north side of 138th Street and the south side of 139th Street were designed by Bruce Price and Clarence S. Luce. The dark brown-brick, neo-Renaissance houses along the north side of 139th Street were designed by McKim, Mead and White.

Nearby, on 138th Street between Lenox and Seventh avenues, is the neo-Gothic **Abyssinian Baptist Church** (1923, Charles W. Bolton), one of the most important institutions in the life of the Harlem community. This was home to the Reverend Adam Clayton Powell, Jr., who became a U.S. congressman, and is now directed by the Reverend Calvin O. Butts (widely believed to be the model for Reverend Reginald Bacon in Tom Wolfe's scathing *Bonfire of the Vanities*). The congregation, founded in 1808, is the oldest black church in New York. The Sunday gospel services are spectacular, and open to all. If you are walking around in the area, you may want to head eleven blocks down Lenox Avenue to number 328, between 127th and 128th streets. This is **Sylvia's** restaurant, Harlem's most famous eating place and the city's foremost bastion of black southern cuisine.

2 CHURCH OF THE INTERCESSION (Episcopal)

550 West 155th Street, southeast corner of Broadway
1914, Bertram Grosvenor Goodhue

AUDUBON TERRACE

Broadway, from 155th Street to 156th Street
Master plan: 1908, Charles Pratt Huntington

MUSEUM OF THE AMERICAN INDIAN

1916, Charles Pratt Huntington

HISPANIC SOCIETY OF AMERICA

West building: 1908, Charles Pratt Huntington
East building, west building additions: 1910–26, Charles Pratt Huntington, Erik Strindberg, and H. Brooks Price

AMERICAN NUMISMATIC SOCIETY

1907, Charles Pratt Huntington

AMERICAN ACADEMY AND NATIONAL INSTITUTE OF ARTS AND LETTERS

South building: 1923, William M. Kendall of McKim, Mead and White
North building: 1930, Cass Gilbert

CHURCH OF OUR LADY OF ESPERANZA (Roman Catholic)

1912, Charles Pratt Huntington

BORICUA COLLEGE

1911, Charles Pratt Huntington

Goodhue's own favorite among his churches is long, narrow, high towered: a wildly picturesque, random ashlar composition, based on fourteenth-century English perpendicular. It is a kind of cross between Goodhue's St. Vincent Ferrer (1914–18, 17.8) with its ruggedness, and St. Bartholomew's (1914–19, 10.10), with its romantically variegated brickwork, both begun the year Intercession was completed. In the north transept is the tomb, sculpted by Lee Lawrie, of Goodhue himself. The church complex—including cloister, parish house, and vicarage—is set, appropriately, in the northwest corner of the eastern half of Trinity Cemetery (Riverside Drive to Amsterdam Avenue, bisected by Broadway, 153rd to 155th streets.) No other church in Manhattan has as much of a country-church feeling. The cemetery (planned in 1876–81 by Calvert Vaux) is the resting place of John James Audubon, Clement Clarke Moore, Eliza Jumel, and Alfred Tennyson Dickens (Charles's son), among others. From the eastern edge, as at City College, there are splendid Harlem River vistas.

In the block north of the western half of the cemetery stands Audubon Terrace, a compact, unified complex of important museums and other institutions. This was the site of the country estate of John James Audubon. The complex was established, beginning with the Hispanic Society museum, in 1906 by the philanthropist and Hispanophile Archer M. Huntington, who commissioned his cousin Charles Pratt Huntington to plan the group and design most of its buildings. The six institutions that compose the Audubon Terrace unit are housed in buildings designed in an Italian Renaissance style, and are disposed around a common court, with continuous Ionic colonnades of Indiana limestone. The court features sculptures by Anna Hyatt Huntington, Archer's wife. At the southeast corner of the site is the Museum of the American Indian, now part of the Smithsonian Institution. It is the largest American Indian museum in the world. To the west is the Hispanic Society museum, one of the little-known gems among New York's museums, featuring masterpieces by Velazquez, El Greco, Zurbaran, and Goya. Simone de Beauvoir wrote

2 *Audubon Terrace*

of the Hispanic Society in 1947:

> I was amazed on going through a door to find myself in the very heart of Spain; the quiet rooms smelt of Spain; they are decorated with majolica, carved panelling and fine stamped leather; hanging from the walls of the gallery which runs round the central hall are Goyas, Grecos and Zurbarans: some of them look of doubtful origin . . . Americans, no doubt, are too avid for Old Masters to be over-particular.

(It seems not to have mattered to this great phony that a disproportionate number of this century's greatest connoisseurs of European art have been Americans.)

Next west is the American Numismatic Society, the only museum in the world devoted exclusively to coins. At the southwest and northwest corners of the site are the two buildings of the American Academy and National Institute of Arts and Letters, the only two Audubon Terrace buildings not designed by Huntington, and America's rather feeble attempt to emulate the Académie Française. (Are Norman Mailer, Susan Sontag, and John Kenneth Galbraith truly among our fifty most important guardians of the English language?) To the east of the American Academy's north building is the Church of Our Lady of Esperanza, a

Roman Catholic church built by Archer Huntington with donations from King Alfonso XIII of Spain. At the northeast corner of the site is the building that until 1971 housed the American Geographical Society, with the largest collection of maps in the Western Hemisphere, now located in Milwaukee. The building is now home to Boricua College, a private four-year college founded in 1974 for Spanish-speaking students. It is an interesting irony that this complex, conceived as a monument to Hispanic culture, was built at a time when no Hispanic people lived in this neighborhood. Today, of course, this is a largely Spanish-speaking community.

Audubon Terrace is everybody's favorite example of a great institution overoptimistically built far from the center of town. Urban critics from Lewis Mumford to Nathan Glazer have maintained that throughout its planning and zoning history, New York City has placed far too great an emphasis upon the intensive development of its center. And while the center has long possessed a unique allure, it has done so, in a way that is surely less true of London or Paris, at the expense of outlying areas of the city, such as Washington Heights and Harlem, not to mention the outer boroughs. Glazer writes:

> Had city officials made an effort to maintain the attractiveness of areas outside the present dense center, New York would be a better and more livable city today. Once it was assumed that the city would expand outward, and great institutions were built in outlying areas: a grand campus of New York University on University Heights in the Bronx, Yeshiva University on 187th Street, a group of museums at 155th Street, a complex of academic institutions between 116th and 122nd streets, the New York Academy of Medicine and the Museum of the City of New York on 103rd and 104th streets. In recent decades we have watched in dismay as many of these institutions, which once represented confidence in the city and its neighborhoods, have shrunk or been transformed, or have escaped to the center where safety is hoped for.

The museums of Audubon Terrace are stupendously underattended. Most New Yorkers know of them only by hearsay. That is why the American Geographical Society moved to Milwaukee where it would be a major, well-attended museum. It is why the Museum of the American Indian has

been hankering to leave. There is no reason places like City College and Audubon Terrace should have to be thought of as refuges from their surrounding communities. But walk a couple of blocks west of the City College campus, or a couple of blocks east of the Audubon Terrace group, and you will see spectacular examples of neighborhoods that once had enormous potential.

Speaking of desertion, about three blocks east of Audubon Terrace on 155th Street is the site of the Polo Grounds baseball park (built 1912), once the home of the New York Giants and the place where Christy Mathewson and Willie Mays, among others, became superstars. The New York Giants are now the San Francisco Giants, and the site is occupied by the **Polo Grounds** public-housing project.

3 SYLVAN TERRACE

From 160th Street to 162nd Street
1882, Gilbert Robinson, Jr.

MORRIS-JUMEL MANSION

160th Street, northwest corner of Edgecombe Avenue
1765; remodeled circa 1810

Another Harlem enclave. Between Jumel Terrace and St. Nicholas Avenue and 160th and 162nd streets is Sylvan Terrace, a street—narrow and romantic and utterly unlike anything else in Manhattan—of twenty wooden row houses, restored with federal funds in 1981 to something like its original appearance. At its Jumel Terrace end stands the historic Morris-Jumel Mansion, a lovely Georgian country house that is Manhattan's only extant pre-Revolutionary War dwelling. Built by Roger and Mary Philipse Morris, the house, made of wood worked to simulate stone, has a white, airy, two-story Palladian portico with four widely spaced, slender Tuscan columns and a broad peaked attic. In 1776, it served briefly as George Washington's headquarters (Washington is believed to have been at one time romantically involved with Mary Philipse Morris). It was purchased by Stephen and Eliza Jumel in 1810, and after Stephen's death in 1832 became the home of Madame Jumel and her new husband, Aaron Burr (who reputedly married her for her money). It is like something from the Hudson River Valley—in fact, this part of Manhattan kind of *is* the Hudson River Valley.

HIGH BRIDGE

High Bridge Park at 174th Street
1839–48

HIGH BRIDGE TOWER

High Bridge Park at 173rd Street
1872, John B. Jervis

High Bridge is a great Roman aqueduct, a granite arcade marching across the Harlem River with magnificent purpose and simplicity. (The steel central span was added in 1923, sadly interrupting the march.) It was built to carry water from the Croton Lake in Westchester County into Manhattan. The water was stored in the neo-Romanesque, two hundred-foot-high, octagonal, rockface, granite tower with its peaked cupola, one of the most romantic sights in town. An adjacent reservoir was turned into a public swimming pool in 1934. The tower was taken out of service in 1949, exactly one hundred years after the establishment of High Bridge Park. More great river vistas. The bridge once had a pedestrian walkway—Edgar Allan Poe was a frequent visitor, and the poet of darkness would survey what was later to become the South Bronx. The walkway was closed many years ago to deter crime.

5 LOEW'S 175TH STREET THEATRE (now the United Church)

Broadway, northeast corner of 175th Street
1930, Thomas W. Lamb

Once one of New York's great movie palaces, back in the days when spectacular theaters could be found not only in midtown, but throughout the neighborhoods. It is now the church of the Reverend Ike, one of the pioneering televangelists. What a piece of work! It seems to be some kind of combination of classical, Byzantine, and Mayan elements, but I defy any student of architecture to identify all the various styles from which Lamb has borrowed. Whatever his inspiration, the result is an improbable—and improbably well-maintained—cliff of ornate terra-cotta rising like an hallucination on an otherwise-bedraggled stretch of Broadway. It is worthy of Cecil B. DeMille. Around the corner, at 21 Wadsworth Avenue at the northwest corner of 174th Street, is Carrère and Hastings's Wren-Hawksmoor Baroque **Fort Washington Presbyterian**

5 *The United Church, formerly Loew's 175th Street Theatre*

Church (1914), an inferior companion to the First Church of Christ, Scientist (1903, 16.26), also by Carrère and Hastings, on Central Park West.

6 GEORGE WASHINGTON BRIDGE

178th Street and Fort Washington Avenue
1931, Othmar H. Ammann and Cass Gilbert
Lower level: 1962

When built, the thirty-five hundred-foot-long span of this suspension bridge connecting Manhattan with Fort Lee, New Jersey, more than doubled the previous record for a single span (held by the Benjamin Franklin Bridge, completed in 1926, over the Delaware River between Philadelphia and Camden, New Jersey). The span is framed by two openwork steel towers rising 604 feet above the water. The design of these towers can almost be called stripped classical because of their monumental arches,

6 *George Washington Bridge*

which, at the equivalent of seventeen stories high, are undoubtedly the largest arches in New York. The bridge's pedestrian walkway can be taken from Manhattan to the Palisades State Park along New Jersey's Hudson River waterfront.

At the eastern end of the bridge, at Fort Washington Avenue between 178th and 179th streets, is the famous Italian architect/engineer Pier Luigi Nervi's flamboyant George Washington Bridge Bus Station (1963), its form reminiscent of a flock of seagulls. Whatever its merits as a piece of engineering, its big blank walls have an utterly stultifying effect on the surrounding streets, creating desolate byways that are the last thing this neighborhood needs. On the riverfront in Fort Washington Park in the shadow of the bridge is the Jeffrey's Hook Lighthouse, better

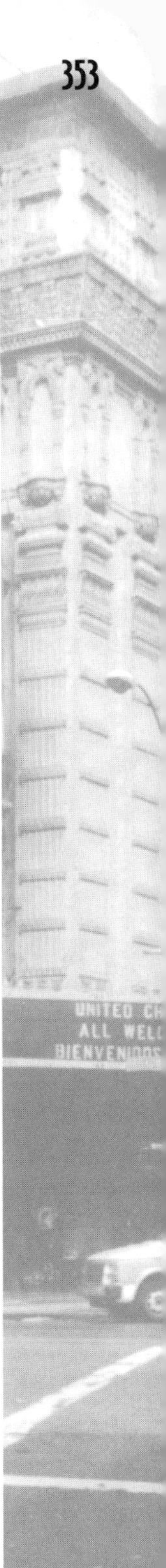

known as the Little Red Lighthouse, the subject of Hildegarde Swift's classic children's book, *The Little Red Lighthouse and the Great Gray Bridge* (1942). The lighthouse was built in 1880 and originally stood in Sandy Hook, New Jersey. It was moved to its present location in 1921 and was in service until 1951.

Just north of the bridge, along Fort Washington Avenue between 183rd and 185th streets, in Bennett Park is the highest natural point on Manhattan Island, 268 feet above sea level. Atop this rocky outcropping stand a pair of huge apartment complexes commanding spectacular Hudson River overlooks. Castle Village, along Cabrini Boulevard between 181st and 186th streets, is a group of fourteen-story red-brick towers interspersed with lush lawns, opening onto a private Hudson promenade. It was designed by George F. Pelham, Jr., and completed in 1938. The neo-Gothic Hudson View Gardens, along Pinehurst Avenue between 183rd and 185th streets, is a group of seven-story buildings, designed by George F. Pelham (father of the architect of Castle Village) and completed in 1925. This is a fascinating area in which to walk around, with startling, precipitous variations in topography and cascades of buildings that make this Manhattan's nearest equivalent to an Italian hill town.

7 YESHIVA UNIVERSITY

Amsterdam Avenue, from 183rd Street to 187th Street
Main building, 2540 Amsterdam Avenue, southwest corner of 187th Street: 1928, Charles B. Meyers Associates

Like the Audubon Terrace museum group (20.2), Yeshiva University is another august institution that staked its ground way uptown back when there was no reason to expect that an area like this wouldn't become one of the most civilized places on earth. This is the oldest and most distinguished Orthodox Jewish university in America. The main building is one of those flamboyant Near Eastern Romanesque/Byzantine/Moorish pastiches that designers once tried to establish as a kind of official style for Jewish architecture. The Yeshiva University Museum, located in the library building (1967, Armand Bartos and Associates) at 2520 Amsterdam Avenue between 185th and 186th streets is worth a visit to see, among other things, its collection of excellent models of historic synagogue buildings around the world. The campus is linear, with none of the enclave quality of City College (20.1).

7 *Yeshiva University*

8 CLOISTERS

North end of Fort Tryon Park, near Riverside Drive and Dyckman Street
1934–38, Charles Collens of Allen, Collens and Willis

On a rocky outcropping with sweeping Hudson vistas, a miragelike country setting beside the pounding city, is the bulk of the Metropolitan Museum of Art's medieval collection. In 1930, John D. Rockefeller, Jr., donated the land that is now Fort Tryon Park (sixty-six acres, 1935, planned by Frederick Law Olmsted, Jr.; 192nd to Dyckman streets, Broadway to Riverside Drive) to the city, with a corner set aside for the Metropolitan Museum to display the considerable remnants of the cloisters of five French monasteries built from the twelfth to the fifteenth centuries. The cloisters are incorporated into a design by Charles Collens, who was the Rockefellers' house architect (he was one of the architects of Riverside

Church, 19.8) before Wallace K. Harrison. This is one of the few remaining New York institutions—with the Frick Collection (17.11), the Pierpont Morgan Library (9.11), and perhaps others—of unspoiled, unapologetic high-cultural prestige. Among the many highlights are: the Fuentiduena Chapel from twelfth-century Spain; the cloister of the twelfth-century Benedictine monastery of Saint-Michel-de-Cuxa in the Pyrenees; the cloister of the fourteenth-century Cistercian abbey of Bonnefont near Toulouse; the cloister of the fifteenth-century Carmelite convent of Trie, also near Toulouse; and the arcade of the fifteenth-century Benedictine priory of Froville in France. Do not miss the Hall of the Unicorn Tapestries, with its six medieval tapestries. Rockefeller went so far as to purchase the Palisades land on the New Jersey riverfront across the Hudson from Fort Tryon Park, so that the views from the Cloisters would not be spoiled by development. Suggested background reading: *The Name of*

8A *Cloisters*

8B *Interior of Cloisters*

the Rose by Umberto Eco, and *Monks, Nuns, and Monasteries* by Sacheverell Sitwell. Across Dyckman Street from Fort Tryon Park, at the northwest corner of Broadway and 204th Street, is the Dutch-style **Dyckman House** (1783), the only remaining eighteenth-century farmhouse on Manhattan Island.

CHAPTER 21

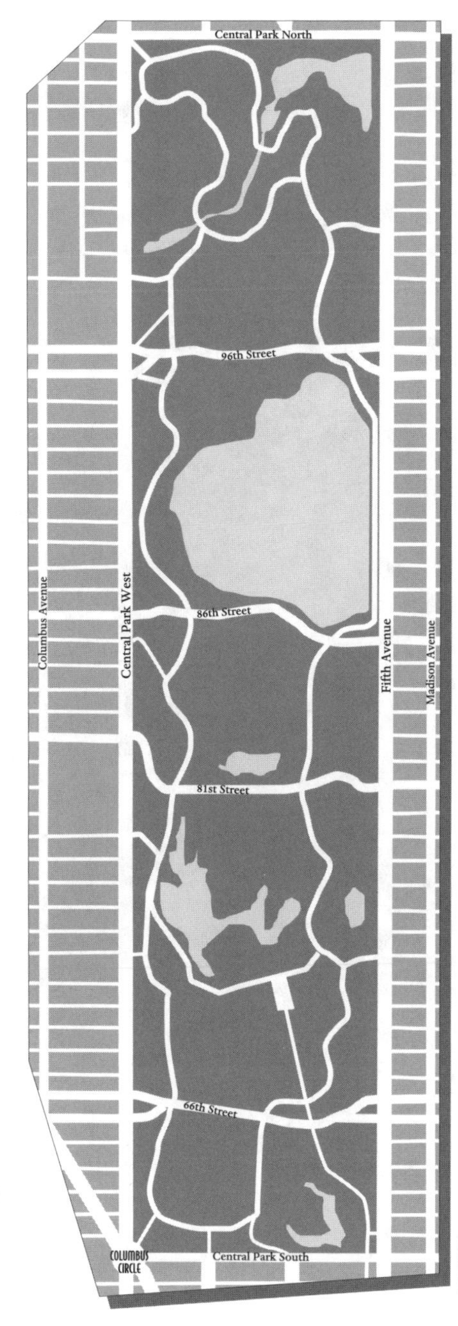

Central Park

1[A] *Central Park*

Chapter 21

Central Park

1 CENTRAL PARK

The most impressive thing about Central Park is the way Frederick Law Olmsted and Calvert Vaux managed to incorporate several widely varied landscapes into such a compact area. The variety is such that the visitor never feels shortchanged by any one landscape, never feels a locale to be cramped and constricted for its purposes. At the same time, one is continually surprised, pleased, and energized—much as in the best of the city beyond—by sudden revelations of new landscapes, new vistas, new experiences. The art of Central Park is in this balancing act—and do not forget that the whole thing is man-made, that it was designed down to each subtle ripple of earth. Like a great free-verse poem, Central Park succeeds not by virtue of its adherence to formal rules, but by its creators' uncommonly acute sense of proportion.

Not having been around in the days before the park was loaded down with all sorts of modern facilities, I am not competent to judge whether it is no longer as fine a place as it once was. What I can say, however, is that Olmsted's and Vaux's magnificent balancing act is not on show over the full 843 acres of the park, and where it isn't, it is not the fault of Olmsted and Vaux, but rather of those who came later and thought they were improving the place. The park may not have easily adapted to all the modern facilities, but it has, more or less, accepted them, as we, the park's users, have accepted them. The Wollman Skating Rink, for instance, is ugly and gives its part of the park something of the feeling of a construction site. But the rink is not only heavily used, but with its wondrous skyline views, it rivals Rockefeller Plaza as the city's most romantic skating site. The playgrounds, most of which were installed by Robert Moses, are also heavily used, and, with their mothers and nannies and toddlers, have, like the rink, become something quintessentially Manhattan, as well as something their users would not easily give up.

Where modern intrusions seem the most egregious is in the transverse section of the park, beginning directly behind the Metropolitan Museum of Art (17.20). The museum's modern additions obtrude into the park not only with horrendous bulk, but with a design based solely on the museum's interior requirements, these buildings do not even attempt to be graceful objects in the park. The other modern intrusion that does its best to destroy the park is not something built, but something brought—actually worn—into the park, i.e., roller blades. I have nothing against roller blades. They can provide stimulating sport. But there are days—including every nice one—when the infernal fraternity of exhibitionistic roller bladers seems to utterly take over the park's walkways. The automobiles on the transverse roadways are by comparison a benign presence. Olmsted's and Vaux's philosophy of park design was based on the heartwarming ideal of a place where people could retire from the hurly-burly of their workaday lives in order to be alone with their reveries. But the roller bladers are proof that mere design does not possess the power to withstand our present breakdown of public decorum.

The city purchased the bulk of the land for the park in 1856. The land was occupied by squatters forcibly evicted by the police (try that today), and was surveyed by Egbert Viele. In 1858, Olmsted and Vaux won the competition for the park's design. The designers were greatly influenced by recent movements in English landscape design, especially the pastoral romanticism of Lancelot "Capability" Brown (1716–83), who eschewed the classical tradition of English garden design, with its formal axes and sculpted topiary, in favor of a kind of Wordsworthian naturalism, exemplified in particular by the undulating landscape. Up to twenty million people use the park each year, which cannot help taking its toll. A major restoration program was begun in 1980, and is scheduled for completion a few years after this book is published.

The most popular entrance to the park is at Grand Army Plaza, Fifth Avenue and 59th Street. To the east is the Central Park Zoo, opened

1B *Central Park Ice Skating Rink*

in 1935, but which had become something of a dump before it was redesigned in 1988 by Kevin Roche John Dinkeloo and Associates. It is one of the happiest things to happen to New York in recent years. I particularly recommend the penguins. To the west is the pond. To the north and west of the pond is the Wollman Rink, and, continuing northwest, one comes to the Sheep Meadow, an expansive open area popular for sunbathing, that some believe offers the most spectacular land-based view in Manhattan, with the towers of Central Park South, Central Park West, and Fifth Avenue visible across the park's greenery. To the east of the Sheep Meadow is the Mall, one of the formal elements Olmsted and Vaux incorporated into their collection of landscapes. Between the south end of the Sheep Meadow and the south end of the Mall is John Quincy Adams Ward's bronze Indian Hunter (1866). At the south end of the Mall is Ward's bronze statue of Shakespeare (1870).

The Mall leads to Calvert Vaux's and Jacob Wrey Mould's Bethesda Terrace (begun in 1862). In the center of the terrace is the Bethesda Fountain, and in its center is Emma Stebbins's bronze angel (1868). The terrace, with the angel in the background, is a popular place for fashion shoots. Just north of Bethesda Terrace is the lake. By walking west along its shore, one comes to Calvert Vaux's romantic cast-iron Bow Bridge (1859), one of the loveliest structures in Manhattan. The bridge crosses

Bridge in Central Park

the lake into the Ramble, a densely planted glen and the best place in the park for getting away from the roller bladers and fashion models. Fanciful Belvedere Castle (1869), just north of the Ramble, is set on a hill with clear views skyward, and is one of the locations favored by birders in the park. One may not think of an urban park as prime birding territory, but in fact Central Park offers excellent viewing, as many coastal species fly over or stop off here on their migratory routes. Directly north of the Ramble is the Great Lawn, a large open area that probably hosts more corporate softball games than any other piece of land in America, and is the site of Central Park's occasional free concerts involving megasuperstars of the pop music industry. To the east of the Great Lawn is the Metropolitan Museum of Art. Nearly ten blocks of the park, from Fifth Avenue to Central Park West, is taken up by the reservoir north of the Metropolitan Museum and the Great Lawn. The 107-acre reservoir is a still-active receptacle in the Croton water system, and is ringed by what may be the most popular jogging track in the city.

Just to the north and east of the reservoir is one of the loveliest things in Central Park, indeed in all of New York: the Conservatory Garden, which can be entered off Fifth Avenue at 105th Street. This is the one indisputably wonderful thing added to Olmsted's and Vaux's design many years later. Robert Moses commissioned and Thomas D. Price designed the three formal gardens composing the Conservatory Garden in 1936 as a Works Progress Administration project. For most New Yorkers, however, this area did not come to life until 1983, when the long-neglected and decayed garden was beautifully restored by the Central Park Conservancy. The Conservancy replanted the impressive perennial gardens, and sowed fifteen hundred wildflowers in the South Garden. The Conservatory Garden is one of the few formal areas in the park—it is much more classical than Capability Brown. The North Garden, French classical in style, features Walter Schott's recently restored Untermeyer Fountain (1947) with its three lifesize bronze "diaphanously clad nymphs [who] dance with enough abandon to turn the heads on every military monument in the park—and in the city, for that matter" (Carter Wiseman). This wonderful fountain ranks with Matisse's great painting *Dance* (1909) at the Museum of Modern Art as an expression of pure joyous abandon.

As it has evolved, Central Park is a magnificent civic amenity, but only isolated spots within it—the Ramble, the Conservatory Garden—offer genuine respite from the hurly-burly of metropolitan life. The greater part of the park is a high-energy urban playground. English visitors, in particular, find the park peculiarly distasteful. Here, for example, is what Jan Morris thinks:

> With its gloomy hillocks obstructing the view, with its threadbare and desolate prairies, with its consciously contrived variety of landscapes, with its baleful lake and brownish foliage, with its sickly carillon which, hourly from the gates of its appalling zoo [Morris is writing prior to the spectacular renovation of the zoo], reminds me of the memorial chimes at Hiroshima, Central Park seems to me the very antithesis of the fresh and natural open space, the slice of countryside, that a city park should ideally be.

CHAPTER 22

Downtown Brooklyn and Brooklyn Heights

1 *Borough Hall*

Chapter 22

Downtown Brooklyn and Brooklyn Heights

1 BOROUGH HALL

Court Street, facing Cadman Plaza to the north
1845–48, Gamaliel King
Cupola: 1898, Vincent Griffith and Stoughton & Stoughton
Restored in 1987, Conklin & Rossant

A reminder of the glory that once was: the City, not the Borough, of Brooklyn! (The City of Brooklyn was established in 1834.) This was City Hall, Brooklyn's answer to its sister burg's City Hall (2.10), built forty years earlier. It's Greek Revival—a little bit late, but Brooklyn was never avant-garde. The cupola was added half a century later to commemorate Brooklyn's merger with New York City in the Great Consolidation. Today, Borough Hall faces out onto vast Cadman Plaza, with a handsome fountain and a lovingly recreated IRT kiosk. The designer of Borough Hall was Gamaliel King, who codesigned Manhattan's Cary Building (2.11) and Friends Meeting House (now Brotherhood Synagogue, 8.7). Each is a very different though excellent building. King only designed buildings on the side. He was a grocer and a carpenter. It makes you wonder if it's any wiser to have career architects than career politicians.

2 CADMAN PLAZA

Bounded by Cadman Plaza West, Court Street, Joralemon Street, and Adams Street
1950–60

When the old Fulton Street El, which crossed the Brooklyn Bridge and gave downtown Brooklyn so much of its flavor, came down, the city gave us this whopping urban renewal project; it was the largest postwar civic-center development in the country. There are eight acres of open space surrounded by government buildings, courthouses, and housing. And, for good measure, they threw in what may be the most boring war memorial in the country. Cadman Plaza is a stew, and it was lambasted at the time of its construction, but I wonder if it hasn't mellowed a tad in the years since. There is, for example, the beached limestone whale of Shreve, Lamb & Harmon's **Supreme Court Building** (1957): those strip windows, straight out of Le Corbusier, now seem almost hip. (The same firm designed the Empire State Building twenty-six years earlier.) The best thing on the plaza, by far, is John Quincy Adams Ward's statue—atop a base by Richard Morris Hunt—of Brooklyn's own Henry Ward Beecher. It is one of the best statues in New York, even if, like so many of our nineteenth-century civic monuments, it is a little on the politically incorrect side: Beecher, known for his ministering to the unfortunate, is depicted with an African American

2 *Supreme Court Building (Cadman Plaza)*

girl reaching up from the side of the base to place palm branches at his feet. No question who's master here. Such implications aside, however, savor the superior modeling of the figures, then turn around and take in the fine long view of Borough Hall with its fountain, and wonder how wonderful Cadman Plaza might have been.

For a 1990s updating of the urban-renewal philosophy, walk a block or so east on Johnson Street to see Metrotech, a joint public-private business development centered around Brooklyn Polytechnic University: eight new buildings, three renovated buildings, sixteen acres, a billion dollars. And, as hoped, it seems to be breathing new life into downtown Brooklyn. One off-shoot is that downtown Brooklyn is getting a brand-new Marriott hotel—the first major hotel to be built in Brooklyn since before World War II.

3 GENERAL POST OFFICE

271 Cadman Plaza East, northeast corner of Johnson Street
1885–91, Mifflin E. Bell
North half: 1933, James Wetmore

This granite pile is as bravura an example of the High Victorian Romanesque, massive and arched and dormered and turreted and rough-textured, as there is in New York. Its brethren are the Federal Archives building (5.17) in Greenwich Village and parts of the American Museum of Natural History (16.18); all three buildings were at one point under construction simultaneously.

4 JAY STREET FIREHOUSE

365–67 Jay Street, between Willoughby Street and Myrtle Avenue
1892, Frank Freeman

Freeman was the Louis Sullivan of Brooklyn. Most of his work was in the borough, and a lot of it has been pulled down. This hasn't, and it's one of his best. It has all the earthy robustness we associate with the Chicago School or H. H. Richardson. The surfaces are a sensual delight, with their play of rough-textured red sandstone, yellow Roman brick, and terra-cotta. Both this and the General Post Office (22.3) are in the Romanesque vein, though the latter achieves its effects through massiveness, with little variety in color or materials; here, at a much smaller scale, it is all color and texture.

6 *Brooklyn Chamber of Commerce Building*

5 TRANSPORTATION BUILDING

370 Jay Street, northwest corner of Willoughby Street
1950, William Haugaard and Andrew J. Thomas

"Simplicity itself," said Lewis Mumford of this building, and boy, was he right. This may be my favorite modern building in the city. You may look at it and say: What?! But staring at it is like chanting a mantra—it works on you and purifies your soul. Mumford praised it as a machine for office work. It's ideally proportioned, he said, for natural light and ventilation, and, indeed, it seems all about good, clean living. But there's some fun here, too, in those corner subway arcades and especially those lighting stanchions with their graceful stylized lettering. I cannot, however, abide Mumford's view that "a business district that consisted mainly of buildings of this type would be far more efficient and far more handsome than anything the rest of the city could show. . . . We could cheerfully trade the imitative classic monumentality of the old civic centers, with their reliance on columns and cornices . . . for some of this honesty, this straightforwardness, this matter-of-fact decency." Mumford—I'll say it—was weird.

6 BROOKLYN CHAMBER OF COMMERCE BUILDING

75 Livingston Street, northwest corner of Court Street
1927, A. F. Simberg

This thirty-six-story office building (now apartments) is one of the best and most dramatic towers of the Golden Age of the New York skyscraper. It is also the least known—unmentioned, amazingly, even in the encyclopedic *AIA Guide to New York City*. It's Gothic, like the Woolworth Building (of fourteen years earlier), but instead of Woolworth's gleaming white terra-cotta, here's buff brick sparklingly accented by terra-cotta. The setback massing is complex, with the main elevation (on Court Street) stepping back fewer times than the corner facing diagonally across Livingston Street. The tops of the setbacks are adorned by terra-cotta parapets, and the culminating pyramidal top is ringed at its base by massed smoke-flues. It's Jazz-Age Gothic, as jazzy as any Art Deco tower. And, so far as I can tell, architect Simberg was a one-hit wonder.

7 BROOKLYN HEIGHTS

Bounded by State and Court streets, Brooklyn Bridge, and the East River

Brooklyn Heights is one of those neighborhoods, like SoHo or Park Slope, that is better experienced as a whole rather than for its individual landmarks. It is a remarkably intact nineteenth-century urban residential neighborhood, in general lovingly tended by homeowners who appreciate both its relative tranquillity and its history. Conceived as an upper-class suburb of New York City, the Heights has long maintained that status, though parts of the neighborhood drooped at times. Today it is as desirable a neighborhood as there is in the city, a bastion of Wall Street honchos who live one subway stop from their offices just on the other side of the river. It is also the home of an entrenched—if waning—Brooklyn bourgeoisie, of old families with very close community ties, living in some of the most beautiful houses on some of the most beautiful streets on the eastern seaboard. The gentility and charm that are hallmarks of the West Village are actually in greater evidence here, less encroached upon by development and fashionable lifestyles.

The charm is manifest not only in the picturesque cul-de-sacs, the romantic row houses, and the peek-a-boo vistas of the Lower Manhattan skyline, but in the very names of the streets: where else can you find Orange Street, Pineapple Street, Cranberry Street? Or how about the main shopping strip, Montague Street? It's named for the original bluestocking, Lady Mary Wortley Montagu (1689–1762), who married into the Pierrepont clan, which owned much of Brooklyn Heights (and for whom not one but two streets here are named).

8 MUNICIPAL CREDIT UNION BUILDING

185 Montague Street, between Court and Clinton streets
1930, Corbett, Harrison & MacMurray

Pure, ultra-jazzy Art Deco from the hand of the master, Harvey Wiley Corbett. It's massed like the punching horns of Count Basie's orchestra and features some of the most delicately traceried Art Deco relief work you'll ever see, combining, as only Art Deco could, floral with mechanical motifs.

9 CITIBANK (originally People's Trust Company)

183 Montague Street, between Court and Clinton streets
1903, Mowbray & Uffinger
Addition to north: 1929, Shreve, Lamb & Harmon

You want a bank? Here's a bank. A marble Roman temple, and exactly the sort of building Louis Sullivan had in mind when he said, in an attempt at withering comment, *If we design our banks to look like Roman temples, then why don't bankers wear togas?* To which the obvious retort is: Why, it would be cool if bankers *did* wear togas!

10 CHASE MANHATTAN BANK (originally Brooklyn Trust Company)

177 Montague Street, northeast corner of Clinton Street
1915, York & Sawyer

Citibank above is grand, but this is one of the great banks of New York, by the greatest firm of bank architects the country ever produced. The exterior is based on Curtoni's Palazzo della Gran Guardia in Verona (seventeenth century), substituting a Corinthian for Curtoni's Doric order. It's a powerhouse composition of an engaged Corinthian order atop a rusticated base of vermiculated limestone. Curtoni was Sanmichele's nephew and

8 *Municipal Credit Union Building*

9 *Citibank (originally People's Trust Company)*

pupil—Stanford White's glorious Tiffany Building (9.6) is modeled after a Sanmichele building. Edward York and Philip Sawyer borrowed from a wide range of models for their banks, and this is probably the best exterior they ever did. Inside, it's the tepidarium of the Baths of Caracalla (Rome, third century)—a perfect model for a banking room, whatever Louis Sullivan might have said. (Charles McKim's late, great Pennsylvania Station concourse was based on the central hall of the Baths of Caracalla, adjacent to the tepidarium.) But maybe my favorite things here are the bronze lamp standards out front, better even than those in front of the New York Public Library. The bases feature griffins and turtles: griffins (or gryphons), with eagles' heads and wings and lions' bodies, symbolize strength and vigilance; turtles are a universal symbol of longevity and down-to-earthness—and, one might infer from these turtles, strong backs. In Henry Hope Reed's classic book, *The Golden City,* this bank is shown on facing pages with Skidmore, Owings and Merrill's 1954 Manufacturers Hanover Trust (13.2), in Reed's attempt to expose the poverty of modernist architecture.

11 ST. ANN AND THE HOLY TRINITY CHURCH (Episcopal)

157 Montague Street, northwest corner of Clinton Street
1847, Minard Lafever

The St. Ann's restoration project has become more famous than the church itself, as, over the years, fund-raisers and artisans have cooperated or quarreled over the direction of the fight to preserve this historic church. It's clearly one of Lafever's best, but it is other features that have energized people, such as the stained-glass windows by William Jay Bolton, which are among the earliest examples of quality stained glass to be produced in New York, and the reredos by Brooklyn's great architect Frank Freeman.

12 BROOKLYN HEIGHTS PROMENADE

East River, between Remsen and Orange streets
1950–51, Clarke & Rapuano

Along with all the expressways, beaches, playgrounds, and housing projects, this is part of the legacy of New York's twentieth-century czar of public works, Robert Moses. The promenade is cantilevered over the Brooklyn-Queens Expressway, allowing the most stunning views there are of the

Lower Manhattan skyline and the glorious Brooklyn Bridge (2.13). I remember well the evening in May 1983 when the city celebrated the centenary of the bridge. I stood with my wife and tens of thousands of others on the promenade as Grucci fireworks were shot from the towers of the bridge in a reenactment of its opening-night festivities a hundred years earlier. As one of the most dazzling fireworks displays in history took place, traffic on the expressway below the promenade came to a complete standstill as motorists got out of their cars and stood in the road to watch the fiery show in the clear night sky.

On the other side of the promenade, facing out over the river, are the rears and backyards of the houses that front on Columbia Heights. These are substantial, even palatial, houses, and it should come as no surprise that, with their spectacular views, they are among the most desirable—and expensive—dwellings in New York. It was from a house that stood at 110 Columbia Heights (the site is now occupied by one of the many Jehovah's Witness buildings in the area) that Washington Roebling, stricken with the bends, watched and supervised the construction of his Brooklyn Bridge. It was in the same house that, half a century later, the great American poet Hart Crane composed his masterpiece, *The Bridge* (1930).

13 84 PIERREPONT STREET

Southwest corner of Henry Street
1890, Frank Freeman

This is one of Freeman's—and Brooklyn Heights'—best houses, a real in-your-face affair of rock-face sandstone, delicate foliate carving, turrets, and bay windows. In addition, it has one of the most fascinating provenances of any New York house. Built for the industrialist Herman Behr, it later became—now, *this* is impressive—the brothel operated by Xaviera Hollander, alias the Happy Hooker, and then—no kidding—a Franciscan brothers residence!

14 APPELLATE DIVISION, NEW YORK STATE SUPREME COURT

Monroe Place, northwest corner of Pierrepont Street
1938, Slee & Bryson

The style has been called "Depression Doric." It's a very severe classical style that flourished in the 1930s at a time when "forward-looking" architects were looking to the International Style and the Bauhaus for inspiration. With the ascendancy of modern architecture, a latter-day example of classicism such as this came to be regarded as a hopeless *retardataire*. It's only since the 1980s, with that decade's mongrel aesthetics, that a building like this can once again be openly admired for what it is: a handsome and entirely apposite step up the classical ladder from its vernacular classical surroundings.

15 BROOKLYN HISTORICAL SOCIETY

128 Pierrepont Street, southwest corner of Clinton Street
1881, George B. Post

Like Park Slope's Montauk Club (23.7) and Manhattan's Jefferson Market Library (5.9), this is a building that came from the bastardization of the ideas of John Ruskin. Here we have earth tones in terra-cotta and Philadelphia pressed brick, and that whole grab bag of broody Victoriana. But note: this is actually a *classical* building. The entrance on

15 *Brooklyn Historical Society*

Pierrepont Street features a Corinthian order. How different from the Corinthian of the York and Sawyer bank above or of Post's own New York Stock Exchange (1.14)! Another lesson in the infinite expressive adaptability of the classical language of architecture.

16 WILLIAMSBURGH SAVINGS BANK BUILDING

1 Hanson Place, northeast corner of Ashland Place
1929, Halsey, McCormack & Helmer

Okay, so it's not exactly in the neighborhood. Here's what you do. Have lunch at the historic **Gage and Tollner Restaurant** (372 Fulton Street, between Smith Street and Red Hook Lane), with its splendid 1892 interior. Be sure to order the clam bellies on toast, prepared, I suspect, as they were in 1892 (though the price has changed). Skip dessert. Walk east six blocks (some of them are kind of long) or so on Fulton Street to Flatbush Avenue. Have dessert—the world's most famous cheesecake—at Junior's Restaurant, on this site since the 1950s. After your cheesecake, turn right onto Flatbush for a look at a confection of a different, though equally rich, kind: the Williamsburgh Savings Bank Building, one of the great skyscrapers of New York. It can be *seen:* it is not only the tallest building in Brooklyn, but there is nothing remotely so high anywhere near it. Like the McGraw-Hill Building (12.1), which was built way west on 42nd Street in the expectation that it would be the first of many skyscrapers in the area, the Williamsburgh was built in a rare burst of optimism about the future of downtown Brooklyn. But nobody followed suit.

Besides being Brooklyn's tallest, there are other superlatives attached to this building. For one thing, it is said that it houses more dental offices than any other building in the world. For another, it has, near its top, what was once the largest four-faced clock in the country (since supplanted by one in Milwaukee). I have always wondered how many Brooklyn apartments have a clear enough night view of the illuminated clock face to be able to tell time by it. The number is certainly in the hundreds.

The building itself is decked out in Byzantine-Romanesque style and does not so much soar as bore its way skyward, culminating first in that clock tower, then in a marvelous quasi-Moorish dome, so unusual for a 512-foot-high skyscraper. Helmut Jahn says that the dome atop his Cityspire (14.6), built in 1987 on West 56th Street, was directly inspired by the Williamsburgh Savings Bank. At the base are high, arched, traceried windows with an undeniable ecclesiastical cast. The building is so finely detailed, so dignified, so self-assured, that it is, in my opinion, one of the ten greatest skyscrapers in New York.

Adjacent, on the southeast corner of Ashland Place and Lafayette Avenue, is the handsome **Brooklyn Academy of Music** (1908, Herts & Tallant), one of the great old concert halls in America. It is home to the famous Next Wave Festival, a showcase for the self-defined avant-garde. Just beyond BAM, north of Fulton Street, is the fine residential neighborhood of **Fort Greene,** which in recent years has taken on some of the prestige enjoyed by Harlem in the 1920s as a center of African American creative activity. Many leading as well as up-and-coming African American artists, writers, and filmmakers (including Spike Lee) call Fort Greene home. Don't miss the lovely **Fort Greene Park** (bounded by DeKalb and Myrtle avenues and Edwards and Washington Park streets), with its wonderful views. Laid out by Olmstead and Vaux in 1867, the park was modified in 1908 by McKim, Mead & White, at which time their **Prison Ship Martyrs' Monument**, a high Doric column with sculpture by Adolph A. Weinman, was installed.

16 *Williamsburgh Savings Bank Building*

CHAPTER 23

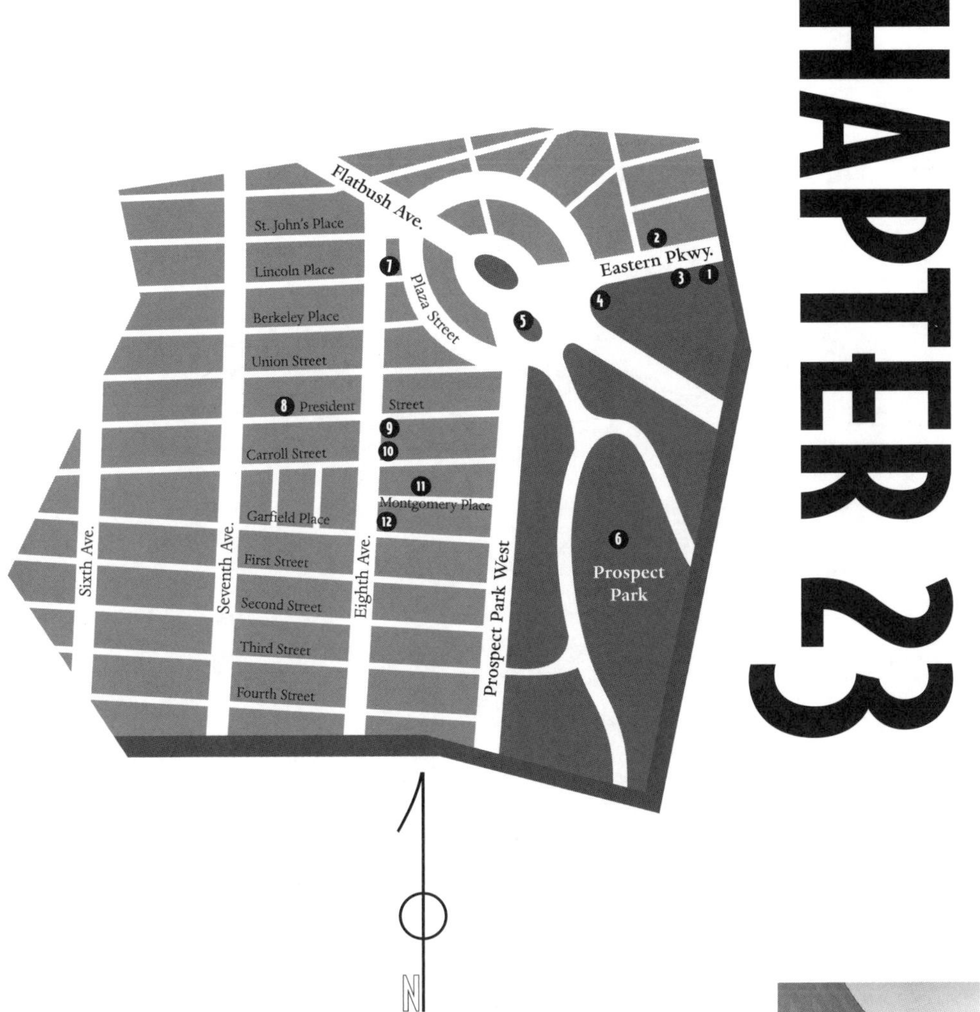

Park Slope and Prospect Park

1 *Brooklyn Museum*

Chapter 23

Park Slope and Prospect Park

1 BROOKLYN MUSEUM

200 Eastern Parkway, southwest corner of Washington Avenue
1897–1924 McKim, Mead & White
Addition: 1978, Prentice & Chan, Ohlhausen
Addition: 1987, Joseph Tonetti
Expansion begun in 1987, Arata Isozaki with James Stewart Polshek & Partners

The Brooklyn is one of the largest museums in the world, and had it been completed according to plan, it would have been the largest. When it was conceived, Brooklyn was still an independent city—the third largest in the country. Brooklyn viewed herself as a bastion of gentility in contrast to New York City (Manhattan). It was only right that she should have a great museum. And, in the 1890s, it was a no-brainer that she'd get McKim, Mead & White to design the thing.

But only a quarter of their museum got built. This had in part to do with the fact that in 1898 the Great Consolidation took place, in which Brooklyn was swallowed up into New York City. New York City already had its great museums; no need to complete this one. Which only begs the question: if this is only a quarter of what was conceived, whence the *megalomania* of certain Brooklynites?

Even in its unfinished state, Charles Follen McKim's building is grand and was grander still before a cockeyed, make-work WPA project lopped off its front stairs in the 1930s. The main lobby had been on the second floor; since the 1930s it's been on the ground floor in an austere modern space fashioned by William Lescaze.

The collections are encyclopedic, with choice specimens of just about everything. The strongest suit here is Egyptology, in which the Brooklyn's is ranked among the three or four best collections in the world. (Oddly, another of the three or four best is that of the Metropolitan, meaning that in order to master Egyptology, it is necessary to come to New York.) There are strong collections in African, Asian, and Native American arts and artifacts, and a fine collection of American paintings from the eighteenth to the twentieth centuries, including outstanding works of the Hudson River School. The Art Reference Library and the Wilbour Library of Egyptology (the latter housed in a funky space designed by William Lescaze) are important metropolitan resources.

For me, however, some of the most thrilling works of art at the Brooklyn Museum are the façade sculptures along Eastern Parkway. The massive female figures on either side of the entrance were originally placed at the Brooklyn end of the Manhattan Bridge (2.17) in 1916 but were moved here in 1963 when the approach was widened. They are the work of Daniel Chester French. The figure on the left represents Manhattan; on the right is Brooklyn. Manhattan bears such symbols as the winged globe on the woman's lap, representing progress and dominion, and the peacock on the right is a traditional symbol of pride—surely the greatest of Manhattan's sins. Brooklyn, by contrast, is seen with such items as a nude child reading a book. To the woman's left is a church, Brooklyn being known as "the borough of churches." These sculptures speak to why some of us regard Manhattan as a nice place to visit but prefer to live in Brooklyn.

The pediment sculptures date from 1913 and are by Daniel Chester French and Adolph Weinman. A remarkable group of thirty figures ranges along the cornice. Installed in 1909, these are works by several sculptors, including Edward Clark Potter, Augustus Lukeman, Attilio Piccirilli, Charles Keck, Karl Bitter, Daniel Chester French, and Herbert Adams. The first figure to the left of the pediment is Keck's Mohammed; I wonder why Moslem nations petitioned the State of New York to remove the statue of Mohammed from the top of the Appellate Courthouse (8.4) at Madison Square Park but have never, to my knowledge, complained of Brooklyn's Mohammed. (Islam is an iconoclastic religion that forbids representations of Mohammed.) Ancient Greece gets its due to the right of the pediment, with figures of the epic poet Homer, the lyric poet Pindar, and Athena, goddess of wisdom, by Daniel Chester French; and figures of the philosopher Plato, the sculptors Phidias and Praxiteles, and the orator Demosthenes, by Herbert Adams. The building itself draws from both Greek and Roman sources: the central Ionic colonnade and the abundant antefixae are Greek elements; the dome and rotunda are Roman.

The Brooklyn Museum is engaged in a long-term expansion according to designs of the Japanese modernist architect Arata Isozaki. Isozaki's auditorium with its undulating ceiling is in place, though most of the rest of the master plan is still to be carried out. Isozaki plans an addition surmounted by a broken obelisk form that, in the view of many local residents, will compromise the lovely view of the museum's dome from across Prospect Park. On a more promising note, there are plans to rebuild the front steps that were so senselessly demolished in the 1930s. My own feeling is that expansion would have been a splendid opportunity for the museum to hire a classical architect to carry out further elements of McKim's original design, or at least to add to the building in like style. But the museum board has chosen instead to go with a chichi architect whose works, I assure you, will not have the staying power of Charles McKim's.

2 EASTERN PARKWAY

1870–74, Olmsted & Vaux

The broad avenue running in front of the Brooklyn was created in the 1870s to the plans of Olmsted and Vaux. It was part of their larger plan for Greater New York in which magnificent parks would be connected by landscaped parkways. Only two of the parkways ever got built: this, which leads from Prospect Park to no one is quite sure where; and Ocean Parkway, which leads from the other side of Prospect Park to Coney Island. This was the first park-and-parkway system conceived in the United States, and served as the model for the most comprehensive such system in the country, in Chicago (which in turn served as the model for Berlin). Olmsted and Vaux were themselves influenced by the then contemporary rebuilding of Paris by Baron Haussmann, though some puritanical American streak kept commerce off our parkways, unlike Paris, where shops and cafés are essential elements of boulevard life. This shunning of commerce has no doubt played a significant role in the steady decline over the years of our boulevards and parkways, which, with only a few exceptions, are mere husks of their former genteel selves.

3 BROOKLYN BOTANIC GARDEN

Eastern Parkway, between Washington and Underhill avenues
Opened in 1910, Harold Caparn, chief landscape architect

Next door to the Brooklyn Museum on Eastern Parkway is the handsome Art Deco gate at the entrance to the Brooklyn Botanic Garden. Opened in 1910, the Botanic Garden is compact—fifty acres. It doesn't contain virgin forests or anything like that. But its small space is superbly designed, and this is, indeed, one of the great botanical gardens in the world as well as one of the best places to visit in New York, especially at cherry blossom time in early May. There are thirteen specialized gardens containing 13,000 species of plants. There's much here that is Japanese, including a traditional Japanese garden and pond (built 1914–15, designed by Takeo Shiota); the magnificent esplanade of Kwanzan cherry trees; and one of the largest bonsai collections in the world. As a result, the Botanic Garden appears to be on the itinerary of many Japanese when they visit New York, and there are days when it seems there are more Japanese than Americans here, which ought to shame Americans. The Administration Building, designed by McKim, Mead & White, was built in 1918. The Steinhardt Conservatory was completed in 1988.

The person most responsible for the design of the Botanic Garden was Harold Caparn, an English-born landscape architect who studied at the Ecole des Beaux-Arts in Paris. It is to him that we owe the formality, cogency, and beauty of the garden layout.

4 BROOKLYN PUBLIC LIBRARY

Flatbush Avenue at Eastern Parkway
1941, Githens & Keally

Another reflection of Brooklyn's past status as an independent city is that the borough's public library system—one of the largest in the nation—is still completely separate from the New York Public Library. This is the main branch of the Brooklyn Public Library, and if it's not exactly Carrère and Hastings' masterpiece on Fifth Avenue, it is nonetheless a very impressive structure in its own right. The building on this site was conceived as early as the turn of the century—at around the same time as the Brooklyn Museum down the street. But it was not completed until

4 *Brooklyn Public Library*

1941. Foundations were dug and part of the skeleton erected for a Beaux-Arts edifice designed in 1908 by Raymond F. Almirall. But financial problems postponed its completion, and by the time the project was back on track in the Great Depression, a new aesthetic sensibility prevailed, and Githens and Keally were brought in to redesign the building, with the constraint that they had to make use of the existing foundation and partial skeleton. Hence, their building has a distinctly Beaux-Arts form and presence, even though it's outfitted in characteristic 1930s Art Moderne garb. The result is a kind of streamlined Beaux-Arts, and it's wonderful—indeed, it's one of the most underrated buildings in New York. Facing the monumental open space of Grand Army Plaza, the library holds its corner strongly, with a broad sweep of steps leading to a concave main façade festooned with richly gilded reliefs by Carl Paul Jennewein, whose gilded reliefs can also be seen at the entrance to the British Empire Building of Rockefeller Center (13.18) and whose lunette murals can be seen in the lobby of the Woolworth Building (2.9). Inside, the wood-paneled, semi-elliptical, three-story-high, clerestoried and galleried main catalogue room is a spectacular space.

5 *Grand Army Plaza*

5 GRAND ARMY PLAZA

Intersection of Flatbush and Vanderbilt avenues, Eastern Parkway, and Prospect Park West
1870, Olmsted and Vaux

The sequence from the Brooklyn Museum, along Eastern Parkway to the Brooklyn Public Library, thence to this open space at the entrance to Prospect Park, is one of America's best architectural sequences.

The pièce de resistance, of course, is America's greatest (by far) monumental arch, known as the **Soldiers' and Sailors' Monument** (1892) and designed by John Hemingway Duncan, who also designed Grant's Tomb. Henry Hope Reed calls it "the finest triumphal arch of modern times, second only to the Arc de Triomphe in Paris" (erected 1806–36). The architectural critic Ian Nairn remarked that the Arc de Triomphe "may have had Roman models, but it feels French to its fingertips." Just so, the Roman (and French) models for Brooklyn's arch yield to a sense that is purely—and triumphantly—American.

It is a monument to the Union dead of the Civil War. The magnificent, Rococo-flavored bronze groups on either pier, by Frederick

MacMonnies, represent, on the left, the Union Army, and, on the right, the Union Navy; they were installed in 1901. The Army group is particularly breathtaking. MacMonnies said he wanted it to seem like an explosion. He also said he was inspired by Delacroix's painting *Liberty Guiding the People* (1830). The foreground figure with raised sword is a self-portrait of MacMonnies. In the Navy group on the other pier, the commanding officer in the foreground resembles the Admiral Farragut in Madison Square (8.4), a work by Saint-Gaudens, who was MacMonnies' mentor. The great quadriga on top, also by MacMonnies, shows four horses, flanked by female figures of winged victory, pulling a chariot bearing a figure of America, holding high the Roman rod of triumph; it dates from 1898. Brooklyn native MacMonnies worked on these groups while living in Paris near the Arc de Triomphe. The spandrel reliefs, between the Army and Navy groups, are by Philip Martiny, whose works so excellently adorn the Surrogate's Court/Hall of Records (2.11) across the river. On the walls of the underside of the arch are equestrian reliefs in bronze, one of Lincoln, one of Grant. Installed in 1895, the human figures are by William O'Donovan, and the horses are by America's greatest painter, Thomas Eakins. The Lincoln, by the way, is believed to be the only equestrian sculpture of the president ever made.

Henry Hope Reed puts it better than I can: "Standing at the entrance to Prospect Park looking north at the arch, the spectator sees one of the nation's great works of art. The brio of the two groups, especially that of *Army*, and the splendid figures and horses of the quadriga are breathtaking."

Just beyond the arch is an oval island with an elaborate sequence of steps and terraces set amid a double ring of sycamores. Here you will find the Mary Louise **Bailey Fountain** (1932) by the sculptor Eugene Savage and the architect Egerton Swartwout. With its conch-shell-blowing Tritons and trident-bearing, open-mouthed, surly Poseidon, this is one of those improbable excrescences of the Beaux-Arts spirit run amok, and impossible not to like. At the north end of the oval is New York City's only official memorial to John F. Kennedy; dating from 1965, the bust is by sculptor Neil Estern and the base is by architect Morris Ketchum.

Back on the other side of the arch, the formal entrance to Prospect Park is marked by what the *AIA Guide to New York City* calls "a necklace of classical ornaments," dating from 1894, with four Doric columns conceived by Stanford White and surmounted by MacMonnies-designed eagles. MacMonnies also did the statue on the left side of the park entrance of James S.T. Stranahan, the Brooklyn pooh-bah who led the movement to create Prospect Park and Eastern and Ocean parkways, and who has been called the Baron Haussmann of Brooklyn. The pair of twelve-sided Tuscan-columned gazebos also were designed by Stanford White.

6 PROSPECT PARK

Bounded by Prospect Park West, Prospect Park Southwest, and Parkside and Flatbush avenues
1866–74, Olmsted & Vaux

By far the best point from which to enter the park is Grand Army Plaza. The sequence worked out by Olmsted and Vaux is one of the most celebrated bits of landscape planning in the world. You are greeted by hillocks and berms and clustered trees that frustratingly foil your view in every direction. The situation becomes so bad that, as you bear right towards the Meadow Port Arch, you are thickly canopied by trees and feeling very closed in. Then you walk through the tunnel; at the other end you can see light and green and you know you will emerge onto something at least a tad more open. But you've been teased. At the end of the tunnel, the **Long Meadow** of the park bursts upon your senses with a release more intense than the Cyclone roller coaster at Coney Island. Before you is a broad vista of gracefully undulating green, enframed, as in a Barbizon painting, by clustered trees. It is one of the most beautiful sights in North America, and something that perhaps no other urban park can match—certainly there is nothing remotely so fine in Manhattan's Central Park.

Simply put, Prospect Park is one of the greatest works of art of the nineteenth century.

And there's much besides the Long Meadow and its approach. The park is an architectural and horticultural wonderland, and I can here note only a few highlights, mostly architectural. Any proper treatment of the park and its treasures would occupy an entire book. (By the way, I strongly recommend *Prospect Park-Central Park: A New Perspective* by M.M. Graff, 1985.)

At the eastern end of the park, near Ocean Avenue and on axis with Park Slope's Ninth Street, is the formal garden called the **Concert Grove**.

Among its ornaments are several busts of great composers; Calvert Vaux's **Oriental Pavilion** (1874); and Henry Kirke Brown's statue of Lincoln (1869), originally placed at Grand Army Plaza. From the Concert Grove you can walk north through Calvert Vaux's barrel-vaulted **Cleft Ridge Span** (1872), believed by many to be the first poured-concrete structure ever erected. To the right after emerging from the tunnel is the park's most famous tree, the spectacularly gnarled **Camperdown Elm**, immortalized in the poem of the same name by Marianne Moore, who spent much time in Prospect Park. Just beyond this tree is the white terra-cotta **Boathouse** (1905), designed in the Palladian style by Helmle and Huberty, whose wonderful bowfront house at 105 Eighth Avenue is described in entry 23.9.

At the very southern tip of the park, where Ocean Parkway emerges from the intersection of Parkside Avenue and Prospect Park Southwest, is **Park Circle**, featuring *The Horse Tamers* by Frederick MacMonnies. Dating from 1899, the two bronze groups are MacMonnies at his flamboyant best and contain some of the best animal sculpture you'll ever see. Nearby, facing onto Parkside Avenue, is Stanford White's **Grecian Shelter** (1906), with a Corinthian order executed in limestone.

I could go on and on about Prospect Park, but you get the idea. Take a tour or get the book by Graff and explore on your own. You won't be disappointed, except perhaps by the "deferred maintenance" that has made parts of the park appear unkempt. Alas, in spite of the efforts of many dedicated people, Prospect Park does not command the dollars of

6 *Boathouse, Prospect Park*

7 *Montauk Club*

its sister Central Park, and it is unlikely that Prospect Park will ever be comprehensively renewed in the way that Central Park has been in recent years. And it is a pity; Prospect is far the finer thing.

7 MONTAUK CLUB

25 Eighth Avenue, northeast corner of Lincoln Place
1891, Francis H. Kimball

When the Montauk Club opened in 1891, this part of Brooklyn abounded in private clubs. Indeed, in 1900 Park Slope had the highest per capita income of any neighborhood in the United States. Architect Francis Kimball, whose several outstanding works in Manhattan include the Trinity and U.S. Realty buildings (1.18) and 867 Madison Avenue (17.15), had worked in London for William Burges, one of the most important of the High Victorian architects influenced by John Ruskin. One of Ruskin's favorite buildings was Venice's Ca' d'Oro (fifteenth century), and it's the ostensible model for Kimball's clubhouse. The warm golden color, not unlike that of the Ca' d'Oro, is achieved through the skillful blending of brownstone with tawny brick and reddish brown brick. The superb terra-cotta decorations were executed by the great mason Charles T. Wills, and many of them depict, in classical style, Native American subjects (particularly having to do with the Montauk people). Notice throughout the façades the careful contrasts of solids and voids, the studied asymmetry, and the wealth of symbolic carving. Though not nearly so flamboyant as its High Victorian Gothic cousin, the Jefferson Market Library (5.9) of fourteen years earlier, the Montauk Club is, in my opinion, New York's best building in that vein—and Francis Kimball the city's best architect mining said vein.

8 869 PRESIDENT STREET

Between Seventh and Eighth avenues
1885, Henry Ogden Avery

At the World's Columbian Exposition in Chicago in 1893, the keynote speech was delivered by Stuart L. Woodford, onetime American ambassador to Spain. Following the world's fair, Woodford returned home to

8 *869 President Street*

President Street in Park Slope, to a house very different in spirit from the "White City" promoted by the fair. The façade is stark, with some lovely ornamental brickwork. But what is really showcased are the articulated structural struts of the pair of bay windows—a device derived from Viollet-le-Duc. The overall effect is one of simplicity, handsomeness, and self-assurance. The house is also uncommonly wide for a New York town house—thirty-six feet.

9 105 EIGHTH AVENUE

Between President and Carroll streets
1916, Helmle & Huberty

This limestone house has a remarkable bowed Corinthian portico that looks like it belongs in a William Kent garden. It's an attempt at a winking monumentality in the tight confines of a row-house lot. What's amazing is that it works—completely. We accept its regality even as we know it's make-believe.

9 *105 Eighth Avenue*

10 *119 Eighth Avenue*

10 119 EIGHTH AVENUE

Northeast corner of Carroll Street
1888, C. P. H. Gilbert

C. P. H. Gilbert (no relation to Cass) designed some wonderful houses—the Morton Plant house (now Cartier's, 13.10), the Isaac Fletcher house (now the Ukrainian Institute, 17.18), and the Otto Kahn house (now Convent of the Sacred Heart, 18.9)—in an astonishing variety of styles. Here it's Richardsonian Romanesque, a round-arched style immediately identifiable by its rock-faced masonry (often accented by contrasting materials), and by a sense of massiveness and solidity, conveyed by such means as deep window reveals and broad roof planes. The style is named for Henry Hobson Richardson (1838–86), who worked mainly out of the Boston area. Richardson, a product of the Ecole des Beaux-Arts, was mentor to a generation of American architects: not only Chicago's Louis Sullivan, with whom Richardson's name is often paired, but also Messrs. McKim, Mead, and White—all three of whom worked at one time in Richardson's office/atelier. Another onetime Richardson employee/pupil was, unsurprisingly, C. P. H. Gilbert. This house, built for Thomas Adams (inventor of Chiclets), is, without question, the finest Richardsonian Romanesque building in New York.

Note how the rock-face brownstone plays off the smooth Roman brick, and how the materials work with the massing of the building to communicate strength and power—which exist harmoniously with bits of the most delicate ornamental carving. The Carroll Street façade has a knockout arch with extravagant, almost Sullivanesque, foliate decorations.

11 MONTGOMERY PLACE

Between Prospect Park West and Eighth Avenue

Named for General Richard Montgomery, felled in the Battle of Quebec in 1775, this, as pretty a street as there is in New York, was developed as a unit between 1887 and 1892 by Harvey Murdock. The tremendous architectural variety was intentional. Twenty of the forty-six houses were designed by C. P. H. Gilbert. The total effect is the important thing, but it's remarkable how many of the individual houses are first-rate in themselves. Some of the highlights:

No. 58 (1890, C. P. H. Gilbert) has superb Roman brickwork, including rounded-brick voussoirs and a fabulous sheet-metal cornice. Note, below the cornice, the foliate terra-cotta decorations flanking a human mask.

11 *Montgomery Place*

No. 47 (1890, Rudolphe Daus) is in the French Renaissance style, with a façade of red sandstone and some graceful French decorations. Note the fleur-de-lis in the gable of the steep, tiled pyramidal roof. Architect Daus also gave us the fine Church of Notre Dame (19.2) in Morningside Heights. (Daus was a fascinating figure: a German national born in Mexico, he was educated in Berlin and at the Ecole des Beaux-Arts in Paris, lived in Brooklyn, and died in Paris. He was employed at one time as Surveyor of Buildings for Brooklyn.)

No. 45 (1899, Babb, Cook & Willard) is also French Renaissance but uses very different materials. Here we have a rusticated granite base, with red brick and limestone above. The architects also gave us the Carnegie Mansion (now Cooper-Hewitt Museum, 18.10) and the DeVinne Press Building (6.4) in Manhattan.

Nos. 42–44 (1889, C. P. H. Gilbert) feature elaborate intaglio brickwork and a bold, bracketed, Italian Renaissance-style cornice.

No. 11 (1897–98, C. P. H. Gilbert), built for Harvey Murdock himself, may be the first of the Montgomery Place houses to be built. It has a rusticated rock-face brownstone base, with Roman brick above. Note the beautiful Romanesque arches and the Dutch stepped gable. The vines that have grown over a portion of the façade have only enhanced its romantic appeal.

Montgomery Place is closed at Eighth Avenue by a handsome Art Deco apartment house from the 1940s. Though obviously not part of Murdock's plan, it is impossible to imagine a finer, better-scaled closing to what Elliot Willensky and Norval White, in their *AIA Guide to New York City*, call "one of the truly great blocks in the world of urbane row housing . . . a symphony of materials and textures."

12 CONGREGATION BETH ELOHIM

Eighth Avenue, northeast corner of Garfield Place
1910, Simon Eisendrath and B. Horwitz

Casual grandeur: The synagogue is a really grand building but skillfully sited and scaled so as not to bear too hard upon what is, after all, an ordinary intersection in the residential heart of the neighborhood. It is a measure of great cities that they can pull off this sort of thing. New York does it in spots; London does it all over the place. Park Slope does it here: the synagogue is oriented diagonally toward the corner, with a not-too-grand, not-too-small flight of steps. The building manages the rare feat of seeming larger from a distance than it does close up: from a distance the dome looks really imposing; close up, it is scarcely noticeable, being back far enough from the sidewalk line. It really is beautifully designed. The mock Moorish/Byzantine/Romanesque schoolhouse (1928, Mortimer Freehof and David Levy) across Garfield Place is at home, too, adding its yellowish hue, Art Deco flourishes, and Jewish symbolism to the mix; and, across Eighth Avenue from the temple, a typically handsome Park Slope neoclassical residential building (the Belvedere apartments, 1903, Henry Pohlman) lends its typically well-manicured façade of Roman brick and limestone. It all adds up to the easy urbanity that at times seems to be Park Slope's monopoly in New York.

12 *Congregation Beth Elohim*

Index for Specialists

FEDERAL AND GEORGIAN

GREEK REVIVAL

GREEK REVIVAL TOWNHOUSES

GOTHIC REVIVAL

ROMANESQUE REVIVAL

HIGH VICTORIAN (see also Queen Anne)

VICTORIAN TOWNHOUSES

QUEEN ANNE

ITALIANATE

CAST-IRON FACADES

"RICHARDSONIAN ROMANESQUE"

BEAUX-ARTS

NEO-GOTHIC AND NEO-ROMANESQUE CHURCHES

NEO-RENAISSANCE AND NEO-BAROQUE CHURCHES

MCKIM, MEAD & WHITE

ART NOUVEAU

ART DECO/ART MODERNE

SETBACK SKYSCRAPERS

EARLY MODERN

POSTWAR MIDCULT KITSCH

CORBUSIAN

MIESIAN

"NEW FORMALISM"

MODERN CHURCHES

MODERN TOWNHOUSES

HOUSING PROJECTS

POSTWAR CLASSICAL

1960S

1970S

1980S

STREETS, SQUARES, AND PLACES

DEPARTMENT STORES

Bibliography

Alpern, Andrew. *New York's Fabulous Luxury Apartments,* New York: Dover, 1987.

The Architecture of McKim, Mead & White in Photographs, Plans and Elevations, New York: Dover, 1990. Reprint of the classic folio, first published in 1915, detailing the works of these New York masters.

Barth, Gunther. *City People: The Rise of Modern City Culture in Nineteenth Century America,* New York and Oxford: Oxford University Press, 1980. An examination of the role played by certain capitalist enterprises–e.g., the department store, the metropolitan press, professional baseball–in the assimilation of European immigrants in American cities. One of the most original, stimulating, and mind-changing books of urban history ever written.

Caro, Robert A. *The Power Broker: Robert Moses and the Fall of New York,* New York: Random House, 1974. Unparalleled for its detailed account of the changing physical environment of the city in the 20th century, by way of a relentlessly negative and possibly unfair portrait of New York's public-works czar.

Condit, Carl W. *The Port of New York: A History of the Rail and Terminal System from the Beginnings to Pennsylvania Station,* Chicago: University of Chicago Press, 1980.

———. *The Port of New York: A History of the Rail and Terminal System from the Grand Central Electrification to the Present,* Chicago: University of Chicago Press, 1981. Condit is one of the most rigorous and readable of American architectural historians, and his study of the construction of Manhattan's two great rail terminals is unlikely to be surpassed.

Coppola, Philip Ashforth. *Silver Connections: A Fresh Perspective on the New York Area Subway Systems,* Vol. 1, Maplewood, N.J.: Four Oceans Press, 1988. The first volume of an independently published, highly idiosyncratic, stupendously detailed study of the decor of every station in the New York subway system.

Cromley, Elizabeth Collins. *Alone Together: A History of New York's Early Apartments,* Ithaca: Cornell University Press, 1990. By far the best book on the New York apartment house.

Dunlap, David W. *On Broadway: A Journey Uptown Over Time,* New York: Rizzoli, 1990. A virtual encyclopedia of Broadway architecture. Would that there were such a book for every major street in the city!

Federal Writers' Project, *New York City Guide,* New York: Random House, 1939. Though filled with all manner of period obtuseness, nonetheless one of the most reliable and fascinating general guides to the city ever written.

Fletcher, Banister. *A History of Architecture,* 18th edition, revised by J.C. Palmes, New York: Scribner's, 1975.The best single source I know for tracing stylistic pedigrees.

Gambee, Robert. *Wall Street Christmas,* New York: W.W. Norton, 1990. Forget the title—this book has little to do with Christmas, and a great deal to do with the architectural and corporate history of the Financial District.

Gayle, Margot, and Michele Cohen, *The Art Commission and the Municipal Art Society's Guide to Manhattan's Outdoor Sculpture,* New York: Prentice Hall Press, 1988. An invaluable guide.

Gayle, Margot, and Edmund V. Gillon, Jr., *Cast-Iron Architecture in New York,* New York: Dover, 1974. Essential.

Goldberger, Paul. *The City Observed: New York,* New York: Random House, 1979. An extremely readable and often original guide to Manhattan architecture. The author's catholicity of taste and praise symbolized the demise of narrow modernist aesthetics at the end of the 1970s.

Gray, Christopher. *Changing New York: The Architectural Scene,* New York: Dover, 1992. The first thing I turn to every Sunday in *The New York Times* is Gray's "Streetscapes" column. This book is a collection—I hope the first of many—of those columns.

Huxtable, Ada Louise. *Architecture, Anyone?,* Berkeley: University of California Press, 1986.

———. *Classic New York,* New York: Anchor Books, 1964.

———. Four Walking Tours of Modern Architecture in New York City, New York: The Museum of Modern Art and the Municipal Art

Society, 1961.

———. "The Tall Building Artistically Reconsidered," *The New Criterion,* November 1982.

———. *Will They Ever Finish Bruckner Boulevard?*, New York: Macmillan, 1970. Huxtable is the doyenne of American architectural critics. Supremely readable, vicious, sardonic—and exquisitely unfair.

Jacobs, Jane. *The Death and Life of Great American Cities,* New York: Random House, 1961. A profoundly influential defense of big-city life, published at the beginning of a decade that will go down in history as the time American cities truly began their long downward spiral.

Jordy, William H. *American Buildings and Their Architects: The Impact of European Modernism in the Mid-Twentieth Century,* New York and Oxford: Oxford University Press, 1986. Contains the best concise account of Rockefeller Center.

Koolhaas, Rem. *Delirious New York,* New York and Oxford: Oxford University Press, 1978. A deliriously frustrating blend of *au courant* academic attitudes, outright zaniness, and real love of "Manhattanism," this cult classic made a generation of architecture students appreciate anew much of Manhattan's long dishonored tradition of self-celebratory design.

Kostof, Spiro. *A History of Architecture: Settings and Rituals,* New York and Oxford: Oxford University Press, 1985. Particularly good on the relation of architecture to liturgy in church design.

Krinsky, Carol Herselle, *Rockefeller Center,* New York and Oxford: Oxford University Press, 1978. The best treatment of Rockefeller Center, by a very able and judicious historian.

Landau, Sarah Bradford, and Carl W. Condit. *Rise of the New York Skyscraper 1865-1913*. New Haven: Yale University Press, 1996. There will never be a better book on the subject.

Leon, Ruth. *Applause: New York's Guide to the Performing Arts,* New York: Applause Books, 1991.

Lowe, David Garrard. *Stanford White's New York,* New York: Doubleday, 1992. Lowe's earlier *Lost Chicago* is the book that made me want to start writing about architecture and cities.

Lukacs, John. *Outgrowing Democracy: A History of the United States in the 20th Century,* New York: Doubleday, 1984. The chapter "The

Bourgeois Interlude" is essential reading for anyone who seeks to understand the soul of the 20th century American city. Lukacs is in my opinion not only the greatest living American historian, but the greatest thinker and writer.

Manhattan Office Buildings: Downtown, New York: Yale Robbins, 1985.

Morris, Jan. Destinations, New York and Oxford: Oxford University Press, 1980.

———. *Manhattan '45,* New York and Oxford: Oxford University Press: 1987. Absolutely sparkling prose that is like a magic-carpet ride to the past.

Mumford, Lewis. *From the Ground Up,* New York: Harcourt Brace Jovanovich, 1956.

———. *Sketches from Life: The Autobiography of Lewis Mumford: The Early Years,* New York: The Dial Press, 1982. Mumford was a brilliant urban critic, a graceful prose writer, and one of the leading American intellectuals of this century. Eminently worth reading, though in my opinion his taste is insanely narrow, and his policy prescriptions potentially disastrous.

Office Buildings: Midtown Manhattan, New York: Yale Robbins, 1992.

Okamoto, Rai Y., and Frank E. Williams, *Urban Design Manhattan,* New York: Viking, 1969. Outstanding discussion of Grand Central Terminal as "access tree."

Oliver, Richard. *Bertram Grosvenor Goodhue,* Cambridge, Mass.: The MIT Press, 1985. The only full-scale study of the works of one of the greatest of New York architects.

Pevsner, Nikolaus. *A History of Building Types,* Princeton, N.J.: Princeton University Press, 1976.

Pierson, William H., Jr. *American Buildings and Their Architects: Technology and the Picturesque, the Corporate and the Early Gothic Styles,* New York and Oxford: Oxford University Press, 1986. One of the best books ever on American architecture, particularly for its unparalleled assessment of the Gothic Revival.

Reed, Henry Hope. *Beaux-Arts Architecture in New York,* New York: Dover, 1988.

———. *The Golden City,* New York: Doubleday, 1959.

———. "New York Architecture," in Alan Rinzler, editor, *The New York Spy,* New York: David White Company, 1967. Reed is a great connoisseur and defender of America's glorious, and absurdly maligned, Beaux-Arts tradition.

Reynolds, Donald Martin. *The Architecture of New York City,* New York: Macmillan, 1984. Responsible and readable discussions of selected significant buildings.

Robinson, Cervin, and Rosemarie Haag Bletter, *Skyscraper Style: Art Deco New York,* New York and Oxford: Oxford University Press, 1975. The best book on New York Art Deco. One of three late '70s books from Oxford that had a profound impact on young people's thinking about New York architecture—the others being Koolhaas and Krinsky.

Roth, Leland M. *McKim, Mead & White, Architects,* New York: Harper & Row, 1983. The best book I know on New York's greatest architects.

Ruttenbaum, Steven. *Mansions in the Clouds: The Skyscraper Palazzi of Emery Roth,* New York: Balsam Press, 1986.

Salwen, Peter. *Upper West Side Story*, New York: Abbeville Press, 1989.

Sanders, Ronald. *The Lower East Side,* New York: Dover, 1979.

Stern, Robert A. M., Gregory Gilmartin and John Massengale, *New York 1900: Metropolitan Architecture and Urbanism 1890-1915,* New York: Rizzoli, 1983.

Stern, Robert A. M., Gregory Gilmartin and Thomas Mellins, *New York 1930: Architecture and Urbanism Between the Two World Wars,* New York: Rizzoli, 1987.

Stern, Robert A. M., Thomas Mellins, and David Fishman. New York 1960: Architecture and Urbanism Between the Second World War and the Bicentennial. New York: Monacelli Press, 1995. The three volumes by Stern et al. are as nearly encyclopedic as possible, and indispensable, if a tad unwieldy.

Sturm, James L. *Stained Glass from Medieval Times to the Present: Treasures to Be Seen in New York,* New York: E.P. Dutton, 1982. The author makes the case that in New York today can be viewed the greatest variety of stained-glass art to be found in any city in the world.

Tauranac, John. *Essential New York,* New York: Holt Rinehart Winston, 1979. Useful for its chronological organization.

Taylor, William R., editor, *Inventing Times Square: Commerce and Culture at the Crossroads of the World,* New York: Russell Sage Foundation, 1991.

A collection of essays that together provide the most in-depth history of Times Square.

Trager, James. *Park Avenue: Street of Dreams,* New York: Atheneum, 1990. Positively brimming with information.

Whiffen, Marcus. *American Architecture Since 1780: A Guide to the Styles,* Cambridge, Mass.: MIT Press, 1981. The best "field guide" I know to architectural styles.

White, Norval, and Elliot Willensky, *AIA Guide to New York City,* San Diego and New York: Harcourt Brace Jovanovich, 1988. No other city boasts as fine a reference guide to its buildings. Superbly written, edited, and designed.

Whyte, William H. *City: Rediscovering the Center,* New York: Doubleday, 1988. Close readings of the urban environment by an activist and follower of Jane Jacobs.

Wist, Ronda. *On Fifth Avenue Then and Now,* New York: Birch Lane Press, 1992. A charming and informative combination of architectural history and personal reminiscence of midtown Fifth Avenue.

Wolfe, Gerard. *42nd Street River to River Guide,* New York: 42nd Street E.T.C., n.d.

———. *New York: A Guide to the Metropolis,* Revised Edition, New York: McGraw-Hill, 1983. Excellent for social-historical background.

Wright, Carol von Pressentin. *Blue Guide: New York,* New York: W.W. Norton, 1991. The best general tourist guide to New York. Remarkably accurate, detailed, and judicious.

Wurman, Richard Saul, editor, *New York City Access,* New York: Harper Perennial, 1991. A rich, color-coded, almost phantasmagorical representation of the urban tapestry.

Index

A

B

C

J

K

L

M

N

T